Talking Politics
in Japan Today

To Utai and Iri

Talking Politics in Japan Today

Ofer Feldman

sussex
ACADEMIC
PRESS

BRIGHTON • PORTLAND

2 4 6 8 10 9 7 5 3 1

First published in hardcover 2004; reprinted in paperback 2005 in Great Britain by
SUSSEX ACADEMIC PRESS
PO Box 2950
Brighton BN2 5SP

and in the United States of America by
SUSSEX ACADEMIC PRESS
920 NE 58th Ave   Suite 300
Portland, Oregon 97213–3786

British Library Cataloguing in Publication Data
A CIP catalogue record for this book is available from the British Library.

Library of Congress Cataloging-in-Publication Data
Feldman, Ofer, 1954–
    Talking politics in Japan today / Ofer Feldman.
        p. cm.
    Includes bibliographical references and index.
    ISBN 1-84519-037-8 (h/c; alk. paper)   1-84519-109-9 (pbk.)
    1. Discourse analysis—Political aspects—Japan. 2. Mass
media and language—Political aspects—Japan. I. Title.
P302.77.F45 2004
495.6′0141—dc22
                                                2004007292
                                                CIP

Typeset and designed by G&G Editorial, Brighton
Printed by MPG Books, Ltd, Bodmin, Cornwall
This book is printed on acid-free paper.

Contents

List of Tables, Figures, and Appendices

Preface and Acknowledgments for the Paperback Edition

I have been delighted by the reception that the hardback edition of this book has received and am very pleased that *Sussex Academic Press* has now decided to publish a paperback edition. Over the course of the last year, since I completed the original manuscript, and the last six months, since it appeared in the hardback edition, I have received multiple e-mails and other communications from Japan scholars, political scientists, those that specialize in political behavior and communication research, as well as news reporters. All of these individuals have been either interested in acquiring additional information, asking for opinions, and/or commenting on the analysis and interpretation of facts discussed in the book.

A common thread that runs through the feedback that I have received is that the most important lessons that the book contains are a) the fact that Japan is currently critically in need of leadership that can demonstrate rhetorical skills that allow effective communication with the public; b) that there is no room for the old-fashioned, implicit and vague rhetoric which has dominated policy and public matters and is understood by only a handful politicians, government officials, and news media reporters; and, c) that Japanese political leaders and decision-makers need to distribute more relevant information to the electorate—rather than exploiting a set of conventional metaphors or slogans that create certain images for themselves and their political groups, or justify their activities and policies.

The problem with public speaking in Japan has been the ubiquitous need to decode meaning from what politicians say. Too often Diet members speak in a kind of code that defies lexicographical definition; they speak in general terms, avoid being concrete, and shy away from taking clear-cut positions on hot issues; they equivocate in both national Diet deliberations and during news media interviews; and they use professional jargon that makes it difficult to understand the real meaning of their verbal communications. Accordingly, and for both listener and viewer, it has never been easy to use the discourse of politicians to make sense of politics. These arguments have been further demonstrated in the time period since the hardcover edition of this book was published.

During late 2004 and the beginning of 2005 there were lively debates in the Diet and especially in the House of Representatives' Budget

Committee on a host of contentious issues including political funding and political donations; the support the government gave to the US-led war against Iraq; the involvement and the extension of the Ground Self-Defense Force troops' mission in Iraq; relocation plans for US forces in Japan; Japan's bilateral talks with North Korea on the abduction issue; reform of the social-security system including pension programs; and the privatization of postal services (mail, savings, and insurance). In all these instances, the government, and Prime Minister Koizumi Junichirô in particular, preferred vague statements and evasion capable of interpretation in a variety of ways, rather than plainly disclosing the details of their policy visions and plans.

One example is related to the postal privatization, the main pillar of Prime Minister Koizumi's reform agenda. In his 2005 policy speech to the Diet, Koizumi described postal privatization as "the heart of structural reform," claiming that "the engine for these reforms is every one of the people of Japan, and the success or failure of the reforms rests with the firm resolve and energy of the people." Yet much of the public remained unconvinced about what Koizumi said and did not understand exactly why privatization is necessary. Opinion polls taken at the beginning of 2005 indicated that close to 90% of the public thought the prime minister should "further detail" the reasons for privatization of the postal system and explain where these changes will lead.

Instead of producing specific reform plans and explaining them using plain language, Prime Minister Koizumi—during Diet speeches, a plenary question-and-answer sessions in the Diet, and frequent television interviews—continued to repeat his slogans and catchphrases including that of "no reform, no growth," and "let the private sector do what it can do best." Even against opposition within his own Liberal Democratic Party's members, he vowed to "get it through the current session at all costs," and that "opposing the privatization is equivalent to demanding that someone swim with his hands and legs bound together."

One of the conclusions of this book is that for skilled political communicators, equivocation can be a highly effective instrument of self-presentation and an important element of their political talent. Yet it is time for Japan to also "nurture" "good communicators," that is, politicians and leaders that will provide details to the public on the how, where, and when of public policy and choices. Presumably, such a leadership will elicit more interest, more confidence, and larger active participation of people in politics, thereby guiding Japan through new international challenges. In this sense, I hope that this book opens a niche to further inquiry on the content and style of communications chosen by elected officials, as scholars continue to search for and unwrap the changing nature of the "conventional wisdom" within Japanese politics.

Finally, I am grateful to all the many individuals and organizations that supported this project and helped me to prepare and publish it. I owe a deep debt first to the many political journalists and editors who explained to me at length the changing nature of their newsgathering efforts in the 1990s. Among them are Ishii Tatsuya of *Kyôdô* News, Komatsu Hiroshi of *Mainichi*, and Satô Kazuo of *Asahi*. Saikawa Takasumi of *Kyôdô* was, as ever, an unfailing source of information and clarification on political journalism, providing me with essential details on the dynamics of Japanese politics and its logic. My students Nakamura Kimihisa, Matsumoto Nozomu, Noichi Takako, and Otsubo Tatsunori, along with Kuno Yukie, helped process the data regarding political interviews, metaphors, and political cartooning.

I have also profited enormously from long discussions with Peter Bull of the University of York, the UK, who enriched me with his insights on political communication, especially in regard to the study of political metaphors and live interviews with politicians. My study of political interviews on Japanese television, reported in Chapter 5, would not have been possible without Peter's thoughtful feedback and criticism regarding everything from methods of analysis to explanations of the research results.

Financial support during this study came from various sources. A Grant-in-Aid for Scientific Research awarded by the Japan Society for the Promotion of Science (JSPS), 1999–2001, helped me to gather and analyze the data reported in this book. The Daiwa Anglo-Japanese Foundation (*Daiwa nichi-ei kikin*) awarded me a generous grant in 1999 to travel to the University of York, the UK, to extend my knowledge of comparative aspects of political discourse. I especially appreciate the assistance of Ms. Kôno Junko, the Foundation's Deputy-Director in the Tokyo office. A fellowship from Fulbright Foundation (*Japan-United States Educational Commission*), 2001–2002, facilitated a nine-month stay in Ohio State University, where I researched the nature and meaning of metaphors and symbols used in the international context. Also, the Mershon Center at Ohio State University provided me with additional support and facilities that allowed me to focus on writing the first draft of this book. I wish to express a special debt of gratitude to R. Ned Lebow, the Center's Director, for his kind hospitality and encouragements during my stay at the Center. I recall with particular appreciation the discussions I had with friends at the Center about the world's changing politics and leadership, and want to express my personal regard especially to Don A. Sylvan, Rick K. Herrmann, and Tony Mughan. Ehud Harari, Christ'l De Landtsheer, Linda O. Valenty, Francis A. Beer, Rafi Manory, and Jacob Bercovitch also gave me helpful, insightful, and valuable comments during the writing of this book.

Thanks are due to Joanne Elbinger Higashi for reading earlier drafts of this work and giving me very useful ideas and suggestions, all of which are incorporated in this book. I am also indebted to Anthony Grahame of the *Sussex Academic Press* for his excellent help in producing this book.

To my wife Rie I owe more than I can express, for her constant endorsement, constructive criticism, and confidence during my scholarly pursuits. As ever, our sons Utai and Iri inspired me with the sense of challenge I needed to complete the project. Needless to say, none of the above mentioned persons or institutions bear any responsibility for any mistake or shortcomings in this book—except perhaps Utai and Iri, to whom this book is dedicated.

KYÔTO, JAPAN
March 2005

Note on Citations and Diacritical Marks

Throughout this book, Japanese words in direct quotations are transcribed as they appear in the source cited. Personal names are given in the Japanese order, i.e. family name first. Proper names are italicized according to English usage; all other Japanese words are italicized on each occurrence. Citations from the dailies *Asahi Shimbun, Yomiuri Shimbun,* and *Mainichi Shimbun* mentioned as *Asahi, Yomiuri,* and *Mainichi,* respectively. In Japanese, vowels can either be short or long; a diacritical mark (e.g. ô, û or â) over the vowel indicates that it is a long vowel.

Introduction: Discourse and the Conventional Wisdom of Japanese Politics

This book details certain aspects of political language in Japan and the functions that language plays in Japanese polity. Its particular focus is the political discourse of high-echelon political leaders, government officials, and news reporters in Tôkyô's *Nagatachô* district—the center of Japanese politics. The national Diet (parliament), the Prime Minister's Official Residence, the headquarters of the major political parties, and Diet members' offices are located in *Nagatachô*. It is where lobbyists, government officials, business leaders, Diet members and party leaders negotiate the content of bills and discuss how the nation will be governed. Decisions made in *Nagatachô* affect the whole country. Thus the term *Nagatachô* has come to be synonymous with the nation's political nerve center, like 10 Downing Street in London and Capitol Hill in Washington.

The chapters that follow explore the daily discourse that Diet members use for communicating with each other and with media representatives; rhetoric that politicians use when addressing supporters and when replying to questions during televised political interviews; metaphors used by politicians and the media and how such metaphors facilitate understanding of political processes and roles; newsgathering methods and reporters' relationships with information sources; and how the prime minister is depicted in political coverage in general and in political cartoons in two Japanese national dailies in particular.

This book also discusses how the language that Japanese politicians use to disseminate information and interpret events relates to the broader Japanese culture and political culture. The discussion includes a look at some entertaining aspects of political discourse—such as symbols, slogans, humor, and colloquial names for political groups and events—which, I propose, are significant to the inquiry into the relationship between language and political processes in Japan. In this book, political language, political speech, political rhetoric and political discourse are terms used interchangeably to refer to language and communication related to politics.

Politics as Public Discourse: Officials, the Media, and the Socio-Cultural Setting

Political society is constituted by language. It is an arena in which words are of vital importance as instruments of power. Words are essential tools for winning political office, influencing policy, and mobilizing public support. Through speeches, statements, testimonies, media releases and briefings, press conferences and leaks, politicians and government officials inform others of their political view and the state of the polity, and mold the political agenda. Public figures also identify unfolding events and define them for other politicians and officials, especially through media reporters and commentators who they hope will help them to gain recognition and support from the general public. Decision-makers use language to affect political affairs on both the domestic and international levels. With words they try to influence the behaviors and attitudes of voters, and to shape opinions about political institutions and themselves. Political leaders win or lose office, and inform or mislead the general public, through their use of language. In the broad sense, the essence of politics is talk, and those who control discourse, control society (e.g. Feldman & De Landtsheer, 1998).

Language that obviously deals with political issues cannot be seen in isolation from everyday language. Depending on its use and context, all language has the potential to become political language. By "political language," I mean language that is used in regard to political matters, for political purposes, by people involved in public affairs—such as politicians, government officials, labor union representatives, members of special interest or political support groups, and religious leaders. It includes spoken and written messages, signals, and gestures, all which is concerned with and affects a large number of people, such as a community, a town, city, nation, or even a larger group of people. Political discourse may consist of explanations, instruction, manipulation, propaganda, guidance, advising, or agreements (e.g. De Landtsheer & Feldman, 2000).

Ultimately, in addition to their leadership qualities, negotiation skills, and ability to keep effective working relationships with colleagues and officials, politicians have to demonstrate that they possess sufficient rhetorical skills to be able to communicate effectively. Indeed, very often the public sees rhetoric as the most important feature of its political leaders, and evaluates them more by their words than by their deeds.

Of course, savvy political communicators construct and disseminate their discourse with the intention of affecting the public. They tell voters how they view the significance of political issues, explain their own motives and objectives, and justify their activities to give meaning to the events that take place in the public domain. They do so in order to shape people's attitudes toward, or to create a particular image of themselves and their opponents, political institutions and parties, and the political process, and also in order to affect public debate.

Political communicators' rhetoric also impacts the public's attitudes toward vital social issues such as the economy, which is a particularly central aspect in Japan both because the country allocates much effort to economic matters and because its economy is so important to the rest of the world. In recent years, the words of prime ministers, influential members of political parties, and economic leaders—including the governors of the Bank of Japan—have affected public attitudes toward investment in the stock market, trends in the value of the yen versus other currencies, and other factors related to international trade and economic relationships. Politicians' rhetoric concerning issues like small government, deregulation, privatization, and unemployment has also molded consumers' feelings about economic growth. Often, such talk has resulted in the spread of optimism about Japan's financial and monetary systems. During 2004, the Bank of Japan's governor gave welcome jolts of energy to both the yen and the Nikkei Index of 225 leading issues (the primary Tôkyô stock market index) by commenting after international meetings such as the Group of Seven finance ministers and central bank governors, that Japan's economy is going in a "good direction" and moving toward a "sustainable recovery."

It is worth mentioning that it's not only the language of Japanese politicians and senior officials that affects the Japanese economy and social structures, but even the discourse of non-Japanese politicians is known to do so. Japanese politicians and news outlets have often used *"gaiatsu"* (literally, "outside pressure," most often from the US) as a reason—or some might say an excuse—for making significant changes in domestic policy. *Gaiatsu* typically consists of public comments made by senior US officials or specialists concerning Japanese fiscal or monetary policy, or trade issues such as import restrictions on agricultural products. In America, "Japan-bashing" by government officials can serve as an easy way to deflect discontent among a certain segment of the electorate, while in Japan it can be used to deflect voters' anger when politicians are "pressured" into enacting unpopular measures such as liberalizing imports of agricultural products or allowing the yen to appreciate. There was a time during the 1990s when American outbursts were so common and expected that Japanese political rhetoric depended on using *gaiatsu* to justify short-term responses to American attacks rather than coming up with original solutions to domestic economic problems.

Because politicians have the non-pedestrian aim of affecting the public at large, their style of communication tends to differ from that of the general public. Politicians (and other officials) inform, explain, and interpret events by using explicit, direct appeals, or implicit appeals that sometimes conceal their true thoughts, feelings, intentions. For example, one type of implicit appeal uses metaphors. As explained in **Chapter 5**, by transferring a word, name, or at least part of the meaning that a word ordinarily conveys to something else, the speaker can discuss one area of experience in terms normally used for describing another. Politicians also use slogans and catchwords, often distinctly associated with a political party or other group, to summarize their promises or policies. Both metaphors and slogans can be powerful tools for exciting citizens' emotions if they are applied persistently and systematically.

Political communicators make conscious decisions about the content and timing of their speeches, appeals, and declarations. As revealed in the following chapters, decision-makers tend to focus their discourse on the issues that make them feel most comfortable and competent, and to avoid issues with which they are unfamiliar or which might adversely affect their political agenda or public image. As detailed in **Chapter 4**, regardless of whether they face colleagues, supporters, or an interviewer on a televised political program, politicians favor issues in which they have a special interest, commitment, or engagement, and which are likely to lead to success. Japanese politicians have particularly interesting ways of constructing their rhetoric and of reacting to issues raised by the news media. Unlike Western societies, Japan does not have a tradition of viewing eloquence as a virtue. Rather, the society as a whole favors indirect speech patterns that use ambiguous expressions and allow the speaker to avoid taking responsibility. As detailed in **Chapters 3 and 4**, this might be one reason that Japanese politicians and government officials are inclined to talk vaguely and avoid disclosing their true thoughts and feelings in public even more than politicians in other countries.

Politicians and other public figures sometimes convey their thoughts, plans, and interpretations of political developments directly to their supporters or the general public, but the vast majority of their communication with constituents (and some of the communication among themselves) takes place through "public" channels such as television, radio, newspapers and websites.

As the primary sources of social and political information, the news media, in particular television and newspapers, have been playing an increasingly important role as the primary channels of political discourse. The news media define the news through their selection of issues to report on and their decisions about how to interpret the news and how to frame particular aspects of perceived reality. By reporting on political issues, events, and the activities of legislators, the news media not only inform the public but also affect political attitudes and behavior, and influence the way people (even young children in the process of socialization) construct their images and perceptions of the political world. Because of the growing impact of the news media, politicians and others try to control the scope and nature of information disseminated through these channels. As **Chapters 1, 2 and 3** reveal, political sources in Japan tend to filter the information they give to reporters and exploit the relationships they cultivate with journalists in order to affect media political rhetoric to their own advantage.

Political communication is not a one-way transaction: another significant factor in the political process is the political discourse that "ordinary citizens" use—both among themselves and toward the political elite—to construct and interpret various messages, ideological arguments, and opinions. "Pedestrian" members of the public play an important, dynamic role in the process of reproducing and transforming discourse not only through the language they use in everyday life but also because they can decode messages in ways not intended by decision-makers. They listen to what certain politicians say about specific issues because politics affects vital aspects of their lives, including health care, housing, welfare, and their standard of living. At the same time, the public also responds with language that communicates its needs, wishes, and expectations to those who control the public purse.

The overall social environment has a significant effect on how messages are produced, transmitted, received, and interpreted by both the political elite and the public. Culture dictates what is possible and not possible to say at a given time, and has a great bearing on the meaning and interpretation of messages. Political rhetoric, as this book points out, affects and is affected by the specific culture in which it is produced, shaped, transmitted, and perceived. Background on selected characteristics of the Japanese political culture is the focus of the following discussion.

"The Common Sense of Japanese Politics"

Perhaps one of the most significant concepts in Japanese political discourse is that of "*Nagatachô jôshiki*" (the common sense, or conventional wisdom, of *Nagatachô*), otherwise known as "*Nagatachô ronri*" (*Nagatachô* logic). "*Jôshiki*" is a shared understanding of knowledge and standards. "*Ronri*" means logic. Journalists and political analysts often use the terms *Nagatachô jôshiki* (e.g. *Asahi*, March 30, 1994) and *Nagatachô ronri* (e.g. *Asahi*, September 12, 1997; *Aera*, May 9, 1989) when they explain or interpret the activities or mood of Japanese politics. These terms suggest that common sense and logic are different in *Nagatachô* than they are elsewhere.

Journalists and political commentators employ the term *Nagatachô jôshiki* to imply that because the denizens of *Nagatachô*—Diet members, bureaucrats, policy secretaries, and party officials—have their own "logic"

or "common sense," their activities and agenda cannot always be understood according to the "logic" of "regular people," or the "common sense"
that is reflected in public opinion. To the average citizen, this unique
"logic" appears disconnected from everyday life and operates under a set
of unwritten, incomprehensible rules.

It is true that the activities of decision-makers in *Nagatachô* often do not
reflect the general attitudes or opinions that are prevalent among the
general public. For example, when Prime Minister (1998–2000) Obuchi
Keizô collapsed and was rushed to hospital in April 2000 (a few weeks
before he died), the general public was not informed of Obuchi's medical
condition until more than 20 hours after he was hospitalized. Also,
Obuchi's successor as Liberal Democratic Party [*Jiyûminshutô*] (LDP)
President and Prime Minister (2000–2001), Mori Yoshirô, was not
selected publicly or openly, but was chosen behind closed doors by only
five powerful LDP leaders.

The public was also outraged by Prime Minister Mori's nonchalant
response to news that the US nuclear submarine *Greeneville* had acciden-
tally sunk the *Ehime Maru*, a training ship used by a Japanese high school.
Voters also faulted Mori for his failure to express adequate concern about
Japan's protracted economic stagnation and falling stock prices, or about
a string of scandals involving LDP politicians, including allegations of
bribery, fraudulent use of government money, and questions over the *de
facto* ownership by Mori himself of a golf club membership. This last
scandal surfaced after it was reported that Mori kept on playing golf even
after he heard that the *Ehime Maru* had sunk and nine Japanese were
missing. After he was criticized for continuing his golf game, Mori said
"(What I was supposed to do) was not crisis management. . . because it
was merely an accident." Mori made a series of verbal and behavioral
gaffes (discussed in **Chapter 3**) that led the public to seriously doubt his
aptitude for governing the nation. By February 2001, close to 80 percent
of the public expressed suspicion or anxiety in regard to his administration. Yet the three-party ruling coalition of the LDP, New *Kômei* Party
[*Kômeitô*], and New Conservative Party [*Hoshutô Shintô*] supported him
against a no-confidence motion presented by opposition parties in the
House of Representatives (lower house of the Diet) on March 5. The
motion was rejected in a 274-to-192 vote. In other words, although the
overwhelming majority of the public opposed the Mori Cabinet, close to
60 percent of Diet members ignored them and supported the administration anyway. In other words, *Nagatachô ronri* enabled Prime Minister Mori
to stay in office.

There are several aspects to the special "logic" that characterizes the
behavior and attitudes of decision-makers in *Nagatachô*. One is the notion
that politics is numbers. In the example above, even though the majority
of the public distrusted the prime minister, the fate of his administration

was decided by members of his own political group. The larger the membership of this group, the more influence they could have on the decision-making process and its outcomes, regardless of whether their decisions reflected the general mood of the nation. Former Prime Minister (1972–74) Tanaka Kakuei explained the importance of numbers by metaphorically saying "numbers is power, power is money" ["*kazu wa chikara, chikara wa kane*"], (*Asahi*, December 17, 1993). Indeed, prominent features in the "common sense of *Nagatachô*" includes struggles among different political cliques (political parties and party factions) over both "numbers" and the increasing amount of money that entered the Japanese political system since 1970s. These struggles have led to rivalry and antagonism among political groups, and to the participation of many Diet members in unethical activities. The reflection of these aspects, particularly in political metaphors, is discussed in **Chapters 5 and 6**.

A second aspect of "*Nagatachô* logic" is the idea that political leaders, particularly the prime minister, serve merely as figureheads, while others wield the real power behind the scenes. The selection of Prime Minister Mori through backroom bargaining was by no means exceptional in *Nagatachô*—such bargaining has long typified Japanese politics. Moreover, because prime ministers (along with other Cabinet members and political appointees who lack their own clear policy goals or agenda) come and go while the issues and policies to be dealt with remains almost unchanged, *Nagatachô* is sometimes described as "*karaoke* politics" ["*karaoke seiji*"] or "*karaoke* democracy" ["*karaoke minshushugi*"]. That is, leaders in *Nagatachô* are like singers taking turns on a *karaoke* stage, one after another, while the songs and rhythms remain little changed as they are selected from a limited, static menu (Inoguchi, 1995). Because Japanese prime ministers rarely have original vision or ability to lead the nation, they are called "portable shrines" [*mikoshi*], like the miniature shrines carried on palanquins by crowds of bearers during traditional Japanese festivals. This feature of "*Nagatachô* logic" is discussed in **Chapters 6 and 7**. **Chapter 7** in particular reveals that the prime minister appears in editorial cartoons in two Japanese national dailies as a weak, passive man, relatively indecisive, confused and lacking in leadership ability. By portraying the prime minister in this way, the editorial cartoons reflect the reality of the prime minister's weak position within Japanese polity. They may also play an important role in affecting public attitudes and increasing alienation toward political institutions and leaders in Japan.

Perhaps the most important feature at the core of the "common sense of *Nagatachô*" is the idea that politics—including both political processes and authority—has a "two-layered power structure" ["*kenryoku no nijû-kôzô*"]. In the broad sense, this notion refers to the existence of two distinct aspects of Japanese social interaction: *honne*, meaning honest feelings, or the inner side of a subject that contains genuine intent, and *tatemae*, which is the "surface pretense," or the face that is presented to the outside. The invisible side of Japanese social (and political) processes is often called *de facto*, while the visible side is known as the *de jure*.

This two-sided structure also relates to the nature and importance of roles played by decision-makers, politicians, government officials, and others such as journalists who cover politics for leading news organs. For the most part, the twin concepts of *honne* and *tatemae* reflect the bifurcated quality of Japanese polity, in which everything has a front and a back. The real deal-making and decision-making processes take place in the back rooms. Only the outcomes are shown publicly. Johnson (1980) notes that there is always a discrepancy between formal and actual functioning of political institutions in a politically organized society. In Japan, historical factors caused this discrepancy to become a structural feature around which the polity evolved. Thus, while the discrepancy between façade and substance is found also in other societies, it is more pronounced in Japan and may be the single most important feature to be considered by any political analyst examining Japanese politics. A detailed account on the linguistics implications of these concepts is offered in **Chapter 3**.

The last facet of *Nagatachô* common sense to be discussed here is concerning political journalism, in particular the way political information is gathered from a selected group of sources and the way this information is distributed to the public. I have detailed related features in *Politics and the News Media in Japan* (Feldman, 1993a). The key concept here is that the flow of news is tightly controlled through the Japanese press club system. Each press club is a formal association of reporters who cover one beat, at one location. The press clubs give reporters easy access to sources, information, gossip, and leads. Reporters have relatively easy access to the country's most powerful government officials, including the prime minister. They meet with these individuals not only in their offices and in the Diet Building, but also at party headquarters, government bureaus, in the Prime Minister's Official Residence, and even in restaurants, on golf courses, or in legislators' private residences.

But these privileges are subject to several conditions that oblige reporters to constantly adjust their work to conform to the expectations of their information sources, who end up exercising significant control over the content of political coverage. Politicians expect that most of the information they give reporters about things they favor and support will be passed on to the public. Politicians and officials actively encourage discussion and promote stories about pet issues by explicitly expressing their desire to see related stories in the newspapers or in television reports. They frequently channel the attention of reporters to issues they want put on the national agenda, by leaking information that serves their own ends either directly, or indirectly by distracting attention from troublesome issues. The daily work of Japanese political reporters is characterized by close and constant contact with information sources in *Nagatachô*, by an excessive dependency on these sources, and by a tendency to pay more attention to *who* is talking rather than to *what* is being said. Sources of national political information are limited to a small pool of individuals at the helm of political parties or party factions, and most news-gathering efforts concentrate on covering the select few at the top who have inside information. Long-time association with these sources determines not only the prism through which reporters view the political world, but also the active and crucial role that reporters play in the Japanese political process.

Political Journalism: Reflecting Changes in the Political Landscape

Since the publication of *Politics and the News Media in Japan* in 1993, Japan has experienced significant changes in its administrative structure, electoral systems, and political party configuration. These changes have in turn affected the structure and functioning of political groups and party factions, and the selection of the country's prime minister and other high-echelon politicians. To a certain degree, even the "common sense of *Nagatachô*" has been altered. The resulting changes in political awareness and climate have affected political discourse in the broad sense, including political reporters' newsgathering styles, their interaction with information sources, and the focus of their attention. Several factors contributed to this trend.

First, 1993 marked the end of 38 years of continuous single-party rule by the LDP, and the start of a new era of coalition governments. In August 1993, a coalition of anti-LDP parties formed a government headed by Hosokawa Morihiro. This first coalition lasted only eight months, but it was followed by a string of governments consisting of various combinations of political parties, some of which had fleeting life-spans. The LDP did regain power in 1994, but only in partnership with allies in coalition governments. Since 1993, no single party has managed to steer the government of Japan.

The appearance of various coalition administrations including members of diverse political groups has introduced something new to *Nagatachô*: *a pluralism of views* regarding policy issues and the national political agenda. Throughout the decade that followed the historic fall of the LDP's unquestioned hegemony, members of the various ruling coalitions have engaged in debate and negotiation over policies and legislation to a degree never seen before in Japanese politics.

While the LDP monopolized Japanese political power from 1955 to 1993, just a handful of party leaders determined policy matters, personnel matters, and strategy. This elite included former Prime Minister Tanaka

Kakuei and Prime Minister Takeshita Noboru (1987–89), and former Vice Prime Minister Kanemaru Shin. Special terms described these politicians' power, such as "Kingmaker" [*kingumeekâ*], "Takeshita Calender" [*Takeshita karendâ*], "Kanemaru Whisper" [*kanemaru sasayaki*], "Kanemaru murmur" [*kanemaru tsubuyaki*], or "Kanemaru soliloquy" [*kanemaru hitorigoto*]. The latter three imply that Kanemaru had the power to decide issues or agendas merely by whispering or murmuring.

During that era, conventional wisdom dictated that reporters focus their efforts on only few individuals—including faction leaders, key ministers, and other veteran politicians who were close to the top people—who could provide reporters with detailed information and interpretations of political events. The sources' high positions made the information they provided appear to be very valuable; stories were deemed to be more newsworthy, and thus were more likely to make headlines in the next edition of the news, in proportion to the loftiness of the source. In other words, the "quality" or "weight" of the political language was judged according to *who* the speaker was, rather than *what* was said. Diet members often provided reporters with trivial information that had no significance to daily politics. But because it was obtained from a particular Diet member, reporters tended to attach great importance to such information, and the mass media would use it as a news item. Although some high-level Diet members tended to use abstract, muddled expressions that people could not understand, reporters relied on these individuals and cited them daily in their political stories. One such politician was former prime minister Takeshita, who was ridiculed for his *gengo meiryô imi fumeiryô* (literally, "clear language, unclear meaning"). Well aware of reporters' utter dependence on them for information, senior Diet members took advantage by controlling the perspective of the news that reached the public.

Once coalition governments emerged in the 1990s, authority was no longer in the hands of a limited number of politicians and the situation gradually started to change. Because a number of parties are now partners in a government dominated by the LDP, the LDP has no choice but to discuss and adjust its stance on issues in order to get measures passed. So even the tiny New Conservative Party, which only had 14 members in the Diet as of October 2003, could have a say in the political process and play a decisive role in making certain decisions. The involvement of more political groups and individuals in the political process made reporters' work more complex, as they now need to gather information from all involved parties in order to present adequate political coverage.

Another change since 1993 is a tremendous increase in the political influence wielded by "young" Diet members, i.e. those with less political experience. This has greatly altered reporters' interactions with information sources. Traditionally, the LDP awarded Cabinet posts and committee chairmanships based on the number of times a legislator had been elected. This mirrored other arenas of Japanese society, where, for example, companies promoted employees largely on the basis of the length of their employment. So reporters sought to interview the more experienced politicians, because they were the ones who had direct knowledge and experience of political events, and more access to a wide variety of political information. There was a direct correlation between the number of times a legislator was elected to the Diet and the number of times he or she met with reporters during a given time span (Feldman, 1993a: 37).

After the 1993 elections, however, 129 (out of 511) newly elected lower house Diet members had no political experience at the national level. The newcomers included Shii Kazuo, leader of the Japanese Communist Party [Kyôsantô] (JCP), and Ôta Akihiro, a powerful leader in the Kômei Party. After the election of 2000, only 17 of the 127 Diet members belonging to the Democratic Party of Japan [Minshutô] (DPJ) had been elected more than four times. In their search for political information and clues to understanding the moods within political parties, reporters were forced to rely on less experienced politicians. This influx of younger politicians not only drastically changed the working style of Japanese political reporters, it also affected the nature of the language used in Nagatachô politics both for communicating with other politicians and with the general public.

A second factor that affected political discourse was the weakening of the LDP's factions. Restrictions on donations to individual politicians were instituted in 1994, and a new electoral system was introduced in 1996. These changes reduced the power of LDP faction leaders, and reduced the significance of the role that the factions play in the political process. Detailed discussion in this regard is presented in the following chapter. Factions, which were at the center of the LDP's political framework, effecting the selection of the party leaders and Cabinet ministers, became in fact venues for exchanging information, and in 1999 were recognized as "policy groups" [porishi gurupu or seisaku shûdan]. In 2003 there were eight "policy groups" in the LDP: Heisei Kenkyûkai (Hashimoto Faction); Kôchi-kai (former Katô Faction); Kôchi-kai (Horiuchi Faction); Seiwa Seisaku Kenkyûkai (Mori Faction); Shisui-kai (Etô – Kamei Faction); Kinmirai Seiji Kenkyûkai (Yamasaki Faction); Banchô Seisaku Kenkyûjo (Kômura Faction); Taiyû-kai (Kônô Group). (Two are named Kôchi-kai both claim to be the descendants of the faction that was established by former Prime Minister Ikeda Hayato (1960–64) and which was led by Ôhira Masayoshi and Miyazawa Kiichi). Since 2000, each of these factions has a position such as Chairman of Policy [seisaku iinchô], or Chairman of Policy Department [seisaku kyokuchô] and often discuss policy matters. Factions invite university professors, economics, intellectuals and government officials for lectures and exchange of opinions over policy issues and policy-making, and announce their policy proposals and suggestions for improvements through leaflets, manuscripts, and even books which are sold to the general public. One of such books is "*Hito tzukuri wa kuni no konkan desu! Kyôiku kihonhô kaisei e itsutsu no teigen*" (Creating People its the Country Bare Bones: Five Proposals to Revise the Fundamentals of the Education Law," published by *Chûkei Shuppan*) which was written by members of the Mori faction in 2002.

A third factor that contributed to redirecting reporters' attention and altering their selection of information sources was the emergence of the House of Councillors, or the upper house of the Diet, as a strong factor in the political process. The effects on political discourse resulting from this change are discussed in **Chapter 2**.

Yet another factor was the major reorganization of the central government ministries and agencies that took place in January 2001. This not only affected the political news sources to which reporters gave their attention, it necessitated structural and logistic adjustments on the part of the media as ministries and agencies were reconfigured. The reforms were aimed at strengthening the functions of the Cabinet and making the national government more efficient and transparent. For example, the Cabinet Law was amended to allow "not more than fourteen" Ministers of State (with a provision for appointing up to three more in special situations), whereas in the past the maximum number of ministers allowed had been 20. Each Ministry and Agency now has one or two Parliamentary Vice-Ministers and one Administrative Vice-Minister who help form policies and supervise the workings of the ministry's various divisions and branches.

The 2001 reorganization also established the Cabinet Office [*naikaku-fu*] as an administrative organ with the twofold role of assisting the Cabinet and the prime minister, and administering the Office's affairs, in a manner similar to the other Ministries. The Prime Minister heads the Cabinet Office, with a Chief Cabinet Secretary, Ministers for Special Missions, Deputy Cabinet Secretaries, two Senior Vice-Ministers, and three Parliamentary Secretaries below him. There are also four councils established under the Cabinet Office umbrella. These are the Council on Economic and Fiscal Policy; the Council for Science and Technology Policy; the Central Disaster Prevention Council; and the Council for Gender Equality. The councils are made up of ministers related to each topic and experts appointed by the Prime Minister. The councils are headed either by the Prime Minister or the Chief Cabinet Secretary and are designed to supplement the functions of the Cabinet Office and the Prime Minister.

The last factor which has affected reporters' newsgathering and the nature of their contacts with information sources, as well as other important aspects of the "common sense of *Nagatachô*" and political discourse, was the selection of Koizumi Junichirô as prime minister. Koizumi established new standards for leadership with respect to policy and national politicians' dealings with colleagues, rivals, and especially the news media.

His attitudes *vis-à-vis* political reporters, as discussed in **Chapter 2**, have affected their routine newsgathering methods and led journalists to adopt new practices in their coverage of the national leader.

As prime minister, Koizumi has demonstrated that he has media savvy, communication skills, and vision. He won the LDP presidential race against opposition from the party's old guard because of his promises of reform. Koizumi's reform platform amounted to what he described as a "dissolution of the party." He promised to disband the LDP factions that had long dominated Japanese politics, and to "change the LDP" to make a "fresh start." Rather than allowing backstage power brokers to choose the members of his administration on the basis of the relative strength of intra-party factions (the LDP's traditional method), he personally selected people based on their expertise and suitability for realizing the goals of his administration. Koizumi created a stir by choosing an economics professor with no political experience to determine economic policy and fiscal reforms. Koizumi also broke with tradition in the arena of public speaking by personally deciding on the content of the inaugural policy speech that he gave in the Diet in May 2001. In this speech he reiterated his determination to carry out structural reform of the nation's political, administrative, financial, and social systems "without being constrained by sacred cows." In order to gain the broadest audience for his speech, Koizumi limited it to about 6,500 words, or almost half the length of the speech former Prime Minister Mori delivered in January 2001.

Realizing that both strong leadership and public dialogue are crucial to securing understanding and support for his administration, Koizumi initiated "town meetings" in each of the nation's 47 prefectures. At these meetings, Cabinet ministers explained the policymaking process, in order to increase public understanding and awareness of various issues. Koizumi has paid a great deal of attention to media coverage and engaged in constant dialogue with the public to make himself more visible than any of his predecessors had. In May 2001, he began giving daily press briefings, which had rarely been done before by a Japanese prime minister. Eventually, his snappy sound bites and dapper style made him the hottest topic on television. Television audience ratings of live broadcasts of Diet sessions at which Koizumi appeared were higher than before. In order to extend his contact with the public even further, Koizumi approached sports newspapers and other publications that are not considered mainstream journalism in Japan, and granted them interviews although reporters from such journals are not allowed to attend press club conferences. Most often this gesture resulted in favorable coverage.

Koizumi also launched a weekly electronic magazine called "Lion Heart," named after his distinctive leonine hairstyle. The publication includes a column written by the prime minister himself as well as messages from other Cabinet members and information about the administration's policies. In the initial edition, Prime Minister Koizumi wrote, "Many people only know me as an eccentric with leonine hair. I want you to learn more about the real face of the Koizumi cabinet from this magazine. My cabinet is pushing for reform. Successful reform calls for dialogue with each and every one of you." The magazine attracted 780,000 subscribers for its inaugural issue, with the number quickly growing to more than 2 million and earning a place in the *Guinness Book of World Records*. Public opinion surveys conducted in 2001 and 2003 showed that the percentage of respondents who supported Koizumi's government increased from 70 percent to 90 percent, making him the most well-liked Japanese prime minister ever.

It was during this period of change that I gathered data and wrote this book. The following chapters reflect the political climate of this transitional period in Japanese history—a time of change that has affected not only the structure and function of political institutions, but also the ways in which Japanese politicians and government officials communicate about political matters.

The Nagatachô Beat: Writing with Wolves

As political communicators, politicians use language as an important tool for informing the public about their political views and decisions, for explaining political issues and revealing goals, and in public deliberation. Public debate between rival political groups entails not just disputing facts related to public policy, but also competing to supply the interpretation of a given issue that best resonates with public opinion. This kind of debate frequently focuses on which facts, beliefs, or other considerations are most important. News media play a decisive role in this process as political communicators vie for public attention and support. Over the years, discussion of the role played by the mass media has underlined the fact that the media, especially television and newspapers, have exerted increasing influence over political behavior and attitudes through their reporting on political issues, events, and the activities of politicians. Individual citizens construct their images of, and attitudes toward, the political world and politicians largely based on information received via the mass media.

Obviously, politicians who serve as information sources—i.e. who supply media representatives with information—are able to influence the news so that their views frame the reporting of events. Information sources develop a sense of what kinds of things reporters consider to be news-worthy and 'help' them to collect this information. Not only do they identify events for reporters and provide the information reporters need to write their stories, but they also tell reporters which events might have more significance for other politicians, government agencies or political parties or in the deliberations of the Diet. Decision-makers devote much time and effort to supplying reporters with subtle and not-so-subtle suggestions regarding the understanding and evaluation of political affairs, and the decision-making process. Many experienced politicians realize the value of using the media as a forum for building a personal political following. They know the deadlines for newspapers and the broadcast schedules of the media they consider to be most important, and they endeavor to influence the timing and content of information conveyed to the public.

As high-echelon politicians become experts in the legislative process, they also become adept media manipulators who have cultivated techniques for luring reporters and influencing coverage, as well as for persuading the public. Former Prime Minister Hosokawa Morihiro (1993–94) is an example of a politician who manipulated the media very carefully. He sometimes chose odd hours, such as very early morning, for addressing reporters about policy issues, and he was the first Japanese prime minister to stand, rather than sit, when talking with reporters, which effectively meant talking with the public when a press conference was broadcast live. Hosokawa decided to stand during press conferences because he realized that sitting gave a bad impression. He also changed the curtain at the back of the press conference room in his official residence from light gray to blue, to make his image more conspicuous on television screens. Moreover, Hosokawa was the first Japanese prime minister to use a teleprompter, which allowed him to read his notes while looking straight ahead at reporters and television cameras, without having to look down. This made it look like he was talking to the public directly and spontaneously, instead of reading from prepared memos. In addition, he instructed producers on the positioning of their television cameras, and was sensitive to the angle from which photographers approached him. In order to gain international recognition, Hosokawa produced a 13-minute promotional video in English. Entitled "Morihiro Hosokawa: A New Prime Minister for a New Era," it depicted both his personal life from childhood, and his political ideas and career.

Of course, reporters are not simply passive players in the newsgathering process. They also search out information and exercise their own sense of what is 'newsworthy,' turning their attention toward some topics and away from others. They consider a particular news event's potential effects on the political process from a broad perspective, and often include in their stories their own interpretation of unfolding events and political dynamics. The way they gather their information is of crucial significance to the content of the stories they disseminate to the public, and ultimately to public discourse regarding public affairs. In this regard, it is particularly important to consider *who* dispenses political information to the media, *what* types of information are conveyed, and *how* reporters gather and process information. This chapter and the following one look at newsgathering methods used in Japan. **Chapter 3** goes into greater detail about information sources available to reporters, and which information gets transferred through the news media to the public. These information sources are examined in light of factors that have affected political journalism and discourse in the recent past, including changes in the roles played by LDP factions, the weakening of faction bosses, and the emergence of Koizumi Junichiro as prime minister.

Organization and Structure of the Press Clubs

Japan's political elite interacts frequently and consistently with media representatives, largely through Japanese-style press clubs called *kisha kurabu* (literally "reporters' clubs"). The *kisha* club system is a major cause of "pack journalism" whereby most reporters pursue the same targets most of the time. This system, and the media's desire to maintain an appearance of nonpartisan objectivity (all major Japanese newspapers have pledged to adhere to a policy of "impartiality, political neutrality, and fairness"), have relegated political reporters to the role of messengers who passively convey information from leading Diet members to the general public. This in turn has led to the homogenization of domestic political news in Japan.

A press club is a formal association of reporters assigned to one beat. Each of perhaps 1,000 different divisions of Japan's government, courts, police, political parties and major economic organizations have allocated a large room for use by the reporters who have been assigned to cover that entity for their news organizations. This room is where the "club" meets: it's where reporters gather to receive briefings, handouts, press releases and other communications, where they interact with information sources, and where they write stories about the organization they cover. *Kisha* clubs are often located on the second or third floor of a government agency or party headquarters, near the office of the organization's head—the minister or Secretary General. A club may have as few as a dozen reporters or as many as 400, depending on the nature of the agency and its importance.

Japanese *kisha* clubs are similar to the Lobby, a formal association of journalists working out of the Palace of Westminster, which is considered to be the key mechanism through which political information from government finds it way into the public domain in the UK. But the Japanese *kisha* club is not simply a mechanism for gathering information. It is a social setting to which reporters belong. Within this setting, reporters make friends, pass on gossip, and share secrets. In Japan, the *kisha* club shapes the relationship between information sources and reporters, affects the content of information provided to reporters and from reporters to the general public, and the public discourse.

Unlike press clubs in most other countries, which are organized and sponsored by information sources, Japanese press clubs are organized and managed by news media associations: the Japan Newspaper Publishers and Editors Association [*Nihon Shimbun Kyôkai*], which is entirely independent and voluntary institute funded and operated by the mass media of Japan, or the National Association of Commercial Broadcasters in Japan [*Nihon Minkan Hôsô Renmei*]. Membership in these clubs, and consequently access to important news sources, has traditionally been limited to mainstream journalists, which means the representatives of 153 compa-

nies—111 daily newspapers, four news agencies and 38 broadcasters—
that belong to the above-mentioned associations of the Japanese media (as
of July 2002). Almost all of these 153 companies are affiliated with one of
five media conglomerates, which publish Japan's nationwide newspapers:
the *Yomiuri*, *Asahi*, *Mainichi*, *Sankei*, and *Nihon Keizai*. Together, these
conglomerates circulate 39.6 million newspapers every day (55.9 percent
of the 70.8 million copies circulated by Japanese dailies, or one newspaper
for every 1.09 people, *Nihon Shimbun Kyôkai*, 2002) representing the most
thorough dissemination of newspapers in the world.

These five publishers also own weekly and monthly magazines, sports
tabloids, local newspapers, and television stations. The highly concentrated nature of Japanese media contributes to its collective ability to
control the flow of information and to influence attitudes and behaviors.
In addition, there are four "bloc" newspapers—*Chûnichi*, *Tôkyô*, *Nishi
Nippon*, and *Hokkaidô*—which each serve a limited region, and six major
broadcasting networks—five commercial ones[1] and NHK [*Nippon Hôsô
Kyôkai*], or Japan Broadcasting Corporation, a nonprofit state broadcasting corporation. There are also two news agencies, *Kyôdô* News
Service and *Jiji* Press.

The nine major newspapers mentioned above (i.e. the big five plus the
four bloc newspapers), the nation's six television networks (NHK, NTV,
TBS, Fuji TV, TV Asahi and TV Tôkyô), and the two news agencies
together comprise *jôchû-jûnanasha* (literally, the 17 companies permanently located in the clubs), whose reporters belong to almost every major
press club and dominate the press clubs as a whole. Each company pays a
monthly membership fee [*kurabu kaihi*] of about 600 yen per reporter,
which entitles its representatives to participate in the *kisha* club's activities.

Reporters who work for political parties, religious organizations, unions,
periodicals, and the foreign press have traditionally been barred from
joining the *kisha* clubs. In recent years, foreign news organizations have
loudly complained that it is virtually impossible to gather significant news
from important organizations in Japan without going through the *kisha*
club. As a result, a few *kisha* clubs began allowing non-members, including
foreign correspondents, to attend news conferences.

"Pack Journalism" and the Homogenization of News

Within each *kisha* club, reporters generally face the same access to
resources. All reporters witness the same events on their assigned beat, and
receive the same briefings and handouts. All are exposed to news sources
at the same time, either during formal press conferences or in relaxed background briefings held regularly by top officials. The reporters in each club
take turns handling administrative tasks, with two or three at a time serving

as secretaries (*kanji*), usually for a term of about a month or two. Their work includes mediation and coordination between the reporters and the sources of information—Diet members or government officials—they are covering, and organizational matters related to the reporters' work. In particular, one of the secretaries' task is to collect the questions that reporters intend to ask, especially in advance of press conferences to be aired live on television, presenting these questions to the sources, and negotiating who gets to ask which questions. For their efforts, each secretary gets the privilege of asking one of the first questions.

In the clubs, reporters are bound by certain rules and transgressors of these rules may be punished for "damaging the press club's friendship and honor," sometimes by being excluded from the club [*tôin teishi*]. The specific rules vary, but always are aimed at preventing friction between news sources and reporters, and preventing news sources from feeling discomfort or irritation. Most *kisha* clubs have a "blackboard agreement" [*kokuban kyôtei*]. Each club has a blackboard listing upcoming events related to the agency being covered, including scheduled meetings of the head of the agency, planned press conferences and announcements about topics to be discussed. The "blackboard agreement" stipulates that reporters will not write stories based on the information on this board, including, for example, the fact that an official is scheduled to explain a particular issue a few days later.

Another example of a *kisha* club rule is that reporters respect news sources' wishes regarding identification of the source of specific information. There are various reasons why a Diet member might not want his or her name associated with a particular piece; some of these reasons are explained in **Chapter 3**. Reporters and news sources cooperate to keep sources out of trouble by clearly distinguishing between information that may be openly attributed to the source ["*on reko*" in Japanese journalistic jargon] and information that cannot ["*offu reko*"]. During press conferences, for example, news sources such as the Chief Cabinet Secretary or a particular minister give on-the-record information that may be cited in newspapers as coming from the particular individual. When information is revealed under different circumstances, reporters generally will not reveal the exact source. There are separate rules applied to exclusive interviews with high-ranking Diet members or officials, and reporters exercise special self-restraint regarding information pertaining to the imperial family.

These protocols force reporters to conform with colleagues in rival news organizations, and to cooperate while looking for newsworthy stories. They often discuss current events among themselves, reaffirming their understanding of the news, exchanging information, and collectively composing an outline of the story they will all file. This Japanese-style pack journalism may not produce towering intellectual achievements or investigative coups, but it seems to satisfy editors because no news agency runs the risk of being the only one to run a story that may later prove incorrect. The result of this sharing of collective interpretations of public events in press clubs is a media that is united in its interpretation of reality.

Nagata Kurabu

There are over 40 press clubs in Tôkyô alone. The largest and most important press club is the *Nagata* Club, or the *Kantei* ([Prime Minister's] Official Residence). The club is located on the first floor in the Prime Minister's new Official Residence. Located near the Diet Building in *Nagatachô*, the building was completed in 2001. The press club consists of a huge room about 40 meters long and ten meters wide. It is only a few meters away from the press conference room where the prime minister and the Chief Cabinet Secretary hold important conferences. On the wall just to the left of the entrance, there are two big boards labeled "Cabinet Secretariat Notice Board" [*naikaku kanbô keijiban*] with announcements and information related to the Prime Minister's Office and the schedules of politicians and officials who work in the building, including the Chief Cabinet Secretary and his deputies. On the wall to the right is an electronic display showing the names of the officials who work in the Prime Minister Office—including the prime minister, the Chief Cabinet Secretary, the three Deputy Chief Cabinet Secretaries, the Chief of the Cabinet Legislative Bureau, the prime minister's assistants, members of the Cabinet Office [*naikakufu*], and the five secretaries of the prime minister. When any of these officials enters his or her office in the Prime Minister's Office, their name lights up and all the press club members can see that they are in the building. As soon as they leave the building, the lamp illuminating their name is turned off.

On the left side of the clubroom, there are desks, sofas, armchairs, two televisions sets, and two large beverage vending machines. This is where reporters rest, read the news, watch television, and nap. The right side of the room is partitioned into niches for the various news organizations in the club. Each niche has about ten workspaces for reporters, and a TV set that is usually on whenever reporters are in the club so they can follow breaking news. There is a "common space" in the center of the room that reporters can also use when they write their stories.

Nagata Club is the number one spot in coverage and corresponding visibility for the reporters. It has close to 400 members, representing about 70 agencies of the news media. They are responsible for covering virtually every activity of the Cabinet and the prime minister, and of the politicians and officials who work at the Prime Minister's Official Residence. This includes the Chief Cabinet Secretary, two or three Deputy Chief Cabinet

Secretaries and their assistants, and the Prime Minister's private secretaries (one each from the Foreign Ministry, the Finance Ministry, the Ministry of Economy, Trade and Industry, and the Police, and one personal secretary).

This *kisha* club became more important than ever following the January 2001 reorganization of the central government, especially due to the establishment of the Cabinet Office, with four councils underneath it: the Council on Economic and Fiscal Policy; the Council for Science and Technology Policy; the Central Disaster Prevention Council; and the Council for Gender Equality. Meetings of the most important council—on Economic and Fiscal Policy [*Keizai Zaisei Shimon Kaigi*] that focuses on issues related to economic policies which are central to Koizumi's administration—take place in the Prime Minister Office's, so reporters in the *Nagata* Club are also responsible for covering it.

Hirakawa Kurabu

Second to the *Nagata* Club in importance is the *Hirakawa* Club, which has almost 150 reporters. The *Hirakawa* Club (also called *Yotô*, or "Ruling Party" Club) is located in the LDP headquarters in the *Hirakawachô* district, close to *Nagatachô* and facing the Diet Building. When the Diet is in session, the club members shift their location to one of two press clubs in the Diet Building: one covering the lower house and the other the upper house. On the second floor of the Diet building, the *Yotô* Club uses two big rooms. As in the *Nagata* Club, each news company has its own niche. The clubrooms are connected to another small room where reporters gather daily to hear the LDP's Secretary General give briefings in front of the LDP logo when the Diet is in session.

Traditionally, reporters in the *Hirakawa* Club only covered events related to the LDP and its leading members. Since the advent of coalition governments, however, they also cover the LDP's coalition partners. As of this writing, that means the New *Kômei* Party, with particular focus on the top leaders in this party—the Chief Representative, the Secretary Generals, and the Chairman of the Policy Research Council.

At the top of the list of LDP politicians covered by *Hirakawa* Club reporters are the party's "three leading officials" [*san'yaku*]: the Secretary General [*kanji-chô*], the Chairman of the Executive Council [*sômu-kaichô*], and the Chairman of the Policy Affairs Research Council [*seimuchôsa-kaichô*]. The LDP Secretary General is considered to be the second most important post in the party, following that of the party president (*sôsai*) who is also the prime minister. The Secretary General is in charge of all party affairs, from election-related issues to daily administration of the party. The Chairman of the Executive Council manages the party's basic policies, which includes the adjustment of policies and decisions. The Chairman of the Policy Affairs Research Council is charged with reviewing policies. The next object of the reporters' attention is the Chairman of the Diet Policy Committee [*kokkai taisaku iinchô*], who focuses on the functioning of the Diet and negotiations with representatives of other parties. Last but not least are the LDP faction leaders and rank-and-file members.

Two trends that dramatically affected the *Hirakawa* Club reporters during the 1990s were the decline of the LDP factions and the emergence of the upper house as an important player in the political process.

Weakening of LDP Factions and their Leaders

Since the 1950s, the LDP effectively governed as a coalition of intra-party factions whose bosses had a fair degree of autonomy. Each faction maintained its own internal structure, trained promising members to be the future party president/prime minister, and encouraged identification with the faction and solidarity [*danketsu*] among all members. As a result, Diet members were more loyal to their faction and its leader than they were to the party as a whole. Each faction held regular weekly meetings where they practiced "*itchi kessoku hako bentô*" (literally, building solidarity while eating boxed lunches). This practice symbolized the solidarity and teamwork that was vital to the survival of the faction and its ability to win positions of power and influence.

The LDP was able to sustain about five factions at once because there were multi-seat districts for lower house elections, which meant that different factions could successfully field candidates within the same district. But in January 1994, the Diet introduced a new electoral system that combines single-member districts and regional blocks of seats assigned by proportional representation. This was enacted along with new regulations governing political donations, government funding for political parties, and the institution of a special legal status for political parties. Together, these four reforms stripped the factions of their significance as a source of backing at the district level. They eventually made the factions irrelevant and diminished the authority of faction leaders (often called *oyaji* or "boss"). As the factions lost strength and influence, the media began to pay less attention to them and their bosses.

The LDP presidential election of April 2001 was a good indication of the extent to which the factions have lost their grip on Japanese politics. As leader of the most powerful faction, former Prime Minister Hashimoto Ryûtarô (1996–98) was considered to be the most promising candidate, but was rejected on the grounds that he was "inept." His faction was created by former Prime Minister Tanaka and later led by Prime Ministers Takeshita and Obuchi; it strongly influenced LDP presidential elections for more than 20 years due to its numerical strength and firm solidarity. In

2001, however, Prime Minister Koizumi Junichiro won the overwhelming support of the party without relying on any faction's strength. His victory strongly suggested that the traditional method of electing LDP presidents—by holding a contest of factional strength—was no longer operational.

In September 2003, the Hashimoto faction split over which candidate to support in an LDP presidential election, further highlighting the collapse of the party's old faction-based framework. The Hashimoto faction's 101 members accounted for 30 percent of all LDP members in the Diet, but it failed to field any official candidate because of a disagreement between two of the faction's heavyweights—former LDP Secretary General Nonaka Hiromu and the Secretary General of LDP members in the upper house, Aoki Mikio. Nonaka opposed Prime Minister Koizumi's reform agenda and called for his replacement as party leader, but Aoki wished to see him reelected in light of his popularity among voters. As a result, the faction effectively allowed its members to vote as they pleased although one faction member had announced his candidacy.

Meanwhile, the 51-member faction led by Horiuchi Mitsuo, Chairman of the LDP's General Council, could manage neither to field its own official candidate nor to form a consensus on whom to support. Like the Hashimoto faction, the Horiuchi faction decided to allow its members to vote as they pleased. The formerly strong solidarity of the faction jointly led by Etô Takami, former Management and Coordination Agency Director General, and Kamei Shizuka, former Chairman of the LDP Policy Research Council, was shaken when several members supported Koizumi's reelection although the faction fielded Kamei as its candidate.

Historically, there had been three main benefits from faction membership: support from fellow faction members in elections, a share of the group's funds, and the chance of being appointed to a Cabinet or party post. But the allure of all three was lessened by the reform legislation initiated during the Hosokawa administration. As a result of the 1994 reform of lower house elections, candidates began to have to look to the whole party for support in elections, rather than looking to just one faction. Until 1996, the lower house electoral districts were called "medium-sized," with three to five Diet members elected from each constituency. A party that wanted to win a majority in the lower house and control the Diet had to field multiple candidates in each constituency. This meant that candidates from the same party competed against each other in a single district. This system bred antagonism within the parties and fostered the growth of intraparty factions. The LDP eventually lost its identity as a party and became simply a collection of competing groups, each aimed at helping its leader become the party president (and Japan's prime minister).

The current electoral system includes both single-member districts and a proportional representation system. In a single-member district, candidates compete on an individual basis and the one who receives the most votes represents his or her district alone. Under the proportional representation system, only parties, not individual candidates, campaign for seats. Each party submits a list of candidates who it will send and winning candidates are determined in accordance with the number of votes each party receives. Under the single-seat system, it is not the faction but the party leadership that decides who to field in each district and how to distribute the party's campaign money. This has considerably weakened the authority and influence of the factions.

Tighter restrictions on political donations from individuals have also weakened the influence of the LDP factions by decreasing the amount of funds their leaders can distribute to faction members. Traditionally, faction leaders had tremendous authority in their factions due to their ability to collect money that they distributed to the members of the faction for use in election campaigns and daily political activities. Within the faction, the leader's word was law. The reform package of 1994 imposed strict restrictions on political donations from companies to individual Diet members in order to prevent "money-for-influence" scandals, which were then widespread. To increase the importance of parties within the political system, it was deemed necessary to destroy politicians' sources of financial independence and to increase their dependence on party headquarters for financial assistance. As of January 2000, corporations, labor unions, and other organizations have been prohibited from donating to individual Diet members. Faction bosses had already been scrambling for funding because of the long recession that hit businesses so hard, but now they are no longer allowed to raise funds to distribute among faction members.

As faction leaders lost power, faction members became freer to express their opinions independently, whereas previously they had been tightly constrained. Especially the younger, less experienced members became more outspoken, sometimes even openly expressing frustration with attitudes held by their faction's leader, or criticizing his views. Political reporters rely on these members for inside information concerning the factions.

The last factor that has enfeebled the LDP factions was the loss of their ability to allocate positions of power, such as ministerial posts or executive positions within the party. Formerly, such positions were distributed according to the size of each faction: the largest faction was given the most numerous and most important positions. However, Prime Minister Koizumi has steadfastly refused to accept factional recommendations in appointing Cabinet ministers and party executives. When Koizumi chose his original team in 2001, he shattered LDP tradition by declining to select members based on the relative strength of the factions. Moreover, Koizumi decided not to appoint anyone from the Hashimoto faction (as noted above, the largest and traditionally most influential faction) to any of the three key party executive posts: Secretary General, Chairman of the Executive Council, and Chairman of the Policy Research Council. In addition, Koizumi dramatically changed the LDP's decision-making processes. Traditionally, a handful of party heavy-weights had been able to influence virtually every decision made in the name of the LDP. But in May 2001, Koizumi adopted a new approach that emphasizes the intra-party divisions rather than the unofficial, but powerful party factions. As a result of Koizumi's supra-factional decision-making style, the boundary between mainstream and non-mainstream factions has blurred, and the rivalry between the factions has diminished. This has also affected reporters' work, as explained later. Now called "policy groups," the erst-while factions have been transformed into venues for exchanging opinions about policy issues.

The Emergence of the Upper House as a Strong Factor in the Political Process

Another development that had a major impact on the work of political reporters was the emergence of the upper house of the Diet, traditionally considered less important, as a strong factor in the political process. The two houses of Japan's national legislature have nearly equal powers, and voters directly elect the members of both, but each house has a different basis for qualifications. Although the upper and lower houses share power, the latter predominates in decisions such as appointing the prime minister, drafting the budget, and approving of international treaties, and can secure passage of bills which have been voted down by the upper house with a two-thirds majority. For many years, the upper house was derided as a "carbon copy of the lower house" [*sangiin wa shûin no kâbon copi*], (Saikawa, 1999: 51) and for failing to play a unique role in the Diet. In order to pass a piece of legislation, it is necessary to secure either a two-thirds majority in the lower house, or an absolute majority in both houses. Over the years, the LDP's strategy has been to seek a majority in both houses because winning a two-thirds majority in the lower house was too difficult.

After the 1989 upper house election, however, things changed. Thanks to increasing dissatisfaction among the public regarding politics in general and certain issues in particular—such as the *Recruit* Scandal, the extra-marital affairs of Prime Minister Uno Sôsuke (June–August 1989), the introduction of a consumption tax, and the LDP's agricultural reform policy—the LDP lost its upper house majority for the first time since World War II. Fifty-four LDP seats were at stake in the election, but the party won only 35. The largest opposition party, the Social Democratic Party of Japan [*Shkaitô* or *Shamintô*] (SDP), won 73 seats (up from 41) at the expense of the LDP and smaller political parties. After that, the LDP could not pass laws as easily as it used to. In the 1998 upper house election, the LDP only took 44 seats. Combined with the 46 seats it gained in the 1995 election, this gave the party only gave 90 of the total of 252 seats in the upper house. Even with the help of conservative independents, the New Frontier Party (*Shinshintô*, a short-lived party that disbanded in 1997) and the Liberal Party [*Jiyûtô*] (LP), the LDP was still short of a majority in the upper house. In July 1999, Prime Minister Obuchi invited the New *Kômei* Party (which had nine members elected in 1998) to join the Cabinet as the third partner in a coalition government consisting of the LDP and LP. The birth of a three-party ruling coalition marked a turning point for Japanese politics.

In the 2001 upper house election, the LDP lost 22 seats while the New *Kômei* Party gained 13. The number of New *Kômei* Party lawmakers is critical to the success of the coalition in place as of this writing (which also includes the New Conservative Party) because it provides the government with an absolute majority in the two houses.[2]

The upper house has also gained influence through the power of one of its members, Mikio Aoki, Secretary General of LDP members in the upper house, and a member of the largest LDP faction led by former Prime Minister Hashimoto. Nearly 40 percent of the 112 LDP upper house members belong to this faction. Aoki also has close connections with the New *Kômei* Party, the LDP's most important coalition partner. Aoki was able to exercise influence over various issues, including the content of the Iraq bill, the extension of the Diet session in 2003, and the reselection of Prime Minister Koizumi in the 2003 LDP presidential election. Aoki has been able to choose candidates in upper house elections, organize their campaigns, and have a say on the appointment of cabinet members as well as senior vice ministers. Politicians are so impressed with Aoki's political strength that they say one should be prepared to give up an election and senior party position if competing against Aoki.

As the upper house became more important to Japanese politics, reporters were obliged to allocate more time and attention to covering it. Until 1998, reporters in the Diet Building used the upper house *kisha* club mainly as a place to rest or read weekly journals to kill time while they awaited press conferences and briefings. But the club has become more active now, as reporters focus on Aoki in addition to the upper house steering committee, and the work of the President of the house.

The *Yatô* Club

Another noteworthy press club is the *Yatô* (opposition parties) Club. It is located on the second floor of the Diet building, only 50 meters from the *Yotô* Club, and has about 130 reporters. Each of the main news agencies assigns up to four reporters to cover the activities of all the opposition parties. Usually each reporter covers the activities of one party: the Democratic Party of Japan, Liberal Party, the Socialist Party (SDP), *or* Japan Communist Party (JCP). As the opposition parties became more important, the room became too small, and another room was made available. Reporters focus on the opposition parties' attitudes toward elections, the workings of the Diet, deliberations over proposed bills, party leaders, and public opinion.

Reporters on the DPJ beat focus especially on the Chief Representative, Secretary General, Chairman of the Diet Policy Committee, and the Chairman of the Policy Research Committee [*seichô-kaichô*]. Sometimes the press has to adjust to rivalries within an opposition party, as in the case of the DPJ, when one reporter was assigned to cover the portion of the party loyal to Kan Naoto, while another was assigned to the group led by Hatoyama Yukio.

Another important *kisha* club covers the Ministry of Foreign Affairs: it is named the *Kasumi* Club, after the *Kasumigaseki* district where the ministry is located. It has 180 reporters who cover Japan's relations with other countries, especially the USA, Russia, North Korea, and China. In addition, there are up to 80 reporters in each of the clubs close to the Ministry of Education, Culture, Sports, Science and Technology, and the Ministry of Defense. The latter covers the security treaty between USA and Japan, other issues related to defense, American military bases in Okinawa, and treaties with other countries. Reporters from the political desks of the leading newspapers and the wire services are also assigned to cover the Minister of Health, Labor and Welfare, the Minister of Justice, and the Minister for Public Management, Home Affairs, Posts and Telecommunications

Teamwork in the Press Clubs

Although *kisha* clubs accommodate reporters from various news media, the *jôchû-jûnanasha* (the 17 companies permanently located in the clubs) described earlier (especially those of the print media) usually install a large staff of reporters in each of the main clubs in Tôkyô. In 2003, for example, *Yomiuri* and *Asahi*, the largest among the big five national newspapers, assigned 11 reporters to the *Nagata* Club, including one from each newspaper who constantly followed the activities of the prime minister. The *Asahi* also put two reporters in charge of the Council on Economic and Fiscal Policy, the most important of the four councils established in the new Cabinet Office. *Nihon Keizai*, or *Nikkei*, sends nine reporters to the Nagata Club, while *Kyôdô* News Agency assigned 13 reporters to cover the activities of the Cabinet and prime minister through this club.

In the *Yatô* Club, *Asahi* has five reporters, *Mainichi* and *Nikkei* each have four reporters, and *Kyôdô* News Agency has six. Each reporter generally covers one opposition party, although reporters sometime cover more than one. For example, in 2003, *Kyôdô*'s SDP reporter also covered one of the groups within DPJ.

In order to be able to immediately analyze many aspects of breaking events, the media often assign reporters from various sections—such as political, economic, foreign affairs, or society—to a single club. The major newspapers form teams for the *Kasumi* Club (covering the Ministry of Foreign Affairs) by joining three to five reporters from the political desk with reporters from the economic, society, or foreign desks. The number of reporters in this club varies according to what is happening on the international political scene. In 2003, during the war with Iraq and tension with North Korea over the return of abducted Japanese, news organizations like *Asahi*, *Mainichi*, and *Kyôdô* assigned five reporters—including journalists from the society and economic desks—to cover the Foreign Minister, the two vice foreign ministers, and various bureau chiefs and administrators. Because they specialized in different fields, each of these reporters could provide a different view of the same event, contributing to more in-depth coverage.

A reporter is usually assigned to a press club for one to three years, and is then transferred to a different club. The point of the rotation system is to allow reporters to acquire experience in a variety of fields, so they can write stories that reflect their broader knowledge and understanding. A second explanation for this system is that if reporters work at one club for too long, they may become too friendly with the public figures they cover and might then slant their reporting in favor of their sources. Reporters who spend too much time in a particular *kisha* club may even start to see the world as their sources do.

Team Meetings

Reporters from the same company assigned to a single *kisha* club constitute a team [*chiimu*]. One reporter, who usually has an average of ten years' experience in two or three different clubs, serves as "captain" [*kyappu*], while another with less experience is sub-captain [*sabu-kyappu*]. These two are responsible for supervising the writing of articles. News stories are sent either by telephone, facsimile machine, electronic compilation system [*denshi henshû*], or messenger to the news agency's headquarters, where they are forwarded first to the political desk, which determines news value, then to the make-up desk [*seiri-bu*], which adds heads and subheads and lays articles out on the page. A final editing is done by the correction [*kôetsu*] desk before an article goes to print.

There are several ways in which the activities of *kisha* club reporters from different news agencies are almost identical. First, the major goal of *kisha* club reporters is to know everything that happens in the organization to which the club is attached. This requires regular and constant monitoring. The reporters call at the most important offices daily, talk to many of the same officials and politicians, read the routine reports provided to them by the agency or political party they cover, and attend regular meetings held by leading figures in the organization. They must know and report about the overall activities of the organization, including those that occur outside the building, such as in Diet committees.

Second, each major news organization has its own niche at the *kisha* club, consisting of several desks and chairs. It serves as a kind of mini-headquarters for the news agency at that location, and is the site of daily team meetings.

The reporters usually arrive at the club around 10 a.m. on weekdays (and frequently on Sundays and national holidays). At about that time, each company holds a daily team meeting where reporters discuss the latest political, economic, international, or other events that may have a direct or indirect influence on the political world in general or on the organization that the team covers. The team tries to foresee the implications of impending events, and assesses the kind of developments it must pay special attention to and who might provide various types of related information. Each team is largely autonomous, with the responsibility of deciding what news to cover and how to cover it.

Team meetings are also an opportunity for reporters to be updated about the latest instructions from the main office of their respective news organs, such as the need for certain information, for more details or background data about a given issue for a specific edition, or for a special feature or cover story. Beat reporters are often asked to provide "analysis pieces" [*bunseki kiji*] or "verification, view articles" [*kenshô kiji*] that explain political events or decisions made by the organization they cover, including their own hypotheses regarding upcoming events, or to write special features known among journalists as *hima dane* or *hima neta* (literally, spare-time topics) about politicians or political affairs. These requests are especially common when the desk is not satisfied with the amount of political news, particularly on weekends.

Because of these demands, a political reporter must constantly meet with Diet members and officials to observe any changes in the political dynamics. They must constantly be "in the swim" and know exactly what is going on from moment to moment. They must be ready to supply not only information about what has just happened, but also about contemporary trends and even scenarios of what may occur in the near future. The team meetings help to establish a framework and schedule for the day, and to focus each team in accordance with the main office's needs and with the climate in the organization being covered. When necessary, other reporters from the political desk, members of the editorial desk itself, and unattached "roving reporters" [yûgun kisha] not assigned to any particular press club, can be called in to assist in newsgathering.

Besides meeting regularly with their team, reporters assigned by major news organs to kisha clubs in the Nagatachō district (such as the Kantei, Hirakawa and Yatô Clubs) frequently meet in their company's room at the Kokkai Kisha Kaikan (Diet Press Assembly Hall). This building is located on a corner with one side facing the Prime Minister's Official Residence and the other side facing the Diet Building. Each of the major news organizations has in this building its own room, which serves as something akin to a frontline headquarters close to where major political events occur. Equipped with telephones, television sets, facsimile machines, computers, and a huge board on the wall listing the telephone numbers of all the press clubs the agency has reporters in, these rooms can accommodate meetings with up to 30 reporters from three or four important clubs close to the Diet. Such meetings are often held in the presence of messengers, desk editors, and at times even the political editor and the vice editor.

The major news organs hold this type of meeting at least once a week; Nikkei holds them twice a week, on Monday and Thursday. These meetings are called kyappu-kai (captains' meetings). Team captains from all the major press clubs in Nagatachō—Kantei, Hirakawa, and Yatô—gather with editors from the political desk, including the chief editor of the desk, and with "roving reporters" to coordinate the activities of the various teams covering the political world of Nagatachō for the same company. Participants discuss what news they will follow in the coming days, what might happen in the political world, and how public figures might react to particular developments. As a result, "roving reporters" may be assigned to cover a given development, or the captain or the sub-captain of a particular press club may be assigned to cover a certain politician or political group related to the club, in addition to overseeing the other reporters in the club.

The reporters' regular workday begins after the team meeting and continues until evening. There are occasions, such as Cabinet reorganizations, when reporters stay at the club until late at night or early the following day. On a regular day, reporters spend the morning covering press conferences or listening to briefings given by persons in the organization they cover—such as ministers, department directors, or section chiefs. After lunch they remain at the club until around 2 p.m., writing stories for the evening edition of their newspaper, watching television, reading magazines, playing mah-jong, napping, or moonlighting by writing articles for periodicals. From 2 to 4 p.m., reporters visit officials at the organization they cover. After that, they receive handouts, listen to lectures by representatives of the organization, or write stories for the morning edition of their newspaper. After 2 p.m. one reporter stays at each company's station at the club as the "person on duty," taking phone calls from headquarters and attending any urgent press conferences. Nowadays, of course, each reporter carries a mobile phone and can be reached at any time with news of any urgent developments.

Coverage of Diet Committees

Kisha club reporters also cover the various Diet committees related to the government agency they cover; these committees examine legal bills, budgets, treaties and petitions, and conduct investigations. Reporters who work at the Ministry of Foreign Affairs (*Kasumi* Club), for example, cover the activities of the Foreign Affairs Committee; the meetings of the Education Committee are covered by reporters from the Ministry of Education, Culture, and Science [*Mombu kurabu*]. Representatives of the news media enjoy a privilege not available to the general public in that they are allowed to observe the meetings of all the committees, including discussions, negotiations, debates, and testimony. They do not have access, however, to meetings of the Discipline Committee that is responsible for maintaining internal discipline and punishing misconduct by Diet members.

The Budget Committee is considered to be the most important of the Diet committees. In addition to discussing the national budget, the Budget Committee has become an arena for debate on every possible issue, and questions raised during the main interpellation period often address defense issues, foreign policy, educational reforms, and accusations of misconduct or corruption by Diet members. At times, analysis or explanation of these discussions requires an expert viewpoint. The major news organizations assign reporters from different press clubs to cover this committee together, so they can explain how a measure discussed by the Budget Committee would affect the various agencies they cover, or the significance of an issue from the viewpoints of those agencies.

The national dailies have various names for the team of reporters that cover the Budget Committee (usually *yosan iinkai tantô*, or Budget Committee Team) but employ roughly the same criteria for constructing this task force. The team generally consists of five reporters: a captain, who usually is familiar with the Budget Committee's workings through experience at the Ministry of Finance press club; a reporter from the Defense Agency *kisha* club; one from the Ministry of Finance *kisha* club; and one from the Ministry of Foreign Affairs *kisha* club. A fifth reporter who may belong to any of the other clubs serves as assistant to the others. This team is usually formed when the Cabinet formally presents the national budget to the Diet in the latter part of January of each year, and is dissolved when both the lower and upper house Budget Committees finish their work at the beginning of April. The team works especially intensely during the several days in which general interpellations [*sōkatsu shitsugi*] take place.

During this period, all Cabinet ministers and the prime minister must attend the committee's meetings from morning until evening. The government must answer questions about a variety of political issues, mainly from members of opposition parties. The general interpellation is broadcast live on television and radio, and attracts much public attention. Committee members often use this as an opportunity to raise controversial issues or make provocative statements. As the meetings of the Budget Committee are broadcast live on television, many "lazy" reporters monitor the live broadcast at their *kisha* club, where they write reports about the meetings.

In **Chapter 2**, we take a close look at reporters' methods of gathering political information, and at their contact with sources.

Beat Reporting and the Search for Information

2

Press Conferences

Kisha clubs facilitate the gathering of information through two main methods: press conferences and *ban* reporting. The most important press conferences for political reporters are held at the *Nagata* Club in the Prime Minister's Official Residence. Every two or three months, the prime minister holds press conferences that are broadcast live on television and radio. The prime minister holds also special press conferences before or after elections, following dissolution of the Diet, after the inauguration of a new Cabinet, before leaving for important overseas meetings, and before or after meeting with a world leader. Japan's top leader also meets the press when there is a special need to address issues and answer reporters' questions.

On rare occasions the prime minister calls an urgent press conference to address vital issues or to announce major political decisions. Prime Minister Hosokawa, for example, held several late-night press conferences to reveal his administration's policies. In December 1993 he began a news conference at around 3:50 a.m. to announce that the government had accepted an Uruguay Round proposal to partially open Japan's market to rice imports. In January 1994, he gave a press conference at 12:50 a.m. to declare that he had reached a last-minute compromise with LDP President Kônô Yôhei regarding political reform bills. At another press conference that began at 12:50 a.m., in February 1994, the prime minister unveiled a plan to replace the nation's 3 percent consumption tax with a new 7 percent "national welfare" indirect tax.

Nagata Club is also the venue for equally important press conferences with the Chief Cabinet Secretary, who serves as the top spokesman for the Cabinet and is considered to be better versed in Diet affairs than anyone else. The Chief Cabinet Secretary meets reporters at least twice a day—at around 11:00 a.m. and around 4:00 p.m. When the Diet is in session and regular Cabinet meetings are held on Tuesdays and Fridays, the Chief Cabinet Secretary meets reporters at about 9:30 or 10:00 a.m., right after the Cabinet meeting has ended. The Chief Cabinet Secretary holds the morning press conference earlier than 11:00 also when he or she is called to attend a meeting of a specific Diet committee or to give a testimony on a specific issue in such a committee. Reporters who cover the Chief Cabinet Secretary have to be early risers who know when the next morning meeting with the Chief Cabinet Secretary will take place.

The Chief Cabinet Secretary starts news conferences by briefing reporters, and then answers any questions ranging from domestic politics and the agenda of the Cabinet to foreign policy. One of the Chief Cabinet Secretary's roles is coordinating policies among Cabinet members. As the closest person to the prime minister, he is nicknamed "the prime minister's wife" (see **Chapter 6**) and knows the national leader's thoughts, opinions, and ideas on all issues. Press conferences with the Chief Cabinet Secretary usually last 15–20 minutes, although some meetings do not exceed three minutes.

Cabinet ministers hold press conferences for the reporters in the *kisha* club closest to their agency at least twice a week, usually after each Cabinet meeting. The ministers describe Cabinet meetings from their own perspectives, explain how new programs adopted by the Cabinet could benefit or harm their ministry, and tell reporters their opinions on any other issues they are willing to talk about. Parliamentary and administrative vice ministers from each government agency also meet the press twice a week to discuss new developments. In addition, the Secretary General of the LDP holds important press conferences at the *Hirakawa* Club, and leaders of the main opposition parties—the DPJ, SDP, and JCP—regularly appear before the reporters of the *Yato* Club to update reporters on the views of their parties.

As explained in **Chapter 3**, reporters view press conferences as a useful channel for learning the official positions of leading politicians and government officials. In order to complete their stories, however, reporters try to obtain additional information through *ban kisha* activities.

Beat Reporting

Ban kisha (beat, or literally "watch" reporters) work in groups of five to 17, each from a different news organ. In recent years, a *ban* most often consists of only seven reporters, representing the big five newspapers and the two wire services. In some situations, the *ban* increases to as many as 17 reporters, representing all the major newspapers and broadcasters in Japan. The group's objective is to cover closely and constantly—even after regular working hours—the movements of a leading politician or other figure whose activities are of great significance to the nation's political, economic, or social life.

Some of the most important *ban* are those connected to the *Nagata* Club. Among them are the *kanbô fukuchôkan-ban* (the Deputy Chief Cabinet Secretary beat), the *kanbochokan-ban* (the Chief Cabinet Secretary beat), and the *sôri-ban* or *shushô-ban*, which covers the prime minister.

The *sôri-ban* is important for two reasons. For one thing, it is the first assignment of a new reporter joining the political desk. New reporters serve in this *ban* for one to two years. During this time, the team captain, desk editors and the political editor carefully assess the new reporter's ability to gather information, collaborate with colleagues, and write stories. The reporter's next assignment, which also lasts for one or two years, is based on this evaluation. Usually the second beat is a political party (first a member of the ruling coalition, then an opposition party) or a government agency, such as the Ministry of Foreign Affairs. This is the main reason why "young" reporters are so determined to excel during this crucial period of their career. Of course, the *sôri-ban* is also important because it covers the nation's top leader, who is almost always the president of the largest political party—the LDP.

The structure of the *sôri-ban* differs from that of other beats. Two reporters from the wire services—*Kyôdô* News Service and *Jiji* Press— follow the prime minister from the time he leaves home in the morning until he returns home, late at night. According to an agreement among all the newspapers, only the two reporters from *Kyôdô* and *Jiji* follow the prime minister's car whenever he leaves his office during working hours— whether he goes to the Diet, to party headquarters, to a private meeting, or home. These two are called *ban-sha* (the car beat). They are obliged to inform all the other news agencies about where the prime minister went and what he did, including details such as what time he entered his office, who he met with at what times, and when he arrived back home. This is published by all the major newspapers in a column called *Shushô dôsei* (literally, the coming and going of the prime minister). So the entourage of the Japanese prime minister, while moving in his car in the streets of Tôkyô, always consists of the car he is sitting in, another car with his body-guards in front, and the representatives of the Japanese news media following him by another car behind.

From the time the prime minister enters his official residence at about 9 a.m. each morning until the moment he leaves the building, the *sôri-ban* consists of representatives of all the major newspapers and other news media affiliated with the *Nagata* Club. The team captains from the major news media at *Nagata* Club each assign three to five reporters to the *sôri-ban*. They alternate among themselves every few hours so that at least one reporter from each news agency is always observing the prime minister's movements.

At the old Prime Minister's Official Residence (just next to the new Official Residence), which remained in use until May 2001, members of the *sôri-ban* sat in a room next to the prime minister's private office on the second floor, or in a chamber called *ban-koya* (literally, *ban* hut; *ban* waiting room) near the stairs on the first floor, whenever the prime minister was in the building. The reporters watched everyone who entered or left the building and the prime minister's private office, and closely monitored the movements of the prime minister and his assistants. Whenever the prime minister left his private office, even if it was just to go to the dining room on the first floor, to a meeting room, or to the toilet, the entire *sôri-ban* rushed after him as he walked, and pelted him with questions regarding his schedule, meetings, or political developments that could give them an idea for a story. As they walked they hung on each other's shoulders in order to be able to hear the prime minister's words, a practice known in journalistic jargon as *burasagari* (hanging down). As he walked with 17 or so reporters in tow, the prime minister answered their questions in a rather spontaneous fashion. Since not all of the reporters could hear his words clearly, those closest to the prime minister later told the others what they had heard, and all of them confirmed their understanding by comparing notes in a practice known as *memo awase* (matching memo).

Prime ministers often gave highly significant answers to reporters' questions during *burasagari*. But time after time there were conflicts between reporters and the prime minister when reporters failed to clearly grasp the words and ideas uttered by the prime minister as he walked, and reached their own interpretations during *memo awase*. Misunderstandings about what the prime minister (or other sources who spoke to reporters under similar circumstances) said sometimes damaged his image. Despite such troubles, Japanese prime ministers traditionally cooperated with this style of newsgathering, thereby helping the media to do their job.

Things changed, however, during the administration of Prime Minister Mori, who began to dislike reporters' "dangling" questions in front of him as he walked the halls of his Official Residence. Mori took office in 2000 and became increasingly frustrated as public opinion surveys conducted by newspaper publishers showed his popularity dropping. He repeatedly found himself having to explain his controversial remarks (discussed in **Chapter 3**). In July 2000, after realizing that constant media coverage was hurting his public image, Mori arranged a 20-minute meeting with the *sôri-ban* to tell the reporters that he was displeased with their coverage.

He said, "I have good days and bad days, and it is your job to create an environment that makes it easier for me to talk." He demanded that reporters "study more" and "make your questions shorter and clearer." Mori asked the reporters present not to publish an account of this meeting, and warned that he would not cooperate with reporters who ignored this request. Despite the threat, several dailies, including the two largest—the *Yomiuri* and *Asahi*—printed transcripts of the meeting (e.g. *Asahi, Shushô kotoba*, July 8, 2000: 4). After that, Prime Minister Mori completely changed his attitude toward the media. He declined to brief reporters or answer their questions while walking in his Official Residence or in the Diet building. He ignored their questions and did not even reply to greetings from reporters. For days, reporters were unable to converse with him as he entered or left his Official Residence, or after important meetings in the Diet. Below are some excerpts from the *Asahi* (*Asahi, Shushô kotoba*, July 12, 2000: 4), illustrating how Mori interacted with the reporters of the *sôri-ban*:

> At 9:55 a.m. in the Prime Minister's Official Residence:
> REPORTER: "Good Morning Prime Minister, can I ask you a question?"
> The reporter is met with silence.
> REPORTER: "Very soon you will move to the new Prime Minister's Official Residence, when this will take place?"
> The Prime Minister does not react at all.
>
> At 14:25 p.m. in the Prime Minister's Official Residence:
> REPORTER: "Mr. Prime Minister, let me ask you a question."
> PRIME MINISTER MORI: "No."
> REPORTER: "Can you please answer my question?"
> PRIME MINISTER MORI: "I said 'NO.'"

The tension between Prime minister Mori and the reporters of the *sôri-ban* escalated further after a US Navy submarine sank the *Ehime Maru*—a Japanese high school's training boat—in February 2001. The media criticized Mori for his unhurried reaction to this event. Mori became totally detached from the media's approach in March 2001: he refused to answer questions from reporters, and informed them that he would not "talk about important issues while walking" (*Asahi*, March 16, 2001). Here are some more reports of his interactions with the press (from *Asahi, Shushô kotoba*):

> (March 16, 2001)
> At 10:00 a.m. in the Prime Minister's Official Residence:
> REPORTER: "The stock market is declining in Japan as well as in the USA and Europe. Is there any remark you can make in this regard?"
> Prime Minister Mori does not respond.
>
> (March 16, 2001)
> At 12:20 p.m in the Prime Minister's Official Residence:
> REPORTER: "Regarding the stock market . . . "
> PRIME MINISTER MORI: (replies in a small voice)
> REPORTER: "What did you say?"
> PRIME MINISTER MORI: (no reaction).
>
> (March 30, 2001)
> At 9:20 a.m. in the Prime Minister's Official Residence:
> REPORTER: "How is your back pain today?"
> PRIME MINISTER MORI: "What a nuisance!"

(April 5, 2001)
At 16:45 p.m. in the Diet Building:
REPORTER: "Have any concrete decisions been made regarding preparations for the upcoming LDP Presidential election?"
PRIME MINISTER MORI: (no reaction).

(April 6, 2001)
At 12:10 p.m. in the Prime Minister's Official Residence:
REPORTER: "Mr. Prime Minister."
MORI: "I have decided not to talk while walking."
REPORTER: "Let me ask again, it is exactly a year today since you assumed office, what are your feelings?"
PRIME MINISTER MORI: (no reaction).

(April 6, 2001)
At 18:50 p.m. in the Prime Minister's Official Residence:
REPORTER: "Please let us know your feelings as this is a year since you are the prime minister."
PRIME MINISTER MORI: "I told you I am not going to talk while walking."
REPORTER: "Well, stop walking and talk to us for a while."
PRIME MINISTER MORI: "I have already talked with the captain."

When Koizumi assumed the office of prime minister in April 2001, he immediately informed the *sôri-ban*, using the words of Prime Minister Mori, that he would "not talk to the press while walking." Instead, Koizumi agreed to appear daily in front of reporters to briefly answer their questions about important issues of the day. This was done through "daily television interviews" [*deiri terebi intabyû*]. After the move to the new Prime Minister's Office in May 2002, it was no longer permitted to spontaneously approach the prime minister as he entered or left his private offices, as had been the custom at the old Official Residence. Meetings with the prime minister had to be arranged in advance. These meetings could take place around noon and before the prime minister left his office for the day, at around 6:30 p.m.

So since spring of 2002, the prime minister appears at pre-set times in front of reporters who wait for him on the fourth floor of the new residence. There he answers questions for about five minutes, twice a day. Barring unusual circumstances, he faces the would-be *burasagari* reporters at noon without TV cameras. In the early evening, he meets the media with TV cameras rolling. Koizumi has completely replaced the old, impromptu *burasagari* sessions with interactions in which reporters must pool precise questions and submit them in advance. When he knows what he will be asked, it is easier to keep the press focused on a specific set of issues and he is more likely to leave himself maneuvering room while limiting the danger of being pulled into "uncharted waters."

This type of media strategy has given Koizumi important opportunities to talk "directly" to TV watchers while appearing to be knowledgeable, well-informed, and in control of political events. From the moment of his inauguration, Koizumi strongly emphasized dialogue with the public. His media strategy helped to improve his public image and lift his cabinet's approval rating to over 80 percent as of 2003.

The working style of the *sôri-ban* reporters has also changed since the prime minister moved to new quarters in May 2002 in that the reporters are no longer allowed to move freely throughout the building. The new Prime Minister's Office has five stories above ground and one below. It has two and a half times the floor space of the old two-story residence, but the entire fifth floor—the location of the offices of the prime minister, Chief and Deputy Cabinet secretaries, and other secretaries—are completely off-limits to media representatives.

Reporters who used to be able to hang out by the prime minister's door and eat at the same cafeteria with officials at the old Official Residence cannot watch everyone who enters or leaves the private office of the prime minister, and cannot immediately approach these figure with questions. In the name of security, reporters' movements are restricted mainly to the first floor, where the *Nagata kisha* club and the conference room are. Reporters and television cameras can follow visitors to the main entrance of the building, on the third floor, but they are not allowed to cross a white line to the right of the entrance. They can photograph visitors from behind the white line, but are forbidden from practicing *burasagari* at the main entrance unless a news source approaches them near the white line.

At the new residence, *sôri-ban* reporters monitor visitors to the prime minister from inside the *ban-koya* chamber. In the new building, the *ban-koya* is on the third floor, near the back elevator that leads down to the first floor where the *Nagata* Club is located. The chamber is about 12 meters long and 2.5 meters wide. It has two desks where reporters can write stories, a fax machine, telephones, and an electric board like the one in the press clubroom below, with lamps that indicate which officials are in the building. The most conspicuous feature of the room is a big glass window facing the main entrance of the building, which is only ten meters away. Reporters can see through the glass when the prime minister or a guest enters or leaves the building. As further "compensation" for being prohibited from sitting close to the prime minister's office and questioning visitors, the *sôri-ban* reporters were given a television monitor in the *ban-koya* so they can see who enters the prime minister private's office on the fifth floor. However, reporters complain that the new building has a hidden corridor that allows guests to meet the prime minister in secret, without appearing on this television monitor.

Faction Reporters

The *Hirakawa* Club covers the LDP and the other coalition parties, and its structure deserves special attention because of the club's important role in providing political information to the public. As with other *kisha* clubs, each major news agency assigns a certain number of reporters, which is between six and eight at the *Hirakawa* Club. The idea is to have at least one reporter covering each of the five or six main factions in the LDP, and other reporters covering the New *Kômei* Party and the New Conservative Party, the LDP's coalition partners. In 2003, for example, *Asahi* and *Nikkei* each assigned eight reporters to the club, including captains and sub-captains. *Mainichi* assigned ten, including a captain and a sub-captain, and *Kyôdô* News Service had nine reporters: a captain and a sub-captain, one reporter on each of the six LDP factions, and one covering the New *Kômei* Party. *Kyôdô* had its upper house correspondent cover the New Conservative Party. In addition, the reporter on the lower house beat also covered the former Katô faction.

Reporters assigned by different news agencies to cover a single faction of the LDP together make up a group called *habatsu kisha* (faction reporters). In 2003 there were six such groups. In practice, faction reporters must focus on the activities of the leader or a few top people in the faction. In this way, faction reporters' work is similar to that of the *ban* reporters. Usually, the beats of the *ban* and the *habatsu kisha* overlap. So a reporter who covers the LDP Secretary General's faction also belongs to the *kanjichô-ban* (Secretary General beat), where the main contact is with the Secretary General of the LDP. These reporters must also cover the activities of the boss and other influential persons of the Secretary General's faction. This is also the case for reporters on the *sômukaichô-ban* (covering the Chairman of the LDP's Executive Council) and *seimu kaichô-ban* (the Chairman of the LDP's Policy Affairs Research Council beat). The LDP's three top officials—the two council chairmen and the Secretary General—are usually from three different factions, which facilitates the work of reporters, enabling one reporter to cover both the faction as a whole and the faction member who holds a key party position.

Traditionally, covering an LDP faction entailed close involvement with a group that possessed its own dynamism and rules. For many years, each LDP faction had its own headquarters and a formal structure that included regular meetings, a membership roster, solid discipline, and a clear hierarchy through which the leader dutifully served members by providing political funds, party and government posts, and election support. Each faction resembled a traditional *mura* (village) or extended family, both of which require members to adhere to certain rules that allow the group to function efficiently. Because of these characteristics, reporters invariably had interesting experiences and were exposed to fascinating information.

During the 1960s–1990s, editors paid special attention to the appointment of faction reporters. They were keenly aware that a reporter's success at obtaining information with which to enrich the company's political coverage depended largely on the reporter's personality and ability to adapt to the peculiarities of a given faction. Character, judgment, and the ability to get along with others were important elements of a reporter's ability to establish bonds of trust with faction members and leaders, and to obtain significant information. In journalistic jargon, faction reporters needed to "gnaw into" [*kuikomu*] the faction he or she was covering, in order to gain the trust of faction members. Such reporters virtually became part of the faction in the sense that they share secrets with the faction's members and advise them on various issues ranging from the content of public speeches through the questions to be asked in Diet committees.

As mentioned earlier, however, after 1993, with the changes in the electoral system and the tightening of the laws on corruption, the LDP factions started to lose a great deal of their importance. Prime Minister Koizumi has demonstrated strong determination to disband the factions, which has further weakened the status of factions and their leaders. This has resulted in several changes to reporters' newsgathering styles. First, until the 1990s, a reporter could not cover rival factions simultaneously. Faction reporters maintained constant and close relations with faction members and learned their most important secrets, such as the faction's intended strategies and personal affairs of its members. If such a reporter were to have frequent contact with members of a rival faction, there would be concerns about information leaks. However, in 2001, as pointed out, Prime Minister Koizumi selected his Cabinet and the three key party officials without regard for the relative strength of the factions. Furthermore, in May 2001 he formally adopted a supra-factional decision-making style within the LDP. Since he began working actively to dismantle the factions, the sense of rivalry between them has decreased. Factions are no longer likened to closed villages; they are more open now. They have less interest in power-seeking strategies and focus much more on policy matters. Unlike in the old days, it is no longer rare to find a single reporter assigned to more than one LDP faction at a time.

A second factor that has influenced the work of faction reporters is the declining importance of faction "bosses" as information sources. Until the 1990s, reporters were enormously dependent on faction leaders for information. At the same time, it was extremely difficult to establish close relations with the leader within a short period of time in order to get information from him. The *habatsu kisha* needed to approach faction leaders through aides and secretaries. They had to spend a great deal of time hanging around faction members in order to cultivate strong and reliable relationships with those in key positions. This meant showing up at countless formal and informal gatherings of the faction, chatting with assistants and advisors in the faction's office, and gradually worming their way in until they could meet the "boss" and get information from him.

As the power and influence of the faction bosses gradually faded in the 1990s, however, this process changed in two ways. First, in some cases, the faction boss lost his status as the main source of information sought by reporters. Consider the case of Hashimoto Ryutaro, who is chairman of a faction. His word used to be extremely influential, and he was always seen as a candidate for another term as the prime minister. Now that his status has declined, however, nobody sees him as a future prime minister, and reporters do not pay much attention to what he says or does. Instead, in 2003, they focus on other members of the faction such as the faction's acting chairman (Muraoka Kanezô), and the two vice chairmen (Nonaka Hiromu of the lower house and Aoki Mikio of the upper house). Etô Takami, leader of the Etô-Kamei faction, also stopped attracting attention from reporters as he approached retirement in the fall of 2003.

A second change was that faction leaders have become much more accessible. It is now possible to contact them directly, even within a short period of time. Faction leaders are no longer regarded as powerful gods like they were in the past, but are seen as "regular people." The media actually referred to former prime minister Obuchi explicitly as an "ordinary person" [*bonjin*], suggesting that he did not have any special characteristics that distinguished him from other Japanese (see **Chapter 6**).

A side effect of the waning power of the faction bosses is that their aides have become much more talkative. In the past, reporters relied mainly on the faction "boss" but strove to get additional information from two or three of his closest aides [*sokkin*]. The latter were very wary of divulging the faction's inside information to reporters for fear that the boss might hear about it and intimidate them. More recently, however, faction members are not afraid to talk, and even rank-and-file members who were afraid to talk in the past, including relatively new members who have only been elected a few times, are more vocal about expressing their opinions on everything from policy to personnel matters. Some even openly criticize their own faction's boss, at faction meetings or in front of reporters. As a result, reporters rely less on faction leaders as news sources, and more on other members of the factions.

Informal Newsgathering Methods

Faction reporters and other beat reporters have several characteristics in common in terms of how they gather information. The structure and workings of the *ban* or *habatsu kisha* groups is like that of the larger press club; one might call it "a *kisha* club within a *kisha* club." A *ban* is made up of representatives of the major news agencies that are permanent members of the club, so there are reporters from five to 17 news organs. Each *ban* has two, or occasionally three, secretaries who arrange meetings with the Diet members that the group is covering. The secretaries are appointed for two-month terms: one is from a newspaper and the other from a television network. As in the *kisha* clubs, *ban* reporters work as a group when they meet with sources. Ordinarily, the *ban* groups follow their target—such as the LDP Secretary General, the Chief Cabinet Secretary, or an LDP council chairman—the entire working day. They wait near the source's office in the morning and pursue them wherever they go, even to private meetings with friends or family. The aim is to observe the target closely in order to pick up any hints that will lead to a story. The *ban* shadows leading Diet members so closely that one reporter who followed an LDP Secretary General for a long time gradually began to walk like him (cited in Feldman, 1993a: 88).

Kondan

There are three newsgathering methods that *ban* reporters use much more frequently than other reporters. These are (1) informal chat sessions (*kondan*) in news sources' offices, (2) meetings in sources' homes before or after working hours, and (3) following sources as they move from place to place.

In addition to press conferences where they brief tens or hundreds of reporters, Diet members also hold intimate talks in their own offices with small groups of reporters. Because these reporters cover the Diet member's activities constantly, from morning until evening, the Diet member gets to know each of them well, including their names and the news agency they work for. During *kondan*, reporters obtain broader, deeper, and more detailed information than the same politician provides in press conferences. Diet members also disclose facts in *kondan* that they will not reveal at all in press conferences with many reporters present. *Kondan* are also opportunities for members of the *ban* to verify information they have gathered elsewhere, from other sources.

In many cases, *kondan* with the *ban* (called *ban-kon* for short) are conducted on a daily or weekly basis. The Chief Cabinet Secretary holds a *kondan* with his *ban* almost every day after press conferences. This meeting is known as the *kanbôchôkan-kondan* (friendly talk with the Chief Cabinet Secretary). Many press conferences with the Chief Cabinet Secretary last only three or four minutes, but immediately afterward, members of the *ban* rush out of the press conference hall with the Chief Cabinet Secretary to learn more and to ask detailed questions. This movement of the 17 or so reporters who trail after the Chief Cabinet Secretary as he moves from the press conference hall to a nearby room for the *ban-*

kon is known in journalistic jargon as *kingyo no unko* (goldfish stool).

The LDP Secretary-General also holds *kondan* with beat reporters almost daily. These meetings are called *kanjichô-kondan* (friendly chats with the Secretary General).

In recent years, *kondan* have been held so often that many reporters, ministers, vice ministers, party officials, and section heads in government agencies perceive them as a formal, rather than informal, method for transmitting political information. For example, the Minister of Foreign Affairs conducts formal press conferences twice a week at *Kasumi* Club, and meets representatives of the club in their office for *kondan* at least another two times. The Administrative Vice Minister in the same agency also holds a *kondan* twice a week on a regular basis; usually one day before Cabinet meetings, which are held on Tuesdays and Fridays.

Other high-ranking officials in the foreign ministry tend to hold friendly chats with reporters before important international meetings or while preparing for an overseas visit by a leading Diet member. Most government agencies hold *kondan* daily after Cabinet meetings and during budget deliberations in the Diet, enabling reporters to sense the "real" mood within a given ministry toward the issues being discussed.

Reporters distinguish between two kinds of *kondan*: those that deal with domestic policy [*naisei kondan*] and those that concern political situations [*seikyoku kondan*]. The former focus on new policies of the Cabinet, issues that coalition parties intend to put on the Diet agenda, and the reactions of opposition parties to the ruling coalition's initiatives. The latter addresses things like general political circumstances, trends within parties and factions, struggles for leadership within the ruling coalition, and misconduct or corruption. *Seikyoku kondan* are mainly held by the LDP's three top executives, and by influential members of factions. The domestic affairs *kondan* are generally held by the prime minister or the Chief Cabinet Secretary, although some information of this type is provided during friendly chats with ministers [*daijin kondan*].

Reporters also distinguish between *omote kondan* (literally, surface chat; *omote-kon* for short) and *ura kondan* (*ura-kon*, literally, backside chat). *Omote-kon* include all the members of a particular *ban*. In this case, the *ban*'s reporters decide to meet a certain politician, and one of its secretaries contacts the politician to arrange a time and place. This might be at the news source's office or residence, or at a restaurant. This type of meeting is initiated and attended by all the members of the *ban*. *Ura-kon*, on the other hand, are held with only a few reporters with whom the public figure feels friendly and comfortable. Sometime two or three reporters initiate this type of private meeting with the person they cover. In other cases, the source invites two or three *ban* reporters for a friendly talk. The source may use a mobile phone to specify the meeting time and place, which is usually a restaurant or hotel, and usually asks the reporters not to mention the meeting to other members of the *ban*. The group generally has dinner together as they chat about issues the source would not like to discuss with other reporters.

"Yo- uchi" or "yo-mawari" and "asa-gake"

Access to *kondan* is only one of the privileges reserved for the *ban* group. Another is the ability to meet with news sources outside of their workplace, especially before or after the workday. These meetings are called "night attacks" [*yo-uchi*], "night rounds" [*yo-mawari*], or "morning visits" [*asa-gake*]. Morning visits are gatherings of *ban* reporters held early in the morning, sometimes around 7 a.m., but more commonly around 9 a.m., at the private residence of the Diet member being covered. For example, in 2000, the *ban* of LDP Secretary General Nonaka Hiromu received briefings between 8:30 and 9:00 a.m. almost every morning in the dining room of the Diet dormitory where he lived. This *ban* included reporters from the five national newspapers, two news agencies, NHK, five commercial television networks, reporters from *Tôkyô* or *Chûnichi, Hokkaidô, Nishi-Nippon,* as well as the local *Kyôto Shimbun,* since Nonaka was elected from Kyôto. At the same time, the reporters on the upper house beat used to meet Aoki Mikio, the Secretary General for the LDP's upper house members, in the lobby of his residence for regular morning briefings.

Similarly, "night attacks" refer to gatherings of beat reporters at Diet members' homes after working hours, between 8 and 10 p.m. Meetings held in a leading Diet member's living or dining room allow reporters and politicians to converse with each other in an intimate and relaxed atmosphere. Very often, the politician provides reporters with essential information in a very friendly way, as they drink whisky or eat snacks served by the Diet member's wife or secretary.

A close relationship with a Diet member is a precondition for obtaining exclusive information, and traditionally the level of this intimacy was reflected in the reporter's access to the Diet member's home. A reporter who had just established contact with a Diet member could visit the latter's home to obtain information, but was only allowed to enter the living room. Such reporters belonged to the so-called *ôsetsuma-gumi* (living room group). As the Diet member and reporter got to know each other better, the reporter might eventually enter the kitchen, and even be allowed to take some of the Diet member's food and eat there freely. The reporter then belonged to the *daidokoro-gumi* (kitchen group). A reporter was really "in" when the Diet member felt safe enough to let the reporter move freely through the house and even into the most private back parlor. At that stage the reporter belonged to the *okuzashiki-gumi* (back-parlor group).

Today, however, few information sources live in a house of their own that is big enough to accommodate a large number of visiting reporters.

Among those who do is former Prime Minister Mori, but nowadays he does not let reporters into any part of his house. Most Diet members live either in a small apartment that has no back parlor, or, as in the case powerful Diet members like former Prime Ministers Hata Tsutomu (April–June 1994) and Maruyama Tomiichi (1994–96) and LDP leaders Nonaka and Aoki, they live in Diet housing facilities that are not big enough to host many reporters. Therefore, reporters either wait at the entrance to the building or near the gate to hear briefings early in the morning or at night.

One significant aspect of these "night attacks" and "morning visits" is that very often all the reporters meet with a source together, as they do in the *kisha* club press conferences and in many *kondan*. This means that all the reporters from the various news agencies enter and leave an official's residence together. They chat, ask questions, and receive answers from the Diet member in the presence of colleagues from other news agencies. As is the case with *kondan*, the need for these "visits" or "attacks" depends on the political climate and the need for information to supplement what was collected during the workday. When the Diet is not in session, for example, or when there is nothing particularly important on the political agenda and therefore no urgent information to get, reporters rarely gather at Diet members' homes. So reporters may go for several days in a row without meeting a Diet member, followed by a period during which they go daily to the Diet member's residence.

Usually, all of the meetings described above are prearranged with the information source. In the course of the day, reporters may decide that it would be useful to meet their target Diet member after normal working hours because of something that occurred in the morning or something on the agenda for the following day. In such cases, a *ban* secretary must get the Diet member's approval for the visit. Because reporters often visit several Diet members' homes in a single round of "night attacks," the secretaries must arrange approximate times for each visit. There are times, however, when sudden developments prompt reporters to suddenly want to meet with a certain Diet member. In such cases, one of the *ban* secretaries can telephone the Diet member's home without previous warning and request an immediate meeting to obtain the legislator's views about that particular development.

Shachû-kon

It is important to note that the *ban* reporters meet their information sources not only at their offices and Tôkyô residences, but also when the sources are traveling to remote places far from Tôkyô, including to their home districts. These newsgathering sessions are called *shachû-kon* (literally, informal chat in the car), and can take place in a moving vehicle, especially a train. The term was used most often in the 1950s and 1960s, when reporters routinely joined influential politicians on their way to and from their constituencies and escorted politicians to public lectures in the countryside. Politicians were often surrounded by reporters during *kondan* on a train. The reporters listened to the politician's briefing, asked questions, received answers, and wrote their stories. When the train stopped, the reporters would meet a local agent of their newspaper and filed them their stories; the latter would then send the stories by telegraph, telephone, or fax to the agency's headquarters.

This type of newsgathering is still practiced today, but not as often as it was in the past. In 2000, Nonaka Hiromu, then-Secretary General of the LDP, used to hold often *shachû-kon* on the train as he traveled between Tôkyô and his constituency in Kyôto. From his deluxe seat on the Bullet Train [*Shinkansen*], he would call reporters from the nearest car and they would encircle him as he briefed them on important political issues. Today reporters do not have to wait until the train stops at a station; they can send stories from their laptop computers immediately by connecting via a mobile phone, or even phone a story to the desk while the train is still moving.

Kicuhû-kondan and Dôkô kisha

A similar type of newsgathering is called *kichû-kondan* (literally, chat in the air). This is practiced by *dôkô kisha* (companion reporters; reporters assigned to accompany a source on a journey). Political leaders often travel abroad to participate in international meetings or to meet with leaders of other countries. On these trips, the political leader is escorted by *dôkô kisha*. A group of such reporters includes members of different news media and sometimes members of the same media drawn from several *kisha* clubs, such as *Nagata*, *Hirakawa*, and *Kasumi*. For world summits and some other important international meetings, the team of reporters may be drawn from different sections of a single news organ, such as the foreign, political, and economic desks. Reporters from a single company constitute a team, like the company teams in each press club, with each reporter contributing parts of a story.

In recent years, it is not uncommon for up to 300 reporters to travel on the same flight as the prime minister or a Cabinet minister, sometimes joining the prime minister and his entourage on one of the two Boeing 747-400 jets that serve as official government airplanes. When the prime minister travels on one of these planes, it is called *sora tobu kantei* (flying Prime Minister's Official Residence).[1]

Kichû kondan are conducted most often by the prime minister or one of his close aides. At a previously agreed time, the prime minister gathers the reporters on the airplane and talks not only about issues directly related to the current trip, but also about domestic politics [*naisei kondan*] and other issues. Reporters file stories based on these chats as soon as the plane lands.

Sending reporters overseas is very costly. Some media organizations, such as the bloc newspapers, cannot afford to do so and must rely on the wire services for detailed information. Other news companies spend huge amounts of money to send representatives on such assignments. For this reason, news stories filed by these reporters usually receive greater attention from editors and are allotted more space—particularly on the front page—and larger headlines. In addition to coverage of the routine activities of a public figure on an overseas journey, news companies expect their reporters to file reports on remarks and ideas related to general political issues or policies.

Reporters and their Sources

Prolonged association with information sources through the *kisha* club system encourages reporters to develop a deep rapport with their subjects at the same time that it makes it easy for reporters to obtain information. Understanding Diet members—their thinking, values, interests, and attitudes—is extremely important to a reporter's work, which is based on maintaining smooth and clear communications.

When writing news stories, most Japanese reporters focus on understanding their news source's viewpoint and transmitting the source's thoughts to the public without quoting the source. Direct quotations are extremely rare in Japanese newspapers stories. Instead, reporters use indirect speech to convey their sources' thoughts. This puts the reporter in control of the story's focus and allows the reporter to combine information and words from scattered parts of an interview to present the source's ideas and opinions. For this reason, when meeting with Diet members reporters tend to encourage them to freely discuss the issues they want information about. Rather than communicating through questions and answers, such meetings are designed so that reporters express opinions about a topic in the expectation that the politician will then express their own opinions in an open atmosphere that allows an exchange of ideas. One might say that in Japan, political information sources provide stories, not statements.

Another reason it is important for reporters to have a deep understanding of their sources is that many important political sources tend to speak in a way that leaves their words open to several different interpretations. When a reporter knows how a news source thinks, it is easier to extract the true intentions and meanings from the source's words. Moreover, longtime face-to-face meetings enable reporters to correctly read facial expressions and fully comprehend a news source's opinions on most matters. These concepts are particularly relevant to the discussion in **Chapter 3**.

Two Sides of the Political Coin: Façade and Substance in Public Talk

3

A politician's skill (or lack thereof) at choosing the right words to convey suitable ideas to a specific audience at the right times can make or break a political career. Conventional wisdom in Japan says that real feelings and opinions about politics and personnel are not supposed to intrude on the "front world," where things must be kept calm and controlled and where surprises are not supposed to occur. Unexpectedly candid utterances can invite criticism or even cause political chaos, and the source of such an expression is not appreciated or respected.

In the summer of 2003, a number of politicians became the focus of public condemnation for evoking emotions through symbol-laden, opinionated statements. The problem was not only the substance of what they said, but often the style in which they said it. First, two Diet members outraged many voters and politicians—especially women—by defending gang rapists and suggesting that rape victims had invited rape by dressing provocatively. On June 26, Ôta Seiichi of the LDP said during a discussion of Japan's declining birth rate that gang rapists "at least had a healthy, vigorous," and "close to normal" appetite for sex. Commenting to reporters on this remark, Chief Cabinet Secretary Fukuda Yasuo suggested that women who are raped are "asking for it" by the way they dress. During the same symposium, former Prime Minister Mori Yoshirô also found himself in hot water for suggesting that only women who bear children should be eligible for pension payments in their old age.

On July 11, Kônoike Yoshitada, a Cabinet minister who doubles as *de facto* head of a government panel on the upbringing of juveniles, came under fire for saying "the parents (of a 12-year old boy who had confessed to killing a 4-year old boy in Nagasaki Prefecture) should be dragged through the streets and their heads should be chopped off." "The mass media should show the faces of the boy's parents. Teachers and the parents should appear" in front of media cameras as a warning to parents who do not control their children effectively, Kônoike added. His remarks drew a barrage of criticism from opposition parties who lambasted Kônoike both for insensitivity and for referring to a feudal Japanese method of punishing criminals. Yet he refused to apologize. "I merely talked in parables because I like Toei's movies," he told reporters at the Cabinet Office. Toei Co. is known for its samurai dramas.

Finally, on July 12, Etô Takami, a senior member of the LDP and leader of the party's third-largest faction, caused outrage first by saying that Japan's occupation of Korea (1910–45) should not be considered as colonialism because both sides signed a treaty of annexation. He then went on to say that China's assertion that 300,000 people died at the hands of Japanese troops in the 1937 Nanjing Massacre was "a pure fabrication, a big lie." Predictably, his remarks sparked complaints from South Korea and China.

This foot-in-mouth syndrome is common among Japanese politicians and government officials. Some of the terms used to criticize politicians when they fail to conceal their feelings or hide their thoughts to the "back world" of politics are *hôgen* (indiscreet remark), *bôgen* (violent or abusive language), or *kuchi wo suberaseru* or *shitsugen* (a slip of the tongue, misstatement). In many instances, public figures have been criticized not only by fellow politicians or government bureaucrats, but also by segments of the Japanese public and even by leaders or citizens of other countries, which sometimes causes diplomatic tension.

This chapter discusses the less restrained side of Japanese political culture. It details the conditions and motives that encourage politicians to make careless or offensive remarks. It also examines how circumstances and the intended visibility of events affect the content of political rhetoric, revealing that Diet members' words do not always mirror their real thoughts.

Honne and Tatemae

The speech of Japanese politicians and government officials generally fits either into the category of *honne*, meaning honest and informal, or that of *tatemae*, which is formal, ceremonial, "pretense" designed for public consumption. *Honne*, is the *ura*—the obverse, or the actual, genuine intent, which sometimes means the hidden side of a subject. It relates to *watakushi* (I), and is private, informal and non-ceremonial. *Tatemae* is the "surface pretense," the *omote* (face) of a subject. This is the presented truth, the easily visible side of a given issue. It relates to *ôyake*, which is public, formal, and ceremonial.[1]

A person may discuss a particular issue from either standpoint: *honne* or *tatemae*. When the speaker discloses genuine thoughts, opinions, and judgments, regardless of the expected reception they will receive—that is *honne*. When statements are carefully worded in order to restrict the conversation to official positions, or when the speaker sticks to euphemisms, ambiguous expressions and generalities, without revealing honest opinions or displaying personal feelings, that is *tatemae*. In Japan, *tatemae* is the most common form of public speaking, because it is not socially acceptable to express personal feelings or opinions in a public forum, nor is it considered appropriate to interject personal opinions in public affairs. Therefore it is important to clearly distinguish between public obligation and private matters.

For Diet members, leaders of political groups and government officials, *honne* and *tatemae* are the two sides of the Japanese political coin; they signify the difference between public disclosure and private discretion. Politicians and government officials present their views with varying degrees of openness [*honne*] or fuzziness [*tatemae*], and address or avoid certain subjects depending on the circumstances in which they find themselves. Specifically, when speaking before large public gathering, politicians and officials employ *tatemae* by speaking in general terms and using buzzwords and metaphors to give only the official line of their administration or political group. Before a large audience, ambitious Diet members favor loose statements of philosophy that can be interpreted in a variety of ways. In fact, one linguistic trait peculiar to *tatemae* statements is that the speaker avoids using vocabulary that indicates any judgment or makes a commitment to any position. Such speakers hedge their comments with words like *tabun* (literally "probably"), *osoraku* ("perhaps"), or *hyotto shitara* ("could be"). They frequently use terms like *maemuki ni* ("positively" or "constructively") to give a vague impression that they intend to move on an issue at some unspecified time in the future, *eii* ("assiduous" or "energetic") to convey a sense of effort when prospects for accomplishment are poor, *jūbun ni* ("adequately" or "thoroughly") when stalling for time, and *tsutomeru* ("to endeavor" or "work hard") when they intend to take no personal responsibility. The speaker is thus able to appear to say something, loading their speech with much professional jargon and abstractions, without revealing any personal opinion, and to phrase comments in ways that make it impossible for the listener to determine where the speaker stands on a particular issue, thereby preserving an image of neutrality regarding sensitive issues.

Conversely, politicians (and government officials) speak more concretely, in greater detail, and are more apt to disclose their true intentions when talking to smaller groups, for example of reporters, supporters in their home district, or party or faction colleagues in get-togethers at party headquarters, in exclusive restaurants, or in "study sessions" organized for frank discussion of matters of common concern.

A good example of *tatemae* is the policy speech that a Japanese prime minister traditionally delivers to both houses of the Diet upon establishing a new administration. In these speeches, the prime minister refers to major problems confronting Japan at the moment, and gives his views on key areas such as foreign affairs, trade disputes, educational reform, and the economy. These speeches use strong-sounding words in reference to issues like maintaining social stability, taxation and educational reform, expanding Japan's role on the world stage, and increasing economic cooperation between Japan and other Asian countries. It is part of the "common-sense of *Nagatachô*" that a prime minister's speech before the Diet must be an amorphous speech that "touches everything covers nothing" (*Asahi*, Editorial, May 11, 1994). The prime minister speaks in general terms, expressing his intention to solve various problems, especially through cooperation with other political groups, or with other countries. In these policy speeches, prime ministers eloquently outline their political objectives but fail to substantiate with specific strategies. These speeches are the *tatemae* of each new administration, and politicians and media pundits alike take them with a good deal of salt, because they are famous for not revealing any explicit policies or time frames for tackling issues.

Similarly, at party conventions, political fund-raisers, or other events attended by thousands of people with televisions cameras everywhere, Japanese politicians generally express little beyond official, broadly accepted views, nor do they utter more than the vaguest of opinions, thus avoiding taking any stand. The same is true for the frequent press conferences that Japanese leaders hold. This includes the regular press briefings that the Chief Cabinet Secretary holds at least twice a day, and the meetings that Cabinet ministers and vice ministers hold with reporters at least twice a week. *Tatemae* also characterizes the press conferences that the prime minister holds at his official residence every two or three months, and the special press meetings the prime minister calls before or after elections, following the dissolution of the Diet or the inauguration of a new Cabinet, and before leaving for important meetings with world leaders. Because of their significance, television and radio stations broadcast these conferences live. These press conferences are usually carefully staged events, with the politicians talking in vague terms and trying to appear as neutral as they can about delicate issues. They are primarily occasions for the prime minister or Diet members to expound the official party or Cabinet line. It is accepted in *Nagatachô* that politicians refrain from giving really significant information at such press conferences, or from disclosing their true opinions about any hot issue.

Diet deliberations and Diet committee meetings that are often aired live, are also dominated by *tatemae*. Diet members refrain from expressing definite or concrete opinions in these situations as well. They shy away from clear-cut positions and avoid passing judgment, criticizing, conveying personal emotions, or expressing annoyance in any way that might provoke anger or embarrass others. Toward this end, Diet members use a kind of code that defies lexicographical definition. For example, they often say *ôkiki suru* ("respectfully listen") to mean that they will listen (but probably do nothing); *shinchô ni* ("cautiously") when they intend to do nothing (e.g.

when a situation is virtually hopeless, but they do not want to say so); *hairyo suru* ("consider"), when something is meant to stay tabled indefinitely; *zensho suru* ("deal with appropriately") to avoid saying anything concrete; or *kentô suru* ("look into" or "study") if they mean to kick around an idea without acting on it. One has to understand the hidden meaning of these terms in order to grasp the true intentions of Japanese politicians or bureaucrats at a given time.

Diet members are especially careful to choose vague language when they need to avoid public conflict or maintain cordial relations within their political groups. It is particularly important to avoid "loss of face," which means public embarrassment that results in a loss of self-respect or standing for either speaker or listener. For example, even if a high-echelon Diet member knows that a colleague has done something wrong, such as receiving a bribe, he will not publicly say something like, "I will try to convince the colleague to resign," or "I will take legal action against the colleague." Instead, the Diet member says *ikan ni omou* (literally, "I feel sorry" or "I deplore"). This term is most often used to express personal feelings about political scandal, unsatisfactory responses to accusations, or "slips of the tongue" made by Diet members (e.g. *Asahi*, August 21, 1998). But *ikan ni omou* contains no accusation or personal apology by the speaker, nor any recognition that the speaker should share any part of the blame. One might say that this expression merely indicates that the speaker understands that he or she is expected to "feel sorry" about a particular incident and that's all.

Talking in *tatemae* euphemisms—by blurring opinions, commitments, and emotions, or by presenting only official, widely accepted views—is perhaps the safest way for Diet members and government officials to express themselves and still remain politically viable. *Tatemae* allows them to protect their own feelings, thoughts, and opinions from public scrutiny, to avoid identifying with or advocating particular ideas, and to limit the risk of embarrassing colleagues or offending anyone who holds different political views. Diet members, especially those occupying or aspiring to higher positions, know that *tatemae* is the best method for being accepted and liked—and consequently supported by as many people and groups as possible. Through *tatemae* they aim to be *happô bijin* (liked by everybody) in order to receive maximum support. (Other aspects in this regard are offered in **Chapter 4** on televised political interviews.)

Abusive Language or Political *Honne*?

Slips of the Tongue and Apologies

When Diet members speak too frankly about what is in their hearts they often find themselves under fire from certain sectors of the public, political opponents, or even from within their own political group. On many occasions, opposition parties have utilized slips of the tongue by high-echelon Diet members as ammunition for attacks on the ruling parties; common techniques are boycotting Diet sessions and demanding the resignation of the minister concerned. On May 17, 2000, for example, following Prime Minister Mori's remark that "Japan is a divine nation centering on the Emperor" (see below), four major opposition parties—the Democratic Party of Japan, the Japan Communist Party, the Liberal Party and Social Democratic Party—united in a bid to force Mori's resignation, charging that he was not qualified to be a prime minister.

To further illustrate: On February 28, 1953, at a session of the lower house's most powerful committee, the Budget Committee, a member of the opposition Socialist Party questioned Prime Minister (1946–47, 1948–54) Yoshida Shigeru about his view of international affairs. He repeatedly insisted that he wanted to know not the views held by the leaders of the USA or UK, but "the opinion of the prime minister of Japan." Prime Minister Yoshida could not hide his annoyance and finally muttered, "That's impolite!" ["*burei da*"] followed by "You damn fool!" ["*baka-yarô!*"]. The opposition quickly moved to discipline the prime minister and the plenary session passed a no-confidence resolution. Yoshida chose to dissolve the lower house (in a move known as the "You-Fool Dissolution" ["*bakayarô kaisan*"]) rather than resign (*Shitsugen ô nintei iinkai*, 2000: 34–38).

In February 1988, during a televised debate at a lower house Budget Committee meeting, Chairman Hamada Kôichi, an LDP member, accused Miyamoto Kenji, the head of the JCP, of being "a murderer." He was referring to an infamous incident that took place before World War II, whereby a group of communist leaders allegedly lynched a suspected police spy. At that time, the Communist party was banned and its leaders reportedly engaged in anti-war and anti-government activities underground. Miyamoto was implicated in the murder case but was exonerated due to lack of evidence. The impromptu remark by Hamada moved leaders of the opposition parties to demand his resignation, and he did later resign his post as Chairman of the committee (*Shitsugen ô nintei iinkai*, 2000: 201–11).

One more example took place on January 23, 2003, during a question-and-answer session of the lower house Budget Committee. Kan Naoto, the leader of the biggest opposition party, the DPJ, clashed with Prime Minister Koizumi. Using a diagram to illustrate his points, Kan nagged Koizumi about failing to keep three key campaign promises Koizumi made before becoming prime minister in April 2001: to visit Yasukuni Shrine on August 15, to limit issuance of new government bonds to 30 trillion yen, and to cap government protection of savings deposits as originally scheduled. Koizumi's smile gradually transformed into a glare until he let his feelings out, exclaiming, "It is no major problem if I am unable to stick to promises of this magnitude." Later in the same session, the Prime Minister added, "It may be true that I have not always done what I said I would. However, as prime minister I have to think of much more important things." Following these remarks, Koizumi came under fire from political pundits and commentators both for his excited reaction and for his broken promises.

Numerous Diet members who made a "verbal misstep" were forced to "take responsibility" by either publicly explaining their comments, apologizing, or to submitting their resignation. In a few cases Diet members have even been expelled from their political group because of their public remarks. In April 2001, Tanaka Kô, a lower house member from the DPJ, was expelled from the party for making statements that countered the party's interests during a Chiba Prefecture gubernatorial campaign. Tanaka publicly expressed his personal opinion that his party was excessively dependent on labor unions. The DPJ believed that Tanaka's remarks hurt the party's candidate, and the candidate lost, so Tanaka had to suffer the consequences. Some politicians have been forced to resign from a ministerial position (and were never reappointed to a Cabinet post). Although they resigned from their ministries, not one gave up their seat in the Diet. Most were returned to the Diet in the next election, probably because their use of language was never raised during the campaign (Yamada 2000, cited in Kawano & Matsuo, 2002: 203).

There was one case in which imprudent speech affected election results at the party level. Prime Minister Mori made a series of gaffes just before the national election of June 25, 2000. His verbal indiscretions soured voters on the LDP (especially in the proportional representation vote) to the point that several prominent party members, including former ministers, failed to win a seat and blamed Mori and his mouth for their defeat.

Prime Minister Mori's Gaffes

Prime Minister Mori was famous for his gaffes. In January 2000, while describing his first election campaign in 1969, he said that when he greeted farmers in his constituency from his car, "they all went into their homes and I felt as if I had AIDS." On May 8, 2000, he caused a stir regarding a program to promote ethical and moral education based on Confucian thought in order to establish a firm base for loyalty to the Imperial system. This program eventually culminated in the issuance of the Imperial Rescript on Education [*Kyôiku ni kansuru chokugo,* or *kyôiku chokugo*]. When asked about the growth of violent crime among school children, Prime Minister Mori expressed the view that the Imperial Rescript on Education of the Meiji Period should be revived, saying, "The Imperial Rescript on Education had bad things as well as good things, and it is unfair to say that all of this Rescript was bad." This statement was interpreted as an expression of a deeply held desire to go back to the Meiji Imperial Constitution, i.e. to the good old days when there was more discipline in schools and workplaces, loyalty to the Nation, and a belief that women should stay home to care for children, focus on domestic work, and be submissive toward their husbands.

In a speech given May 15, 2000, Mori made what became known as his "divine-nation remark" ["*kuni no kami hatsugen*"]: "I would like the Japanese people to clearly acknowledge that Japan is a divine nation with the emperor at its center." The remark was made at a meeting of *Shintô Seiji Reimei*, a league of pro-Shintoist Diet members. Opposition parties jumped on this statement as being antidemocratic and contradicting the postwar constitution, which holds the people as sovereign and specifically rejects the notion of imperial divinity. Others accused Mori of stirring dangerous religious sentiments. Prime Minister Mori responded to the criticism on May 16, saying he meant that Japan "has a long history and its own culture and traditions. This does not contradict the principle of popular sovereignty established in the postwar era. With regards to my remarks about the emperor, I meant that he symbolizes Japan's long history and culture." He later apologized for the misunderstanding caused by his remark both before the Diet and in a live, televised interview, but he declined to retract the statement. Mori denied that the emperor is God, stating that, as stipulated in the Constitution, the emperor is the symbol of the unity of the Japanese people. He repeatedly explained that his remark did not refer any specific religion. He added, "it goes without saying that sovereignty rests with the people and that freedom of religion is guaranteed (under the Constitution)."

Three weeks later, on June 3, 2000, Prime Minister Mori gave a lecture in Nara in which he criticized the JCP for opposing the imperial system and the Self-Defense Forces, asking "How could we possibly secure Japan's '*kokutai*' and ensure public safety with such a party?" This remark caused an uproar among the opposition, who claimed the term '*kokutai*' was commonly used to refer to a national policy centering on the emperor before and during World War II. Mori said in a speech later that he had been "scolded for a slip of the tongue"—a comment that was widely taken as an admission that the remark was inappropriate. Yet he insisted that he did not consider the '*kokutai*' remark to be a mistake, adding that his comment was only meant to acknowledge the fact that his use of the term was criticized. Mori said he meant to refer "to the nation's (current) system, and was not connecting it with the old (usage of) *kokutai*."

Several days later, on June 20, Prime Minister Mori put his foot in his mouth yet again, saying he hoped that voters who were still undecided would not participate in the upcoming general election. He said this during a campaign speech in Niigata Prefecture, in reference to public opinion polls published that morning which showed Mori's LDP likely to secure a majority in the lower house but noted that 30–50 percent of voters remained undecided. Mori said, "It would be okay if they remain uninterested in the election and stay asleep. Unfortunately, that's not how it will go" (*Asahi*, June 21, 2000). Mori's remarks were widely interpreted as meaning that the prime minister was hoping for low voter turnout.

Then, in October 2000, Mori made his so-called "abduction resolution remark" ["*rachi dakai hatsugen*"] regarding Japanese nationals allegedly abducted by North Korean agents. Mori raised "the possibility of having the missing Japanese citizens found somewhere outside North Korea," perhaps in Peking or Bangkok, as a compromise solution to the abduction issue (*Asahi*, October 26, 2000). He said this to British Prime Minister Tony Blair when they met at the Third Asia-Europe Meeting summit in Seoul, South Korea. He revealed that three years earlier (in 1997), when he visited North Korea as LDP General Council Chairman, he had suggested to North Korean officials, through another Diet member, that Japanese abductees could be "found" in a third country, thus enabling Pyongyang to save face. The alleged abductions (some of which North Korea later admitted to) had been a major stumbling block in normalization talks between Japan and North Korea. Mori rejected opposition calls for his resignation for this controversial comment.

In January 2001, Prime Minister Mori made yet another faux pas while touring Africa. While addressing a group of Japanese expatriates in Johannesburg, South Africa, Mori commented that he was born in 1937, "the year of the Chinese Incident, and before the Greater East Asian War." Besides the fact that the comment was totally inane, Mori was criticized for apparently not realizing that "Chinese Incident" and "Greater East Asian War" are terms that were used by the militaristic wartime government for what are now known as the Second Sino-Japanese War and the Pacific War respectively. The terms were attempts to justify wars of aggression against China and other Asian countries. Considering that he made this remark some six months after his divine-nation comment had already sparked an uproar, Mori's use of these terms indicates an astounding lack of sensitivity.

Incentives for Mis-Speaking

What motivates politicians to publicly express their ideas and feelings rather than restrain themselves in situations where it is "common sense" to confine controversial thoughts and emotions to the "back" world of politics? In some cases, it is probably a matter of personality. Obviously, some politicians are more prone to explicitly express their "*honne*" without considering the possible repercussions of doing so. Such politicians not only address issues that others avoid, they also wade right in and publicly reveal their views. They are liable to criticize individuals or groups they disapprove of, and to protest if they perceive a lack of appropriate response from social or political entities. Even green reporters know that attending a public speech given by such a politician can result in an interesting headline for the following day's news. Often these particular politicians have trouble controlling their emotions—and thus quite naturally express their frustration or displeasure with colleagues or situations. Prime Minister Uno Sôsuke, for example, was called "an instant water boiler" because he had difficulty hiding his feelings and tended to erupt angrily when a reporter posed a disagreeable question. Kan Naoto, who was Minister of Health and Welfare under Prime Minister Hashimoto Ryûtarô and later became the leader of the DPJ, was nicknamed "*ira-kan*" ("irritable Kan") because of his well-known impatience and irritability (Saikawa, 1999: 328).

Another politician with a reputation for revealing his "*honne*" in public (and for making controversial remarks) is Ishihara Shintarô, a veteran LDP Diet member and the current Governor of Tôkyô. Ishihara is best known outside Japan for his anti-American book, *The Japan That Can Say No*. In April 1977, as Director General of the Environment Agency, Ishihara received a petition from a citizens' group demanding that the government provide aid to victims of Minamata Disease (a degeneration of the nervous system that became common in the fishing town of Minamata. It was caused by methyl mercury poisoning from eating seafood polluted by industrial effluent; the city of Minamata later became known worldwide as a symbol of environmental pollution). After reading it, Ishihara said, "I have no doubts about the content, but this [the petition] appears to have been written by people with low IQs" (*Shitsugen ô nintei iinkai*, 2000: 114).

On another occasion, while addressing Japan's Ground Self-Defense Force on April 9, 2000, Ishihara warned the troops to be prepared for rioting by illegal aliens in the event of a major earthquake. "Atrocious crimes have been committed again and again by *sangokujin* and foreigners who have illegally entered Japan," he said, causing outrage on two counts. First was his use of the term *sangokujin* (literally, "people from third countries," a term used immediately after World War II as a derogatory reference to people from the former Japanese colonies of Korea and Taiwan). Second, his statement was a blatant perversion of history. After the Great Kantô Earthquake of 1923, thousands of Koreans who survived the tremors and firestorms were slaughtered by rioting Japanese who believed rumors that Korean radicals were staging an uprising in Tôkyô. Ishihara was blasted by Koreans and other foreigners, and a citizens' network was established to seek his resignation as Tôkyô governor. (Not to be outdone in the area of xenophobic remarks, while serving as the LDP's Policy Affairs Research Committee Chairman, former Prime Minister Mori noted during the 1992 Los Angeles riots that "Korean workers [in Japan] could cause trouble and form an army," *Yomiuri*, June 9, 1992). In December 2002, Ishihara claimed in a *Shukan Josei* magazine interview that the worst side effect of civilization is the proliferation of "old hags" ["*baba*"]. He explained that "It's meaningless for women to live after they lose their ability to reproduce." He further noted that if women live as long as the famous centenarian sisters affectionately known as Kin-san and Gin-san, "It is quite harmful to the earth."

Another politician who made numerous problematic remarks in public was Watanabe Michio, a former LDP Policy Research Committee Chairman and former Foreign Minister. Standing beside a candidate for Saitama Prefecture Governor at a supporters' rally, Watanabe made his famous "impiety remark" ["*oya fukô hatsugen*"]: "The more social security there is, the more it becomes impiety." This came not long after Watanabe's "cellar remark" ["*ana gura hatsugen*"] in February 24, 1988, when he said that in China's Sanseichô Province "there are still people who dig holes in the ground and live in them." On July 23, 1988, Watanabe said at a party-sponsored seminar in Karuizawa, Nagano Prefecture, that many black Americans often use credit cards, then quickly declare bankruptcy, implying that they walk away from their debts (*Shitsugen ô nintei ünkai*, 2000: 212–14). This remark, dubbed "indifferent" ("*Akkeraka*") caused an uproar in the USA, and the LDP and the Japanese government received a flood of protest letters. Watanabe apparently regretted his remark; since then he had contributed $100,000 every year for scholarships at universities attended mostly by blacks in the southern USA. In December 1991, when Watanabe became Foreign Minister and deputy prime minister, Foreign Ministry officials were afraid of further embarrassment, so they often wrote him memos instructing him what to say in public and how to say it. (Former Prime Minister Mori's advisors used the same tactic after his numerous blunders of 2000. They provided him with memos and instructed him to stick to the script during public appearances.)

One other politician whose verbal outbursts and diplomatic faux pas often made headlines was Tanaka Makiko, who served at different times as Director General of the Science and Technology Agency and as Foreign Minister. On April 14, 2001, while speaking to LDP supporters in Tôkyô, Tanaka ridiculed the late Prime Minister Obuchi Keizo, calling him "*odabutsu-san*," and urged the audience to support Koizumi Junichirô in the LDP's presidential election. Tanaka said Obuchi tried to raise his public approval rating "although he rang up 100 trillion yen in debts during his first year in office." She continued, "Then his (brain) ruptured and he kicked the bucket. He asked for it." Tanaka's speech was met with roars of laughter, but she received a letter of protest from the LDP Secretary General, who objected that her remarks ridiculed and insulted the sincere political stance on which Mr. Obuchi had staked his life (*Asahi*, April 18, 2001).

Personality factors may explain the tendency of specific politicians and government officials toward making these types of remarks. Certain public figures do appear to be more inclined than others to use "abusive language." This makes it necessary to distinguish between this type of utterances and "slips of the tongue." These are two distinct concepts, as some politicians find themselves in trouble for indiscreet remarks that they said unintentionally. Their remarks appear to be "pure misstatement" or "incidental slip of tongue" rather than "violent or abusive language." My point here is to differentiate between unintentional problematic comments and intentional, abusive remarks. I further suggest that it is most often the surrounding circumstances that cause some utterances to have unintended consequences (as in "slips of the tongue"). For example, a politician might make a comment in a closed meeting with reporters in the belief that the comment will be kept off the record. Although the politician had no intention of provoking or offending anyone, some segment of the public may become upset if the remark ends up being reported by mass media. Or it sometimes happens that certain voters are not amused by something a politician intended as a joke. In other situations, politicians may intentionally make insensitive or slanderous comments aimed at provoking others. These two explanations for why politicians make problematic statements—circumstances and personality—are not mutually exclusive, but rather complement each other as reasons why public figures put their feet in their mouths. The following describes three categories of oral blunders.

"Intimate" remarks   The first is remarks made in closed, informal meetings that politicians hold with small groups of colleagues, bureaucrats, or news reporters. In these meetings, Diet members often make controversial remarks without paying much attention to content or wording, or to the possible implications should their words find their way to the public ear. They have no intention of hurting any person or group. If such comments are made public, it is often the politicians themselves who are most surprised and embarrassed, not only because what they thought was a private comment ended up being publicized by the mass media, but because the result is often that they are subject to negative public attention for what appears to be an insensitive comment.

As an example, upon assuming his new position as Minister of Health and Welfare on December 27, 1983, Watanabe Kozo half-jokingly told reporters, "During the campaign, I smoked 80 cigarettes a day. Cigarettes are good for health . . . Smoking tobacco makes one live longer" (*Shitsugen ô nintei iinkai*, 2000: 276). His statement was severely criticized by people suffering from chronic, smoking-related illnesses and by medical doctors. Watanabe himself was stunned by the uproar over his off-the-cuff remark. Or, consider a remark that then-Prime Minister Uno made in July 1989 while drinking with his aides. He said (in light of a scandal over his adulterous relationship with a woman), "As things stand now, I am willing to quit. I never wanted to become prime minister at first place" (*Aera*, July 11, 1989: 14). Confronted by the press the following day, the prime minister felt uncomfortable by the turmoil that his "private" chat had caused. He called the report "absurd," flatly denying he had any intention of resigning.

In September 1990, newly appointed Justice Minister Kajiyama Seiroku briefed reporters about a police crackdown on foreign prostitutes allegedly soliciting customers on Tôkyô streets. In his remarks, Kajiyama compared the women to black Americans who "ruin the atmosphere" when they move into a neighborhood. He said streetwalkers give a bad reputation to orderly neighborhoods "like in America when neighborhoods become mixed because blacks move in, and whites are forced out" (e.g. *Mainichi*, September 22, 1990). Shortly after his words were reported, protests came from the Tôkyô ambassadors of several African countries, as well as from other foreigners. The ministry then issued a correction in which Kajiyama said he meant to say that people living in the area where the crackdown took place "feel insecure" and have been "complaining."

On June 6, 2002, Chief Cabinet Secretary Fukuda Yasuo commented during an informal discussion with reporters on Japan's "three non-nuclear principles" (not to produce, possess, or allow nuclear weapons into the country, which became one of Japan's key national policies). Fukuda said, "If something serious (related to national security) or major changes in international relations should occur, public opinion could shift in favor of this country's having (nuclear weapons)." He probably simply meant to say that any basic policy of a country can be subject to review in light of changing times and circumstances. He did not refer to any government policy, but rather to the possibility of a shift in public opinion. Nevertheless, a great uproar was sparked as newspapers published articles speculating that Fukuda's comment suggested the government might be reviewing the three non-nuclear principles. He was attacked by opposition leaders for having "hawkish" views. In fact, Fukuda never intended to suggest that there was any possibility that the government would change its non-nuclear policy. But his comment received especially extensive attention because it was made just as the Diet was deliberating an LDP-sponsored package of bills aimed at giving the nation more flexibility in its potential responses in the event of a military attack from abroad. In the wake of the uproar over Fukuda's remark, Prime Minister Koizumi reiterated that Japan would adhere firmly to its three non-nuclear principles (*Yomiuri*, Editorials, June 7, 2002, and June 20, 2002).

One can also include in this category troublesome remarks that were caused by a politician's lack of knowledge or information. On September 12, 2001, the day after the infamous terrorist attacks in the USA, Foreign Minister Tanaka Makiko told reporters where US State Department staff members were taking refuge after hijacked plans crashed into New York's World Trade Center and the Pentagon. Citing information from the US State Department, she told reporters that the department was temporary relocating to a training institute in Arlington, Virginia, and that the ad hoc headquarters was being headed by Deputy Secretary of State Richard Armitage. Following Tanaka's indiscretion in front of TV cameras, Prime Minister Koizumi, Chief Cabinet Secretary Fukuda, and the Japanese Ambassador to the USA all expressed anger, and senior Foreign Ministry bureaucrats decided to stop reporting secret information to Tanaka due to fears that she might not keep it confidential. Tanaka expressed regret for her carelessness, claiming that no one had told her the information was not to be made public.

"Entertaining" the audience The second category is gaffes made during speeches with the intent of amusing listeners.

Japanese Diet members regularly address supporters in their constituency, especially on weekends. These meetings serve as important opportunities for Diet members to update supporters on their own activities on behalf of the community, as well as to give their views of current affairs, including inside developments in Japanese politics. A veteran Diet member once told me that when he is surrounded by supporters in his hometown, he always opens up and discusses political events as if he was among family. "Every Diet member knows that our supporters want us to talk about public affairs in simple, easy-to-understand language, and especially to let them know about things that are not reported in the newspapers," he said.

Diet members do everything they can to satisfy this desire, and to tailor their speech to the particular audience in front of them. Rather than limiting themselves to dry facts, they often entertain supporters with anecdotes and details about unpublicized aspects of the political process. They tend to divulge their personal assessment of social issues, international affairs, their own political group, and even personnel issues, and to reveal their true thoughts and feelings regarding a wide range of subjects including colleagues and opponents. After all, shouldn't it be safe to reveal their personal feelings to people they regard as "family"?

Not a few Diet members tend to wax eloquent as they relax. They very often start their talk with interesting anecdotes or metaphors in order to create a relaxed atmosphere in which they can open up and establish a smooth dialogue with their audience. The more they feel relaxed and close to their audience, the more their excitement leads them to talk frankly. This tendency is often reinforced by enthusiastic reactions from the crowd, such as frequent applause, laughter, or encouraging shouts. This kind of atmosphere emerges very frequently when politicians speak in their home district. One former minister explained, "At such times, I always feel the audience wants me to share more and more experiences, and to tell more about my own beliefs and views. And that is what I exactly do."

It is not rare for Diet members to illustrate their discussions of political issues with small stories about recent experiences they had in *Nagatachô* with other politicians or with government officials. They tend to intentionally exaggerate these tidbits in order to keep the audience's attention—at times by emphasizing absurd or amusing aspects of their work, or by spicing their performance with jokes or metaphors in the local dialect to impress the audience with their proximity and friendliness. The leader of one political party put it this way: "No one can lecture about a serious topic like politics for 90 minutes in front of 2,000 people without inserting a joke here and a small story there, maybe even mentioning a bit of gossip or a rumor to keep the talk interesting. Otherwise, everybody will feel bored and go home."

These are the kind of circumstances in which a politician is also prone to utter a harsh or insensitive word or two regarding another politician, a bureaucrat, a political group, or even women in general. Such remarks are intended only to entertain the listeners at hand. That was probably the only reason why Horinouchi Hisao, former Minister of Agriculture, Forestry and Fisheries, said in a campaign speech in July 1989, "Politics is impossible for women" (*Shitsugen ô nintei iinkai*, 2000: 314). He drew sharp criticism for this disparaging statement.

As long as no reporters attend such gatherings and publicize the politicians' words, there is rarely any damage. The audience enjoy their Diet representative's talk and report on the political situation and the Diet member's views on the world beyond the district, and then leave for home. But sometimes the contents of a speech get reported in the media—whether at the local or the national level—and draw criticism as being careless or indiscreet. When these reports cause political ripples, other news organizations inevitably take them up in their own headlines. In this way, a casual remark that a politician makes at a small gathering of supporters can draw massive media attention that results in negative feedback or great inconvenience for the politician, or at times even damaging Japan's relations with its neighbors or adversely affecting the legislative process. There are numerous examples of this, including the remarks cited above involving Prime Minister Mori.

In January 1992, at a gathering of his supporters in Shimane Prefecture, lower house Speaker and former Foreign Minister Sakurauchi Yoshio, said American workers wanted high pay even though were lazy and unproductive. He was discussing a pledge by Japanese carmakers to sharply increase purchases of US-made auto parts. Japanese manufacturers had complained that car components produced in the US were of inferior quality. Probably aiming to entertain his listeners, Sakurauchi claimed "the root of the problem lies in the deteriorating quality of American workers. . .

The American labor force doesn't work hard enough. They want to receive high salaries without working fully." In addition to casting doubt on the quality of US goods, he said, "About 30 percent of the US labor force cannot read well enough to receive written work instructions" (*Yomiuri*, January 21, 1992). While he did get a lot of laughs from the crowd, his comments were slammed the following day in the national and international media.

In another case, in June 1992, former LDP Vice President Kanemaru Shin told a gathering of support groups in his district (Yamanashi Prefecture) that when he met President George Bush a few days earlier, he had told him "Russians are liars," and "Giving money to Russia now is like throwing money away" (*Shitsugen ô nintei iinkai*, 2000: 314). Again, although his remarks were intended to entertain his listeners by his intimacy to the US President, they carried other meaning for the news media.

It should be noted that Diet members, especially those who hold high-echelon positions within their party, regularly give lectures to various organizations in and outside their district. The more outspoken ones are always in demand as speakers. Such Diet members may give three or more lectures in different locations in the course of a single day. On average, they may give two or three lectures a week, amounting to at least 100 lectures a year. In addition, of course, they speak within their party at meetings organized for various purposes in various seasons, including campaign speeches and official greetings, often on behalf of friendly colleagues or candidates. These legislators have connections in various government offices and can exert various kinds of influence. It is not rare for them to say publicly that they can get government offices to do something for the listeners in return for voters' support for a certain candidate. Such remarks may be intended as mere rhetoric, but they attract media attention because of their suggestive nature.

For example, on February 18, 2000, Ochi Michio, Chairman of the Financial Reconstruction Commission (which determines the fate of failing and processes applications from banks seeking public funds), spoke at a meeting organized by his LDP colleague, Hasumi Susumu, in Hasumi's home district of Tochigi Prefecture. The audience included many executives of regional financial institutions. Referring to audits by the Bank of Japan and the Financial Supervisory Agency (which inspects and supervises the financial industry), Ochi said, "Please inform us of any complaints about the inspection, if it's strict . . . I will give the utmost consideration if you make a written request to Mr. Hasumi and he passes it to me" (reported in Kawano & Matsuo, 2002). In other words, he hinted that he would use his influence to soften inspections of financial institutions. Ochi's main purpose was probably to show off his political influence. But as a committee chair assigned an important role in restoring confidence in Japanese banks at a time when confidence was so low, his suggestion that the commission might exercise arbitrary discretion was tantamount to treason. After news media reported this comment, the opposition parties threatened to boycott deliberations on the fiscal 2000 budget, and Ochi was eventually forced to resign from his Chairman position.

Another famous example occurred when Tanaka Makiko (then Foreign Minister) was asked to endorse Yoshikawa Mayumi as the LDP's candidate for a upper house seat. In a speech given in Maebashi, Gunma Prefecture on July 28, 2001, the day before the election, Tanaka jokingly asked, "So what is this candidate's name?" pretending not to know. The candidate showed Tanaka a banner on her shoulder bearing her name, and tried to pat Tanaka's arm, but Tanaka told her not to touch, in an obviously joking manner. This did cause laughter among the audience, but Tanaka was severely criticized, and was blamed when Yoshikawa failed to win the seat. Tanaka later apologized to the candidate she was supposed to have endorsed, admitting she had made "inappropriate" remarks.

Politicians may also get in trouble for "slips of the tongue" made while entertaining within their own political party. In April 1988, for example, in his opening address at an LDP debate on political-economic issues, Mori Yoshirô (mentioned above) made the "spittoon remark" ["*tantsubo hatsugen*"] when said, "(The city of) Ôsaka, otherwise known as the spittoon, is always thinking only about how to make money, and has become in fact a dirty city. If it plans to develop as a city of the 21st century, it should increase its cultural and public affairs" (*Mainichi*, April 24, 1988). And, on December 11, 1993, Ôuchi Keigo, the Health and Welfare Minister, mentioned during a conference of the Democratic Socialist Party in Fukui Prefecture that, "Without wanting to name specific countries, all Asian countries surrounding Japan are AIDS countries." Ôuchi went on to say, "Peacekeeping forces, other than those from Japan, become affected by AIDS and go back home. The world is threatened with destruction more by AIDS than by nuclear disaster." Ôuchi was censured by AIDS patients and organizations that support them, by doctors' groups, and by non-Japanese Asians in general (*Shitsugen ô nintei iinkai*, 2000: 316).

Diet members would even do well to be careful about disclosing their *honne* during "seminars" or "study sessions," with other members of their party or faction. "Seminars" give political allies opportunities to socialize on weekends or holidays, in relaxed venues far from *Nagatachô*, possibly at a resort. Participants informally discuss issues of common concern, and hear lectures about political, social, or international affairs from veteran politicians, scholars, or specialists. These meetings are intended partly to strengthen the cohesiveness of the group. Although they are "closed" to outsiders, details of what was said at such meetings have often been leaked to reporters and revealed to the public, resulting in a public stir. A famous example is the widely reported statement made by former Prime Minister

(1982–87) Nakasone Yasuhiro when addressing an LDP seminar in Shizuoka on September 22, 1986 (Akasaka, 1986):

> No country puts as much diverse information as accurately into the ears of its people (as Japan does). It has become a very intelligent society. Compared to the likes of America, the average level in Japan is far higher. In America, there are many blacks, Puerto Ricans, and Mexicans, and taken on average, America's per capita level of intelligence as gained through education and the mass media is still extremely low . . . Japan is such a dense, vibrant society, a high-level information society, a highly educated society . . .

Many Japanese took Nakasone's remark to mean that he believed Japan's racially and culturally homogeneous society was inherently superior to a mixed society like that of the USA . So Nakasone's remark received little attention in Japan until the Americans made an issue of it. At first Nakasone tried to shrug off criticism by claiming that he had been quoted out of context and that although he may have expressed himself clumsily, he had not meant to malign the US or any ethnic group. Later, Nakasone apologized formally to the American people for the remark.

Just two days after Nakasone made this offending remark, he again suffered a "slip of the tongue" during a special press conference held September 24, 1986. In an attempt to explain the previous remark, Nakasone said, "Because Japan is an ethnically homogenous society, it is easy to reach everyone (in matters related to education)" (*Shitsugen ô nintei iinkai*, 2000: 190). This particularly angered the Ainu, descendants of an indigenous people who now number about 240,000 and are struggling to preserve their cultural traditions and ethnic identity. It is only in recent years that the Japanese government has started to recognize the Ainu's claim that they are a separate people from the majority of Japanese citizens.

Insensitive or slanderous comments   The third type of comments are insensitive or slanderous comments that politicians make about "hot" divisive issues, sometimes with the intention of upsetting a certain segment of the population or foreign communities. Diet members or government officials can anticipate in advance that their remarks may complicate a situation or hurt certain people, yet they go ahead and have their say anyway. Most often they do so out of arrogance, rather than out of naîvéty as is the case with remarks of the first category described above. Comments of the third type are not aimed at entertaining. They go beyond "slip of the tongue," to constitute "violent language" [*bôgen*]. Tôkyô Governor Ishihara's *sangokujin* remark, for example, falls into this category. Another example is a comment made by then-Prime Minister Miyazawa Kiichi (1991–93), who said this in February 1992 in response to a question in the Diet's Budget Committee about the causes of US economic ills:

Many young Americans fresh out of college went to work on Wall Street for extremely big salaries, so there has been a rapid reduction in the number of engineers who make things . . . I have long felt that because of this a work ethic may have been lacking . . . I think in some sense there were elements of this in Japan's so-called bubble economy. (*Asahi*, February 4, 1992)

Miyazawa was perplexed by the fierce US response to his reference to Americans' lack of a "work ethic." He insisted that his remarks had been taken out of context and reported incorrectly. Prime Minister Kaifu Toshiki (1989–91), while refuting criticisms that his political reform proposals would invite the same problems that plague the American electoral system, told the Diet in September 1991, "American candidates do not put sufficient weight on ethics in their elections . . . " (*Shitsugen ô nintei iinkai*, 2000: 315).

Another insensitive (and again racist) remark was made by Hori Kôsuke, Home Affairs Minister and Chairman of the National Safety Commission, who noted on April 26, 2000, that foreigners staying illegally in Japan could use prepaid cell phones to commit crimes. His remark followed the arrest of kidnappers who used a prepaid phone to communicate with the father of their seven-year old victim. The kidnappers were Japanese.

In a lecture at the Foreign Press Club of Japan in April 2001 former Minister for Economic and Fiscal Policy Asô Tarô admitted, "I may be dogmatic and prejudiced, but I think that the best country to live in is the one where rich Jews prefer to live" (*Asahi*, April 20, 2001). During a speech to the national convention of the Japanese Association of Psychiatric Hospitals on November 6, 2002, Kimura Yoshio, Vice-Minister for Health warned, "There are many money-grubbers like Jews who are keeping a vigilant eye on the 30-trillion-yen medical market. We have to coordinate our efforts to stop such people." Kimura apologized to the Israeli ambassador for his remark, after the Simon Wiesenthal Centre, a US-based Jewish human rights organization, sent a letter to Prime Minister Koizumi.

Similar "violent language" expressed by politicians at the local level is rarely taken up by the national media. One exception was when Kokubo Masao, an LDP member of the Hyôgo Prefectural Assembly, said at a March 1993 meeting of the assembly's special budget committee:

I realize there are some stupid Japanese women who would marry those useless people (foreign workers in Japan) . . . I feel strange when I go somewhere where more than 10 Pakistanis or Indians have gathered . . . Have you ever shaken hands with a black person? When I shake hands with a black person I feel like my hands are turning black. (*Asahi*, March 19, 1993)

As mentioned above, "indiscreet" and "violent" remarks made by Japanese politicians have often provoked criticism from outside as well as inside Japan. Three sensitive topics in particular have provoked overseas outrage. The first is "self-other-related remarks" that compare Japanese people with other ethnic groups (such as Jews or blacks) or Japan with other countries (especially the US) and "find" Japan to be superior, more morally pure, and/or having harder-working people. Examples cited above include Nakasone's comment on the higher educational level of Japan (because of its "homogeneity") and that of Miyazawa on the US work ethic. The second topic is defense, which includes questions about the need to change Japan's constitution and the value of nuclear armaments. The third is Japan's historical role in Asia in the 20th century. Diet members have often made remarks to justify Japan's military activities in the Sino–Japanese War and in the Pacific War. Most such remarks were made during newspaper or magazine interviews initiated by the politician, or in columns aimed at letting the public know their true beliefs regarding controversial issues in order to ignite political chaos.

Defense and the Constitution

Since the end of World War II, Japan has remained polarized over defense-related issues, especially Article Nine of the Constitution, which bans the use of force to resolve international conflicts. Several high-echelon Diet members (and public officials) have been criticized for their public statements about these issues. For example, former Prime Minister Kishi Nobusuke (1957–60) declared in an interview with NBC on October 14, 1958, "The time has come for Japan to abolish Article Nine of the Constitution" (*Shitsugen ô nintei iinkai*, 2000: 240). Following criticism in the Diet, he denied having made such a remark. In August 27, 1980, Okuno Seisuke, then Minister of Justice, said in a meeting of the lower house Committee on Justice, "From a politician's point of view, the current Constitution was decided by the Allied Forces. Hopefully the public will discuss the need to create a new Constitution by itself . . . The main political parties completely disagree about Article Nine. So it would be good to change the Constitution in line with the public view" (*Shitsugen ô nintei iinkai*, 2000: 131). Okuno also was condemned for his saying.

Prime Ministers Suzuki Zenkô (1980–82) and Nakasone Yasuhiro were both chastised for remarks on defense issues. After holding official talks with President Ronald Reagan in May 1981, Prime Minister Suzuki was reproved for issuing a communiqué that included the word "alliance" ["*dômei*"]. Suzuki's Foreign Minister Itô Masayoshi resigned to protest Suzuki's refusal to admit that there was a military meaning to this use of "alliance." In January 1983, Prime Minister Nakasone was criticized for several statements he made about defense while meeting with President Reagan. On one occasion, Nakasone declared that Japan should aim for "complete control" of the strategic straits controlling the Sea of Japan "so that there should be no passage of Soviet submarines or other naval activities in times of emergency." In an interview, he referred to Japan as an "unsinkable aircraft carrier" ["*fuchin kûbo*"] that could prevent penetration by Soviet Backfire bombers into Japanese airspace. For many opposition members and private citizens, this expression evoked negative images of Japan as a military fortress (Sakonjô, 1983). Another phrase that Prime Minister Nakasone used in talks with the US president was "common destiny" ["*unmei kyôdôtai*"], by which he apparently meant shared values and interests, but which many Japanese viewed unfavorably as linking Japan and the US military in a "collective security" arrangement.

In 1993, Nakanichi Keisuke was forced to resign from his post as Director General of the Defense Agency in order to resolve a Diet deadlock over a controversial speech wherein he called for a revision of the Constitution. On December 1, 1993, Nakanichi told a study meeting of Diet members from his political party,

> The world is changing rapidly, and whether or not we can adapt will determine whether we survive. Among other things, the Constitution did not foresee participation by our Self-Defense Forces in UN peace-keeping operations. (*Asahi*, December 2, 1993)

This remark was taken as a call to let the Self-Defense Forces become more active in UN peacekeeping operations by amending Article Nine. This comment provoked criticism from members of the opposition parties and resulted in the resignation of the Nakanichi from his position as a minister.

Another controversial remark about defense was made on October 15, 1999, by Vice-Minister of the Defense Agency Nishimura Shingo during an interview with *Playboy*:

> As long as both (India and Pakistan) have nuclear arms, nuclear war will not occur. Countries that do not have them are in the most dangerous situation. Japan is the most dangerous place. It might be better for Japan to get nuclear arms. This must be discussed in the Diet. (*Shitsugen ô nintei iinkai*, 2000: 216)

The governments of South Korea and China lodged formal protests against this statement. Opposition parties called for the head of Prime Minister Obuchi, who had appointed Nishimura, and tried to force a vote of no-confidence in the Cabinet. In the end, Nishimura had to resign due to the criticism.

Reinterpreting History

Finally, another type of remark with which Diet members stir people up is insensitive comments about World War II and Japan's role in it. Through nationalism and ignorance of history, several apparently intentional misinterpretations of historical facts regarding Japan's invasion of its Asian neighbors have provoked criticism from them.

There are two main views of the war in Japan. The "mainstream" interpretation agrees with the International Military Tribunal for the Far East, which prosecuted war crimes on behalf of the victorious Allies. According to this view, Japan committed acts of aggression toward Asian countries and should apologize for those actions. On August 10, 1993, in his first press conference after taking office, Prime Minister Hosokawa Morihiro clearly admitted Japan's "war responsibility" and acknowledged that he personally perceived World War II as a "war of aggression" that was "wrong" (*Asahi*, August 11, 1993). Prime Minister Hosokawa was not the first prime minister to hint at Japanese imperialism and aggression. When asked about the nature of World War II at a plenary session of the upper house in June 1989, Prime Minister Uno proclaimed that it plainly was an act of military aggression. Previously, Prime Minister Takeshita Noboru had said he would wait for the judgment of historians, but later he admitted that Japan acted aggressively. But Hosokawa's remark differed from those of his predecessors in that it was made of his own accord at a news conference. He had positioned a thorough review of the war as one of the top priorities of his new cabinet, deviating from agendas set by previous cabinets (*Asahi*, August 15, 1993). His statement was welcomed by China, South Korea and other Asian states as a long overdue gesture that opened the door to new, forward-looking relations.

In August 1995, Prime Minister Murayama Tomiichi issued a statement expressing his "sincere apology" for Japan's aggression and colonial rule of neighboring Asian countries during World War II. The statement also outlined a series of steps to be taken by Japan to resolve issues stemming from its wartime conduct. In his statement, Murayama referred to these steps as an expression of Japan's "remorse and soul-searching" about the sexual enslavement of women from South Korea, the Philippines and Taiwan who were forced to work in Japanese military brothels before and during World War II (*Asahi*, August, 15, 1994). Prime Minister Koizumi also expressed a "heartfelt apology" to Chinese victims of Japan's wartime aggression on October 8, 2001, while visiting a museum in China dedicated to China's wartime resistance against Japan. Koizumi said: "I looked at the various exhibits with a feeling of heartfelt apology and condolences for those Chinese people who were victims of aggression."

However not all Japanese support Hosokawa, Murayama, and Koizumi's views. There are about three million war dead enshrined at Yasukuni Shrine and about one million war-bereaved families. These families wonder whether their fathers, sons, husbands, and other family members had died fighting in a war of aggression against neighboring Asian countries and if the government is wrong in paying hommage to people who died for their country. These people have with no doubt electoral power which is evaluated by many politicians. Some of these politicians, in contrast to this attitude of Hosokawa, Murayama, and Koizumi, subscribe to the historical view "affirming the Greater East Asia War." They believe the war was aimed at liberating Asia from Western powers, and that Japan's wartime deeds were no worse than those of other countries. And these politicians let their views known in public.

In September 1986, Education Minister Fujio Masayuki angered South Korea by saying in an interview with a monthly magazine that South Korea bore some responsibility for Japan's "annexation" of the Korean Peninsula between 1910 and 1945 (*Bungei Shunjû*, 1986). In the same interview, he said, "There was no invasion by the Japanese Government and it was based on a mutual agreement between Japanese Prime Minister Itô Hirobumi and Jong Go, the Korean representative." Referring to Japan's military actions in China before and during World War II, he said Japan was not the only country that had invaded other countries and that atrocities of war existed worldwide. He also expressed doubts about Chinese estimates that the Imperial Japanese Army slaughtered more than 300,000 Chinese civilians in the "Nanjing Massacre" following the invasion of Nanjing in December 1937. The South Korean and the Chinese government lodged formal protests and Fujio resigned from his position.

In April 1988, National Land Agency Director General Okuno Seisuke justified Japan's military actions against Asian countries during World War II, saying "Japan fought the war in order to secure its safety. . . . Asia was colonized by Caucasians at that time. Japan was by no means an aggressor nation" (*Aera*, May 24, 1988). Okuno opined that the Japanese government "Maintained a consistent non-expansionist policy" in its war with China, so he did not like it to be called a war of aggression. In addition, he claimed that the Marco Polo Bridge incident that triggered full-scale war was purely accidental. Okuno furthermore expressed regret that some Japanese had been "twisted around" by Chinese leader Deng Xiaoping's comment to LDP leader Itô Masayoshi: "China regrets the existence of a handful of Japanese people who do not wish to see improvement in Sino-Japanese relations." Prime Minister Takeshita and Foreign Minister Uno expressed their regrets about Okuno's comments while the major opposition parties demanded his resignation and slammed the Takeshita Cabinet. Eventually, Okuno resigned, taking responsibility for the criticism he aroused by these remarks.

On May 4, 1994, Justice Minister Nagano Shigeto had been in office for only 10 days when he retracted two controversial statements he made in an interview with the daily *Mainichi*:

> It was wrong to define the Pacific War as a war of aggression on Japan's part . . . Japan stood up for its survival because it was in danger of being crushed

. . . Japan thought seriously about liberating colonies . . . allied powers should
be blamed for having driven Japan that far. The aims of the war were funda-
mentally permissible and justifiable at that time.

Nagano also added that he thought the 1937 Nanjing Massacre was "a fabrication."

On August 11, 1994, Environment Agency chief Sakurai Shin explained at a news conference that Japan did not intend to fight a "war of aggression" in Asia. He said that during the war, "Japan did not fight the Pacific War with the intention of invading." As a consequence of the war, he added, most Asian countries gained independence from European colonial rule and, as a result, were able to promote education and boost literacy, thereby attaining momentum for economic recon-struction (*Shitsugen ô nintei iinkai*, 2000: 316). On October 11, 1995, Etô Takami, Director General of the Management and Coordination Agency, commented that "Japan also did some good things for Korea" during its 1910–45 colonization, "including planting trees and building roads." (Etô made similar remarks in July 2003, as mentioned at the beginning of this chapter.) Both Nagano, Sakurai, and Etô were forced to step down from their positions amid the furor that followed their remarks.

And on February 19, 2001, Norota Hôsei, Chairman of the lower house Budget Committee and former Defense Minister, said this at a meeting of LDP supporters in Akita Prefecture: "Faced with oil and other embargoes from other countries (including the USA), Japan had no other choice but to venture out southward to secure natural resources. . . In other words, Japan had fallen prey to a scheme of the United States. This is what many historians are saying." Calling the Pacific War the "Greater East Asia War" as it was called by the Japanese Imperialists who sought a "Greater East Asia Co-Prosperity Sphere" ruled by Japan, Norota added, "Many heads of countries said the Greater East Asia War helped colonialism (in Asia) come to an end, thus helping many areas win independence." His comments were blasted by South Korean foreign ministry officials and Japanese opposition parties, who submitted a resolution calling for Norota's dismissal as Chairman of the Committee.

Silent Political Communicators

Obviously, Japanese Diet members have to pay a great deal of attention to what they say in public, since speaking inappropriately on the "front" side of politics can cause them harm. To prevent embarrassment, public debate, or criticism over what they say, high-level Diet members and public officials often conceal their real thoughts and opinions, preferring instead to comment in a formal manner or to speak vaguely. Ordinarily, they try to control the information they disseminate to the public through the news media so as to avoid being criticized for using indiscreet language.

Senior Diet members (and government officials) tend to volunteer more information and disclose their real intentions to small, select groups of 10–15 media representatives who are invited to informal background briefings [*kondan*]. These include beat (*ban*) reporters who cover their activities exclusively. As detailed in **Chapter 2**, these meetings are attended only by reporters who the Diet member knows very well, and on these occasions Diet members dispense information more openly, explain issues in more detail, and disclose "the story behind the story" and other information that they would not reveal in an open press conference, particularly if it were broadcast live. They volunteer a good deal of information on political events as they develop, the activities of leading Diet members, and their own true thoughts and intentions regarding policy or personnel issues. At these meetings, the privileged reporters are able to chat with their source, ask questions and receive clarification. *Kondan* enables reporters to grasp the real mood in a political group, government ministry or agency regarding specific issues. High-echelon Diet members also speak *honne* when they meet reporters in their homes during "morning visits" (*asa gake*), or "nights rounds" and "nights attacks" [*yo-mawari* and *yo-uchi*]. Diet members' living rooms provide an intimate and relaxed atmosphere for conversation. These very friendly meetings may include alcoholic drinks or snacks served by the Diet member's wife or secretary, and constitute reporters' best chance to gather real information about the core of political events and personnel matters.

Meetings between news reporters and their sources fall into four categories. First are on-the-record meetings at which reporters are free to disclose their source and all remarks. In the second type, the content of remarks can be reported, but must be attributed to an unnamed source such as "a high-ranking government official," "a well-informed source," "a top government official," "LDP executive officer," or "a number of involved people." Thus information disclosed by the Chief Cabinet Secretary will appear in the newspapers as attributed to "a senior government official;" information obtained from one (or all) of the three key officials of the LDP will be attributed to "top-level LDP official": ministerial or vice ministerial remarks during *kondan* will be attributed to either "top-level official in the Ministry of Foreign Affairs" or "top-level official in the ministry of Economy, Trade and Industry"; and news obtained from bureaucrats at the level of division chief or chief of section of a certain ministry will be attributed to "a source in the Ministry of Foreign Affairs" or "a source in the Ministry of Education." The identity of all these news sources is known to everybody in *Nagatachô* and is only concealed from the general public.

In the third type, the content can be used as background for other stories, and in the last type, nothing from the meeting can be reported.

Most intimate meetings between reporters and high-echelon Diet members fall into the latter, completely off-the-record category. Revealing their *honne* only to a close circle of people reassures sources that their information will remain "among friends," and not be leaked to outsiders in an inconvenient way. Because of the limited number of reporters present at off-the-record *kondan*, it is easy to determine who did not respect the speaker's wishes, just by looking at the next editions of the news. So reporters have the opportunity to learn the inside story, but they are not supposed to let the public know.

As a result, political stories in the national media are dominated by coverage of the routine activities of high-echelon Diet members, especially the prime minister. Political coverage focuses on where these people went, who they met with, and what they talked about, mostly in general terms. This is the formal, *tatemae* side of Japanese politics. Such stories are safe for politicians because they rarely involve personal opinions, evaluations, or direct statements. The public thus lacks essential information, and is left to try to read between the lines and decipher what slips through the cracks in order to fathom the real dynamics of the political process and the will of its leaders.

Although information sources are keen to shield themselves for the reasons mentioned above, there have been numerous instances in which high-level Diet members (and senior bureaucrats) were forced to resign due to leaking of information originally given off the record. Some of the off-the-record information revealed to reporters reaches the general public through the "back door of Japanese journalism," i.e. weekly and monthly magazines, as opposed to the "front door" national dailies. Occasionally such information is leaked and appears in the national media where it immediately attracts the nation's (and sometime international) attention. For example, in October 1995, Hoshuyama Noboru, head of the Defense Facilities Administration Agency, made an off-the-record statement that was leaked to the national media. Hoshuyama was forced to resign over an alleged remark to the effect that then-Prime Minister Murayama was "stupid" in the way he handled Okinawa Governor Ota Masahide's refusal to sign orders forcing landowners to renew leases on property used by US military forces. In violation of established journalistic ethics, Tôkyô Broadcasting Service (TBS) reported this off-the-record remark made at an informal meeting. The rest of the news media then followed suit, and played up the issue. A month later, Etô's off-the-record comment that "Japan also did some good things for Korea" was leaked in a similar way, inciting outrage from Koreans and other politicians.

Many politicians blame the news media for taking their remarks—whether on or off-the-record—out of context, or for blowing them up to the extent that cause them trouble. Reporters call this "passing the buck" [*sekinin tenka*], i.e. transferring one's responsibility to someone else. In fact, many politicians view the media as the source of their image troubles, and openly blame the media accordingly.

Here are few examples: at a gathering with his supporters in his constituency in November 3, 1992, Watanabe Michio criticized the mass media and said it behaves "exactly like gangsters" ["*bôryoku dan*"]. In May 1994, Ozawa Ichirô, leader of the now-defunct New Frontier Party [*Shinshintô*], said he thought the mass-circulation daily *Asahi* was either "a red newspaper or black journalism" (*Asahi*, May 17, 1994), when it ran an article based on second-hand information without checking the facts with him. Ozawa blasted the daily for "slandering" him, apparently in reference to an April 26, 1994, *Asahi* story in which he was quoted as saying, "It doesn't matter which woman one sleeps with." The remark was allegedly made in reference to the SDP's departure from the ruling coalition in reaction to the formation of an LDP alliance in the lower house. Speaking of the new alliance as if it were an extramarital affair, Ozawa reportedly told reporters in the Diet building, "It doesn't matter which woman someone sleeps with. . . If the SDP felt jealous of the new alliance, they should have come and joined us. The SDP is putting up irrational resistance." The comment was later criticized by Diet members and women's groups as being indiscreet and demeaning to women. And famous gaffe-maker Prime minister Mori often blamed reporters for exaggerating his remarks and emphasizing his controversial comments. On October 25, 2000, he criticized reporters for reporting his controversial proposal for securing the return of Japanese abducted by North Korea (see above). He angrily told reporters that the responsibility was theirs, because they were in such a hurry to publish what they heard about the matter (*Asahi*, October 26, 2000: 2).

In a June 2000 debate aired on TV Tôkyô, LDP Policy Chief Kamei Shizuka tried to explain the high level of disapproval towards the Mori administration by saying "more than 90 percent is the fault of the mass media." He added that it is obvious to everybody that Mori was not thinking of restoring the type of regime that ruled before World War II as he said the media claimed. "Mori is Japan's boss. Japan does not need a leader like Napoleon. The Japanese prime minister is like a chairperson. He himself has no power on his own. If he does his work properly, that is enough" (*Asahi*, June 4, 2000).

4 ▶ "Yes, But ... Well ... Maybe ... They Say So ...": Analysis of Replies during Televised Political Interviews

One of the most important and perhaps the most interesting aspect of political rhetoric in Japan is the communicative patterns of Japanese politicians during televised interviews. In recent years, televised interviews with politicians have gained importance as a means of political communication in Japan. Several television stations have allocated significantly more time in their news programs and special features to interviews with Diet members, government officials, and public opinion leaders. These interviews enable the public to become more familiar with opinions and ideas held by leading politicians and decision-makers on important political and social issues. Such interviews also serve as a significant source of information about the nation's political agenda and the ways that politicians and officials are thinking of responding to issues. These interviews have the potential to affect viewers' attitudes and behavior toward the administration, government bureaucracy, political parties, and politicians.

Televised political interviews are in fact performances arranged to be "overheard" by an audience that may number in the millions (Heritage, 1985). They are conducted in a distinct social situation that affects the interviewers and interviewed politicians alike. Because the politicians' replies are intended not only for the interviewer but also for the listening audience, interviewers tend to make uncommon use of what are called "listener responses," i.e. signals of continued listener attentiveness. Interviewers are also inclined to use several techniques termed "formulations" (Heritage, 1985) to restate for the audience what an interviewee has previously stated. These latter include clarifying earlier responses, underlining the significance of comments, or probing or challenging declared positions. Because so many people are watching and listening, interviewed politicians tend to consider the potential effects of their remarks on the general public.

In this chapter I will examine the extent to which this awareness is reflected in the politicians' replies. Specifically, the aim of this chapter is to show how leading Japanese politicians handle a wide range of questions posed to them during interviews. There is a growing body of evidence, consistent with the popular view, that politicians in the USA, Canada, and the UK do not reply to a large proportion of questions they are asked during political interviews (e.g. Bavelas et al., 1988). The following discussion measures and explains thus the degree to which Japanese politicians respond to interview questions, after deliberating on such issues as (1) criteria for identifying questions and replies, and (2) ways that interviewers and interviewees present their propositions.

Theoretical Considerations

Research into political interviews has been heavily influenced by the pioneering studies of Janet Bavelas and her colleagues (Bavelas et al., 1988; Bavelas et al., 1990), who noted frequent use of equivocation during interviews. They defined equivocation as "nonstraighforward communication; it appears ambiguous, contradictory, tangential, obscure or even evasive" (Bavelas et al., 1990: 28). (Hamilton & Mineo, 1998, define equivocation as the "intentional use of imprecise language.") Bavelas and her associates theorized that individuals typically equivocate when they are placed in an "avoidance–avoidance conflict," whereby all possible replies to a question have potentially negative consequences, but a reply is still expected.

In many everyday situations, individuals find themselves forced to choose between being hurtfully honest or mercifully misleading. This kind of dilemma can often be managed through ambiguity. For example, if a person is asked to comment on an unsuitable gift from a well-liked friend, the person could say falsely that he or she likes the gift, or the recipient could say honestly that he or she does not, at the risk of hurting the gift-giver's feelings. Bavelas and her associates (1990) proposed that when possible, the recipient will avoid both of these negative alternatives—especially when a hurtful truth serves no positive purpose. Instead, the recipient will evade the question, perhaps by saying, "I appreciate your thoughtfulness" without mentioning any opinion of the gift itself.

The argument underlying the work of Bavelas et al. (1990) is that equivocation does not occur without a situational precedent. In other words, although it is individuals who equivocate, they do so within the context of—one might say as a result of—their communicative situation. This important notion helps explain the responsive patterns of Japanese politicians during interviews.

Bavelas et al. state that, "Communication always involves a sender, some content, a receiver, and a context" (1990: 33). A message is equivocal if it exhibits ambiguity in at least one of the following dimensions: sender (unclear as to who is expressing a point of view); content (unclear as to what is being expressed); receiver (unclear as to who is the intended target of the message); or context (does not address the preceding message). In the content dimension, the sender may provide insufficient information or use contradictory messages that contain "but," "although," or "however" clauses. In the sender dimension, the communicator may refrain from using "I," attribute their viewpoint to another source, or use anonymous pronouns such as "some people." Examples of equivocation along the receiver dimension would include changing the referent from a person to a behavior (e.g. "you performed poorly" becomes "the performance was poor") or shifting the referent from the message recipient to people in general ("everybody in the class did poorly"). With regard to the context dimension, a communicator can change the topic slightly, postpone giving an answer, or merely hint at an answer (1990: 34–44).

To define equivocation more precisely, Bavelas and her research team (1990: 35) have used the following approach:

1. Sender: To what extent is the message *the writer's (or speaker's) own opinion?*
2. Content: How clear is the message, in terms of just *what is being said?*
3. Receiver: To what extent is the message *addressed to the other person in the situation?*
4. Context: To what extent is this a *direct answer to the (implicit or explicit) question?*

Bavelas rated responses along these four dimensions and found that responses to "avoidance–avoidance conflicts" were judged as significantly more equivocal. It is easy to select a message (or a reply) when there is only one positive alternative (i.e. a non-conflict situation) or when one must choose from among several positive alternatives (an "approach–approach conflict"). However, message production is problematic when one must select from alternatives that are all negative ("an avoidance–avoidance conflict"). Thus it is "avoidance–avoidance situations" that lead to equivocation.

Political Interviews

The theory developed by Bavelas and her team is not restricted to any particular social setting. Yet they claim that "avoidance–avoidance conflicts" are especially prevalent in interviews with politicians. Politicians as a group are well-known for equivocating, but this is typically explained by saying that they are reluctant to commit, or that they have devious, sly, and deceitful personalities that cause them to equivocate whether conflict is present or not. Goss and Williams (1973), for example, argued that politicians who need to address an audience that is known to disagree with them on some issues will often use deliberate vagueness as a rhetorical strategy. In such cases, a politician may respond clearly to questions about non-controversial issues but equivocate regarding controversial issues. Because listeners tend to interpret statements in ways that are congruent with their own attitudes, they may judge an ambiguous speaker more favorably than a speaker who makes disagreeable statements (Williams & Goss, 1975).

However, Bavelas and her team propose a situational explanation for political equivocation; they say it is the nature of political interviews that creates equivocation. They argue that one of the main reasons politicians equivocate during interviews is that they are often placed in avoidance–avoidance conflicts (where all possible replies are negative, but nevertheless a reply is expected). Political interviewers rarely pose questions that do not create avoidance conflicts, because they are interested in controversial and sensitive issues that divide the electorate rather than issues over which consensus exists. Thus politicians frequently find themselves having to avoid making a commitment or giving a direct reply that could alienate part of the electorate by taking a stand on a particular issue (Bavelas et al., 1988).

Other reasons for equivocation during political interviews include conflicts of interest between political parties and voters, and discrepancies between aspects of a party's platform or between the candidate's stance and that of the party, or between previous party promises and current practices. Political candidates and politicians must try not to appear inconsistent over time, at odds with their party, or insensitive to contradictions. Sometimes a politician must conceal or even deny facts in order to protect confidential information related to a question she or he is asked. Sometimes there are facets of the interview process itself that cause equivocation; for example, a time limit may force the politician to give an oversimplified or incomplete answer to a question regarding a complex issue, which may make the politician appear to be evasive. Lastly, when a politician lacks knowledge of an issue being addressed, she or he has to choose between acknowledging the lack of information or fudging, perhaps even fabricating, an answer (Bavelas et al., 1990: 246–49).

Within the context of the above equivocation theory, this study analyzes televised interviews with Japanese politicians and investigates their attitudes toward answering or not answering particular questions, and the reasons behind these attitudes. One could assume that questions about intra-party or intra-faction personnel matters, and questions about controversial policy issues, would create the kind of avoidance–avoidance conflict described by Bavelas et al., and that Japanese politicians would equivocate in response to such questions.

When looking at Japanese politicians' responses to interview questions, it is important to remember the cultural context in which these exchanges take place. The Japanese are famous for emphasizing agreement and harmony in their communications, and for going to great lengths to avoid embarrassment. Precision, clarity, and forthrightness are not necessarily seen as virtues in Japan, even in many situations where those qualities are valued in the West. Japanese, in general, limit themselves to implicit and even ambiguous language, avoid taking extreme positions, and even regard vagueness as a virtue. According to Mizutani (1981: 54) a considerable percentage of the Japanese people find an ambiguous speaking style acceptable. To avoid leaving an assertive impression, Japanese tend to depend more frequently on qualifiers such as "maybe," "perhaps," "probably," and "somewhat." Since Japanese syntax does not require the use of a subject in a sentence, "qualifier-predicate" is the dominant form of sentence construction. Omission of the subject often creates a great deal of ambiguity. In addition, Japanese tend to prefer understatement and hesitation, and avoid using superlative expressions (Akasu & Asao, 1993; Imai, 1981)

Methodology

Data

The study examined spontaneous responses by politicians, made during interview sessions that were televised live (i.e. not taped or edited). The data came from interviews conducted on two weekly television programs during a period of one year—from January through December of 2000. During this time, interviews were conducted with a large number of politicians, as well as with non-politicians. On occasion, three to seven politicians from different political parties or party factions were gathered at the studio at the same time. Often, interviews took place with politicians who were out of the studio, in their constituencies or at party headquarters. In order to follow the course of questions and answers, the study only examined political interviews with a single interviewee. In the examined period, only 67 out of a total of 202 interviews were with individual politicians. Of these, I analyzed 59 interviews with 22 different Diet members, including the prime minister (Obuchi and Mori), political parties leaders, the Chief Cabinet Secretary, and Cabinet ministers; and eight interviews with three prefectural governors. Several of these politicians gave multiple interviews during the study period (see Appendix 4.1).

The television programs at the center of this study were Fuji TV's *Hôdô 2001* (Broadcast 2001) and Asahi TV's *Sandei Purojekuto* (Sunday Project). These two television programs are regularly aired live and invite public figures such as Diet members, local politicians, government officials, and other decision-makers from various social and economic sectors. Both programs are broadcast nationwide every Sunday, except for rare occasions when they are replaced by coverage of special events like the high-school baseball championship games held each summer. *Hôdô*

2001 airs between 7:30 and 9:00 a.m., and *Sandei Purojekuto* is broadcast from 10:00 to 11:45 a.m. Both programs focus on "hot" political, social, or economic issues. In both programs, questions are posed mainly by prominent journalists, but additional questions are also presented by scholars or experts in such areas as public policy, social affairs, or economics. Both programs attract considerable public attention, with clips from the interviews often being introduced later in the day on news programs. Remarks made by politicians on these programs often show up the next day as headlines in the leading national newspapers. Of the 67 interviews analyzed in this study, 33 were aired on *Hôdô 2001*, and 34 were from *Sandei Purojekuto*.

Each interview had its own characteristics and time frame. The length varied according to the importance of the issues discussed, the respon-siveness of the interviewees, and the amount of time available due to logistical considerations. The longest interview during the period covered by the study (with Tôkyô Governor Ishihara Shintarô) lasted 70 minutes and 51 seconds; the shortest (with Fuyushiba Tetsuzou, Secretary-General of the New *Kômei* Party) lasted only nine minutes and 40 seconds. The number of questions per interview ranged from eight (in an interview with DPJ leader Kan Naoto) to 95 (with Hatoyama Yukio, another leader of DPJ). In total, there were 1,631 questions asked during the 67 inter-views, with an average of 24.3 questions per interview. The average length among the 67 interviews was 24 minutes and 29 seconds.

Procedure

Interviews from the two programs were recorded using a VHS-format videocassette recorder. A transcript was made for each interview. During the pre-study stage, samples of taped interviews were shown to small groups of graduate and undergraduate students attending social psychology courses. The students discussed characteristics of the inter-view sessions, the content of questions, and the responding style of the interviewees. Further discussion followed after the students had read tran-scripts of the interviews. Several pilot studies were conducted during 2000 after which two coding sheets were developed specifically for this study. The first analyzed the structure and content of interviews based on the verbal behavior of the interviewer, while the second focused on the inter-viewees' replies. Criteria for identifying questions and responses to questions were also determined in these sheets.

Coding Sheets

Identifying questions   The first coding sheet focused on the interviewer and the ways he or she affected the interviews. In order to measure the extent to which politicians answered interviewers' questions, care was taken to identify questions posed during the interviews. "Questions" refer to utterances made by interviewers in order to elicit information from interviewees. This study examined all questions posed by interviewers on the two television programs. In the first program, Hôdô 2001, questions were usually posed by three interviewers: journalists Kuroiwa Yûji and Yoshizaki Noriko, and political commentator Takemura Kenichi. In the second program, *Sandei Purojekuto*, questions were asked mainly by one journalist, Tahara Sôichirô. In the sample exchanges reproduced below, "Kuroiwa," "Yoshizaki," and "Tahara" refer to these interviewers. In both programs, however, questions were also frequently asked by other guests on the program including political critics (e.g. Iwami Takao), economic critics (e.g. Takarabe Sei-ichi), university professors (e.g. Kusano Hitoshi), journalists (e.g. Takano Takeshi), and TV personalities (e.g. Shimada Shinsuke).

The first major task of the study was to identify questions and distinguish them from other utterances. If questions were defined simply as utterances that take an interrogative form, this would have been easy, as in the case of this exchange between Tahara and Katô Kôichi, a former Secretary-General of the LDP:

> TAHARA: The level of public disapproval of Prime Minister Mori's administration is about 76 percent. Something should be done in this regard. One factor we can think about is that so-called public opinion is completely different from the common sense of *Nagatachô*, isn't it?
> KATÔ: It looks different.
> TAHARA: Do you see it this way?
> KATÔ: Yes. (*Sandei Purojekuto*, November 19, 2000)

In this sequence, two clear "questions" are posed to Katô: both take the interrogative form and end with rising intonation. But when we define "question" as a request for information, it does not necessarily require interrogative syntax. Consider the following example from an interview between Kuroiwa and his partner Yoshizaki, and Ishihara, the Governor of Tôkyô:

> KUROIWA (in reaction to Ishihara's criticism of a newspaper's editorial about the LDP): You are talking about the editorial that was published three days ago. Ee, is that right?
> ISHIHARA: Nobody would be inspired by that [editorial]. It does not have any new message or anything new.
> YOSHIZAKI: Yet it mentioned Mr. Katô [Kôichi] as the next prime minister.
> ISHIHARA: Well, I hope he keeps up his efforts but I do not know if this will happen. Mr. Kamei Shizuka [another LDP Diet member] would be more interesting. (*Hôdô 2001*, October 29, 2000)

In this sequence, Yoshizaki challenges Ishihara's contention that the editorial contained nothing new by pointing out that the piece did in fact contain new and intriguing information, namely that Katô would run for prime minister. Although there was no interrogative syntax in the remark, Ishihara took it as a question and replied with the suggestion that another candidate would be more "interesting." This is an example of a declarative question that is not even accompanied by rising intonation, although its function is clearly to elicit a response.

Some questions, usually asked at the beginning of an interview, function as greetings before the actual interview begins. The following interchange between Tahara and JCP chairman Fuwa Tetsuzô is an example:

TAHARA: Where are you now?
FUWA: At party headquarters. (*Sandei Purojekuto*, June 18, 2000)

We considered this type of question to be a greeting and therefore excluded it from analysis.

In line with Jucker's (1986: ch. 5) approach, this research classifies interview questions into two large groups according to their syntactic expression. The first group consists of prefaced questions. In most cases, these are prefaced by a main clause referring to the speech act of the interviewer and in which the main prepositional content of the question appears in indirect form in a subordinate clause. This group includes questions such as "What do you think?" "What do you feel?" "Are you saying . . . ?" "Are you suggesting . . . ?" "Will you explain . . . ?" "Could you say what . . . ?" And, "Can I ask you . . . ?" The second group consists of non-prefaced questions. Possible forms for these are interrogative questions, including Yes/no, that is "questions which seek a 'yes' or 'no' response in relation to the validity of (normally) an entire predication" (Quirk et al., 1972: 52, cited in Jucker, 1986: 109), and WH-questions: start with one of the "five Ws or H words" (What, Why, Who, When, Where, or How); and declarative, imperative, or lacking a finite verb and thus moodless questions.

Analyzing Politicians' Replies – *The Equivocation Typology*: The second coding sheet used in this study focuses on how Japanese politicians replied to the questions they were asked. The explicitness or vagueness of responses was evaluated by analyzing answers in relation to the questions that produced them. The method used in this study replicates the research method used by Bavelas and her research team (1990) with several modifications. Bavelas noted that equivocation is not a unitary dimension, but "communication always involves a sender, some content, a receiver, and a context" (1990: 33). Her group proposed that there are four distinct ways in which people can equivocate: in terms of the clarity of the message content (referred to as the *clarity dimension*); the extent to which the message reflects the speaker's own opinion (*sender dimension*); the extent to which the message is addressed to a particular other person (*receiver dimension*); and the extent to which the message is a direct answer to a question (*context dimension*). The important point is that a message can be equivocal on any of these four dimensions. So the content may be perfectly clear (unequivocal in terms of *clarity*), but not a direct answer to the question (equivocal in the *context* dimension).

The second coding sheet used in this study examined the extent to which Japanese politicians responded to interviewers' questions in terms of each individual dimension. The study analyzes dialogues between individuals in a particular situation, i.e. in televised interviews, rather than analyzing one or two simple sentences as Bavelas and her associates did. Because the present study is more complex, the coding sheet and the method employed have been modified in several ways, compared to the original study by Bavelas and her team.

Specifically, the second coding sheet offers six possible answers in Likert form, ranging from 1 through 6, for each of the four dimensions. "Neutral" was not among the possible responses, in order to force a selection. The Likert form was used to determine (1) how clear the answer was, (2) the extent to which responses reflected the interviewees' own opinions, (3) whether a message was addressed to the interviewer, and (4) the extent to which responses directly answered questions. Using a scale of six points for each dimension, trained coders evaluated each answer that a politician gave to each question that was asked.

To assess *clarity*, the question was "How clear is the message in terms of what is being said?" The six differentials in the answer scale ranged from (1) "Straightforward, easy to understand, only one interpretation is possible," through (6) "Totally vague, impossible to understand, no meaning at all." When the coders assigned a differential other than (1), they also had to specify what made the reply vague by choosing at least one of the following reasons for the lack of clarity: (1) "The interviewee's speech includes vocabulary that is difficult to comprehend," (2) "The speech is inconsistent; it contains contradictory messages," (3) "The speech consists of long and complex sentences," and (4) "The ideas expressed are difficult to follow." Bavelas and her team did not include this kind of explanation.

For the *sender* dimension, the coding sheet used the same question employed in the original Bavelas study: "To what extent is the response the speaker's own opinion?" The scale consisted of six differentials ranging from (1) "It is obviously his or her personal opinion, not someone else's," to (6) "It is obviously someone else's opinion."

Regarding the *receiver* dimension in the original study (Bavelas et al., 1990: 39), the rater asked, "To what extent is the message addressed to the other person in the situation?" Because the original scales were developed for question–response sequences in a conversational context, it was generally clear who the intended receiver was. In broadcast news interviews, however, there are multiple receivers. When an interviewee answers a question, it is not always clear whether the intended receiver is the interviewer, the general public, a particular segment of the public, or another politician or group of politicians. Interviewees sometimes even address others in the studio, such as journalists. Heritage (1985) calls all these "overhearing audience." The coding sheet in this study handled the problem of multiple receivers by designing two questions:

I "To what extent is the message addressed to the person(s) who asked the question?" A scale of six options was used here, from (1) "Obviously addressed only to that person," through (6) "Addressed to other people."

If the answer was not (1), then the coders asked another question:

2 "To whom does the message seem to be addressed?" Raters indicated who they thought was the intended target of the message by choosing among these responses: (1) "TV viewers," (2) "Government/ bureaucracy," (3) "Members of the speaker's own political party," (4) "Members of other political parties," (5) "Mass media," (6) "Other ———. (specify)," (7) "Not clear to whom the message is addressed."

In this study, a message was considered to be equivocal only if the intended recipient was unclear (category 7). That is, if the message is clearly addressed to, for example, TV viewers, it is not equivocal.

This second question represents an important modification from the Bavelas group's (1990) treatment of the *receiver* dimension. Their study failed to deal with the issue of multiple addressees, which is a key feature of televised political interviews.

Lastly, like Bavales et al. (1990), this study recognizes explicit equivocation along the *context* dimension when a politician failed to give part or all of the information requested in a given question. Of course, politicians are famous for equivocating in several ways that can be identified and categorized, as Bull & Mayer (1993) noted, they define these as "types of non-replies." Some of these are described below, but this study does not attempt a detailed analysis of these modes. Rather, an interviewee was simply perceived as equivocating when he or she failed to answer a question for any reason. The question used to measure the *context* dimension was, "To what extent is this a direct answer to the question?" Six differential aspects ranging from (1) "This is a direct answer to the question asked," through (6) "Totally unrelated to the question," were used to code the replies.

Distinguishing replies from non-replies: Several examples to demonstrate how answers were coded according to the above criteria as set out below:

(a) *Yes/no answers*: As noted, yes/no questions are those "which seek a yes or no response in relation to the validity of (normally) an entire predication." Yes/no questions invite a yes or no, so when one or the other response was given, it was coded as an explicit reply. Other words besides "yes" or "no," may be used to adequately convey affirmation or negation, e.g. "certainly," "of course," "not at all," and "never." In the following exchange between the interviewer and Mori Yoshirô of the LDP, Mori clearly answered Tahara's question although he did not say "yes" or "no."

> TAHARA (referring to the possibility that the opposition parties will propose to normalize Diet affairs): Will [the LDP] respond positively?
> MORI: It is obvious. (*Sandei Purojekuto*, February 6, 2000)

Another example is taken from an interview with Tanaka Makiko of the LDP:

> YOSHIZAKI (referring to the limited question time that the coalition of ruling parties is given during the Diet's Policy Countermeasures Committee): Is this a tough barrier for you?
> TANAKA: Its terrible! (*Hôdô 2001*, March 12, 2000)

Yes/no questions may also be answered by replies that lie somewhere along a scale of affirmation—negation, e.g. "probably," "perhaps," "it appears so," or "to some extent." The following example illustrating related type of replies, comes from an interview with Noda Takashi, the Secretary-General of the Liberal Party:

> TAHARA: By the way, it may sounds strange, ee, if you establish a new party, will you become the head of the party?
> NODA: Well, I think rather the role of coordinator is more important.
> TAHARA: So then you will be the Secretary-General?
> NODA: This is what I am thinking.
> TAHARA: In that case [former Prime Minister] Kaifu [Toshiki] will be the leader [of the party]?
> NODA: There are some strong voices in this regard, well, I strongly wish it was like this. (*Sandei Purojekuto*, April 2, 2000)

Noda is clearly responding to the questions, but he does not use the words "yes" or "no" in doing so.

It is important to note some linguistic differences between Japanese and English. For one thing, in Japanese one says "yes" or "no" to match the content of the question. So for example, if a politician is asked "You're not going to the Diet today?" he or she may respond, "Yes, that's right" (agreeing with the question's premise) to mean "I am not going to the Diet today." At the same time, Japanese frequently use devices like "isn't it?"

or "aren't they?" (*ja arimasen ka or ja nai ka*) at the end of positive statements, as a way of soliciting agreement. For example, if one says, "That politician's attitude is awful, isn't it?" the question ends with the negative "*ja nai ka*," but the statement itself is positive—and the speaker expects positive agreement. The following example is from an interview between Tahara and Ozawa Ichiro:

TAHARA (referring to a meeting between Ozawa and then-Prime Minister Obuchi in which they failed to agree on having Ozawa's Liberal Party join the ruling coalition): You did not have a fight, did you?
OZAWA: Yes. (*Sandei Purojekuto*, April 30 2000)

By this reply, Ozawa was saying that he did not quarrel with the prime minister.

(b) *Wh-answers*: Wh-questions ask What, Why, Who, When, Where, or How. When the politician supplied the requested information, the response was coded as a reply. When the politician failed to provide the information, the response was coded as an equivocation, as in the following exchange between Tahara and Nonaka Hiromu of the LDP:

TAHARA: By the way, ee, regarding [Prime Minister] Mori's administration, why is its reputation so bad?
NONAKA: Well, it has just begun. Umm, even before it started working, there was an election, and now a summit meeting [with world leaders] is approaching. Let's wait and see what will happen. (*Sandei Purojekuto*, July 9, 2000)

It is clear that Nonaka does not answer the WHY question posed by the interviewer. Instead, he proposes to "wait and see" how things develop. Of course, Nonaka was fully aware of several good reasons for Prime Minister Mori's declining reputation, including nationalistic remarks that had caused a stir. But as Secretary-General of the LDP, Nonaka's job was to support his party's president (the prime minister), so he obviously did not want to give a detailed reply that would be critical of Mr. Mori.

(c) *Alternatives questions*: These questions give the politician a choice of two or more alternative answers. When the politician chose one of the alternatives, that was seen as constituting a reply. However, it is possible to present an additional alternative, which might also be regarded as a reply. Consider the following extract from an interview between Tahara and Nonaka Hiromu of the LDP:

TAHARA (referring to the position of the government): Is it possible that everyone avoided taking on [a specific ministerial position], or that [Prime Minister] Mori, well, wanted to appoint someone out of the LDP [for this minister position]? Which is correct?

NONAKA: No, no, (Prime Minister) Mori wanted to appoint a woman [for this specific position]. (*Sandei Purojekuto*, July 9, 2000)

Another example from an interview with Hatoyama Yukio, the deputy leader of the DPJ:

TAHARA: Let me ask you another question. Umm, in Japan, there is no competition, and the monetary world is a good example. Well, at any rate, there is an increasing opinion to adopt free competition American-style, yet on the other hand, there is a view that free-competition is a scary situation. And there is another way, the European style of free competition, supported by the UK, which helps the weak people in society. Between these two, which does the DPJ support?

HATOYAMA: Both of them. (*Sandei Purojekuto*, May 7, 2000)

In these examples, neither Nonaka nor Hatoyama chose one of the alternatives presented, although they both gave clear replies to the questions. When a politician rejected all alternatives suggested by the interviewer but did not offer any other answer, the response was regarded as equivocation.

In brief, the scale for the *context* dimension distinguished between (1) unequivocal—clear and complete answers, and (2) equivocating answers which, according to the definition mentioned, means "nonstraighforward communication, including messages that are ambiguous, indirect, contradictory, or evasive."

Coding

The coding of both the equivocation typology and of the nature and content of the questions was done by two well-trained postgraduate students. Any disagreements between the two were resolved through discussion with the author.

Results and Discussion

Politicians' Replies

At the center of this study is a sample of 67 interviews with individual politicians (as opposed to interviews with two or more politicians simultaneously) on the two television channels mentioned above. Of the 67 interviews, 33 were aired on *Hôdô 2001*, and 34 were from *Sandei Purojekuto*. A total of 1,631 questions were identified, amounting to an average of 24.3 questions per interview.

The 67 interviews were analyzed in terms of the four criteria used to explore politicians' replies to questions: the *sender, clarity, receiver,* and *context.* The analysis indicates that, on a scale that ranged between one to six, the average scores were 3.39 for the *sender* dimension, 2.79 for the *content* dimension, 1.68 for the *receiver* dimension, and 3.51 for the *context* dimension. In other words, when Japanese politicians replied to questions during these political interviews, more often their responses did not directly answer the questions they had been asked, were not easily comprehensible, addressed people other than the interviewer, and did not reveal the speaker's own views.

Sender Dimension   There were many instances in which Japanese politicians used a pronoun meaning "I" or an expression such as "I think" or "I believe," making it clear that they were expressing their own opinion. The following is an extract from an interview between Tahara and Ishihara, the Governor of Tôkyô:

> TAHARA: By the way, I think . . . , strictly speaking, members of the LDP have not thought about anything [in terms of political objectives] since the party was established. The factions of [former Prime Minister] Tanaka [Kakuei] and *Keiseikai* [the faction led by former Prime Minister Takeshita Noboru] have been powerful for a long time, so the other factions did not think about anything. Nor did *Keiseikai* think about anything. In *Keiseikai*, by the way, [leaders such as] Obuchi [Keizô], Takeshita [Noboru], and Kajiyama [Seiroku] died one after another. Can this change the LDP?
>
> ISHIHARA: Well, after all, [the LDP] must reject the . . . umm . . . dynamics of *Keiseikai*. I think that Takeshita was fully aware of this. He, um, knew that the power that propels politics was people, um, money. He himself rejected the [use of] words, and thus, himself, um, in short, as I previously said, his words were clear but their meaning was vague. I think this is terrible, I do. (*Sandei Purojekuto*, July 16, 2000)

In his reply Ishihara clearly reveals his own thoughts on former Prime Minister Takeshita and his political fashion. Ishihara stresses the fact that HE himself already said things related to Takeshita's use of language in politics, and ends his reply with emphasis that this is his own opinion by explicitly adding the pronoun "I" at the end of his comment although "I" is not generally used when speaking Japanese. (Notably, however, Ishihara's reply does not answer the question. He was asked if the LDP could be changed, but remarked on former Prime Minister Takeshita and his political style. This is a typical example of equivocation along one dimension—*context*—despite clarity in another dimension—*sender.*)

One more example of a politician using "I" to draw attention to the fact that his reply reflects his own views comes from an interview between Kuroiwa and Noda Takashi of the Liberal Party:

KUROIWA: Mr. Noda, we watched the Liberal Party and thought it would leave the ruling coalition of parties, but then the coalition collapsed. That means, when Mr. Ozawa [Ichiro, the leader of the Liberal Party] declared that he intended to leave the coalition, Mr. Obuchi [Keizo, the Prime Minister and the President of the LDP] dropped out. Did you know in advance that it would happen that way?

NODA: Well, though it was not unexpected, there was a tedious mood, information came from sources [close to] the prime minister, [from] LDP sources, or New Kômei Party sources. Not once, frequently [this mood continued], and I gradually felt the emergence of an impatience. (Hôdô 2001, April 2, 2000)

In this reply, Noda specifies that he himself "felt" the emergence of a special "political mood" that eventually led to the disintegration of the coalition. It is clear that it was he, himself, who detected this mood based on information he received.

On the other hand, there were 638 replies (39.1 percent of all replies) in which politicians used no personal pronoun at all, leaving it unclear whose opinion they were expressing, or in which they used expressions that did not pinpoint the sender, such as "we," "our party," "politicians," "it seems. . . " or "it is said. . . " The following example comes from an interview with Kanzaki Takenori, the representative of the New Komei Party:

TAHARA (regarding the fact that New Kômei Party used to say a lot about public works but recently said little on the subject): Now when [New Kômei Party] joined [the coalition] with the LDP, did [the party's] way of thinking change?

KANZAKI: Well, the way of thinking is the same. Yet, we emphasize revision, the [need] to stop waste in public works . . .

One reason for politicians to avoid clarifying the *sender* by using a personal pronoun has to do with a peculiarity of Japanese culture and language. Although there are multiple pronouns that mean "I," there is a definite tendency to avoid their use as much as possible (e.g. Suzuki, 1989: Ch. 6). Also, Japanese tend to use expressions like, "many people say. . . " and "it is said. . . " in order to express an opinion without making a personal commitment to it (e.g. Kitao & Kitao, 1989: 52–53). This might explain why, in this study, the politicians equivocated regarding the *sender* dimension in close to 40 percent of their replies. In other words, there were only 993 replies (of the 1,631, 60.9 percent) in which a politician clearly identified the views being stated as his or her own.

Despite this tendency, it should be noted that there were no politicians who equivocated on this dimension in every case. Nor was there any one politician who always specified that the views being expounded were his or her own opinion. There were, however, specific politicians who had a more pronounced tendency than others to reveal their own opinion and specify it as such. Even without using first-person pronouns, they made it clear that they were expressing their own thoughts. Among these were Ishihara Shintarô, Kanzaki Takenori, Ôgi Chikage of the Conservative Party, Hatoyama Yukio of the DPJ, and Koga Makoto, the Secretary-General of the LDP.

For example, Koga was asked 38 questions during an interview with Tahara (*Sandei Purojekuto*, December 10, 2000), and in 32 of his replies (84.2 percent), he left no room for doubt that he was disclosing his own opinions. Of the 15 questions that Ôgi was asked in an interview with Tahara (*Sandei Purojekuto*, June 18, 2000), she made it obvious in 12 of her replies (80 percent) that she was giving her own views (most often by emphasizing the pronoun "I"). But even these politicians sometimes concealed their own views. This can be, as mentioned, the outcome of cultural norms or for other reasons.

The type of question asked, for example, also seems to have a bearing on the extent to which politicians will disclose their own opinion. They will clearly reveal their own judgments in response to certain questions, while relying on the ideas of another person or group—or invoking "(Japanese political) common-sense" to reply to other questions. There are even some questions that politicians will answer with both their own opinion and the views of others.

The problem, of course, is to identify certain patterns that politicians follow. In other words, to identify why politicians tend to give their own views when replying to certain questions but not when answering others. Part of the answer may lie in personality-related factors, considering that some politicians usually equivocate while others usually disclose their own views. But the fact that not one politician always revealed (or concealed) his or her own views suggests that it is probably not a matter of persona alone, but might be related to the question asked (as suggested in the original theory of Bavelas et al.). In other words, the nature of the reply may depend on nature of the question and the politician's readiness to talk about a particular issue.

An equally important factor, besides the cultural aspect suggested above, is related to the type of work politicians do. Politicians who are invited to be interviewed on television generally occupy leadership positions. Interviews via mass media represent opportunities for them to publicize their own opinions and, more importantly, to inform the public of the views that are prevalent in the political groups they represent and most often lead. One example of this appeared above in the interview with the New *Kômei* Party's Kanzaki, revealing his party's attitude toward public works. Interviews with the media also present these leaders with good opportunities for explaining the general mood within their group, the group's stance toward various issues, and its intentions regarding other political groups, the government, and the bureaucracy. Indeed, interviewers often ask for comments about the behavior, intentions, or thoughts of a politician's colleagues, especially of those who belong to the same groups. Consider the following extract from an interview with Koga Makoto of the LDP:

> TAHARA: This is also about a newspaper article, ee, [Prime Minister] Mori has [taken] a strong stance, [claiming] that if this story [about his relationship with gangsters] is published, he will sue. Perhaps you have not talked with Mr. Mori about this, [but] what would his lawsuit be about?
>
> KOGA: I did not hear anything about whether he would sue or not. But he thinks that if there are errors of fact, they should be addressed legally. I wonder if it would be good for him to respond quickly or not. It depends on the content. (*Sandei Purojekuto*, December 10, 2000)

Koga, as Secretary-General of the LDP and as a close colleague of Prime Minister Mori, was being asked to reveal what Mori thinks about a certain issue, and Koga did cite Mr. Mori as the source of part of his reply. Another example from the same interview shows another type of question that political leaders are often asked:

> TAHARA: (about the future of the LDP) . . . Mr. Koga, I think you have the same ideas [as Nonaka Hiromu, former Secretary-General of the LDP]. Well, what part of the LDP you think should be changed and how do you plan to do it?
>
> KOGA: I think the starting point for changing the LDP is that each Diet member has to recognize, take responsibility, and have a sense of mission about the future of Japan, about self-reform, and about being a member of the LDP. I think that is the starting point.
>
> TAHARA: Are [members of] the LDP not doing those things right now? [Is there a] lack of such things?
>
> KOGA: I think so [that they are not doing such things sufficiently].
>
> TAHARA: The LDP Diet members are remiss in this respect?
>
> KOGA: Yes. (*Sandei Purojekuto*, December 10, 2000)

In this extract, Koga, as secretary-general, is asked about how to change his party and about the general readiness within the party to tackle necessary changes. The exchange is an example of how leading politicians tend to discuss not only their own private thoughts and beliefs, but also those of others within their political group. These politicians tend to talk beyond their personal views even when they are not specifically asked about the whole group. As mentioned above, because high-echelon politicians see interviews as opportunities to inform the public about their group, they naturally see it as part of their job to reveal information regarding the ideas and intentions of group members.

Considering this tendency, it may be necessary to modify the *sender* dimension in future research. Political talk is not private talk. High-echelon, experienced politicians in particular, who are invited for televised political interview, are likely to be asked about the views of members of those group they represent or lead. These politicians are naturally expected to reveal not only their own personal views and stances on important issues and events, but also those of members who they work with. In analyzing political interviews, thus, this aspect should be taken into consideration. That is, high-echelon politicians who appear in interviews are expected, and probably see as part of their job, to reveal the opinion and intentions of followers and others within their groups, and thus to disclose views beyond their own. To better understand politicians' attitude while communicating politics, the *sender* dimension in future studies should thus specifically examine the extent to which interviewed politicians disclose their own stances and opinions, *vis-à-vis* their followers', in replying to interview questions.

Content Dimension   The meaning of the reply was not clear in 1,093 of 1,631 cases (67 percent). Interviewees tended to construct vague, ambiguous, imprecise messages, sometimes contradicting themselves and sometimes using understatements. The reasons for the lack of clarity was as follows: 486 (44.5 percent of the 1,093 unclear replies) replies included words or expressions that were difficult to comprehend; 344 (31.5 percent) consisted of long and complex sentences; 215 (19.7 percent) expressed ideas that were difficult to follow; and, 47 cases (4.3 percent) were inconsistent, containing contradictory messages. There were 183 replies that contained both long, complex sentences and difficult jargon.

Consider the following example from an interview between Kuroiwa and Yamazaki Taku, former Chairman of the LDP's Policy Affairs Research Council:

KUROIWA (about a supplementary budget proposal): Is there a possibility that you will oppose it, Mr. Yamazaki?

YAMAZAKI: No, I will not oppose it. But the framework of the supplementary budget was provisionally decided and on the day it was announced the stock market collapsed. Basically, the decision about the supplementary budget should be finalized. Its scale, looks very big, 11 trillion yen. Usually, when such a big budget is announced, stock prices go up, but this time they went down. There are various reasons why they declined, 200 million stocks went down, there were many reasons why they did not go up. But I think [that is because] there is additional 200 million yen worth of treasury bonds to fund the budget, finally, the global stock market determined that this government cannot do financial reconstruction and they sold their holdings. I think foreign players started to sell. That means, the credibility of national bonds has decreased.

KUROIWA: Mr. Yamazaki, basically you oppose the supplementary budget, don't you?

YAMAZAKI: Well, there are a lot of unnecessary items. I think this budget was constructed without concern.

KUROIWA: Despite this, would you support it in the Diet? (*Hôdô 2001*, November 5, 2000)

In this example Kuroiwa reformulated his first question because, while Yamazaki stated he will not oppose the supplementary budget proposal, his reason for supporting it are not clear. Yamazaki also said that he thought the supplementary budget was a bad idea. His reply is not clear at all and many parts of it are loosely connected to the extent that the interviewer asked again about Yamazaki's stance toward the budget, and asked a third time after Yamazaki did not provide a satisfactorily clear reply the first two times. Yamazaki's replies consisted of long, complex sentences, and his ideas were difficult to follow.

Another example illustrating difficult-to-follow ideas comes from an interview with Nukaga Fukushirô, Director of the Economic Planning Agency:

KUROIWA: Well, although I do not want to think about a financial crisis, have you made any decision regarding the use of public funds should such a situation occur?

NUKAGA: As I said before, ee, banks are making efforts to merge, to increase their own competitive strength and so on. So equity capital ratios become more important. We recognize that [the banks' situation] would improve. As for the stock market, as I said before, one must look first at business revenues or the fundamental economic situation, and evaluate our attitudes toward making a strong Japanese economy in the future, while aggressively implementing structural reform deregulation. Also, our economy is inevitably tied to the economies of the USA and other parts of Asia. Last weekend, the NASDAQ market made repulsion. I do not think the market will decline for a long time. [The Japanese economy] is going to be correctly evaluated. From the intermediate-term standpoint, because there is a cautious view, we must watch and decide. But the Japanese economy—and corporations know this—cannot survive without structural reform. From the standpoint of the administration or policymakers, implementing such reform in particular will be a precondition for the 21st-centurian, for winning the 21st century. And we will absolutely carry it out, so we [the ruling coalition of parties] hope [the people] will feel secure. (Hôdô 2001, December 24, 2000)

Not only is it difficult to follow the ideas Nukaga expressed in this reply, but his use of difficult jargon (e.g. equity capital ratio, enterprise revenue, and implementing structural reform deregulation) made his reply even more unclear. On the top of this, he was not answering the question he was asked (whether to use public funds if a financial crisis occurs).

Again, there is a cultural explanation for the large extent to which politicians' replies were not clear (close to 70 percent). As mentioned, Japanese, in general, limit themselves to implicit and even ambiguous language, do not explain or express things precisely or pointedly and often use indirect expressions (e.g. Akasu & Asao, 1993).

Nevertheless, the fact remains that one-third of the replies (33 percent) analyzed contained explicit, easy-to-understand remarks. The politicians whose speech was cited above as examples of unclear language or contradictory remarks made very clear responses to other questions during the same interview session. So once again we see that politicians' replies are not always muddy. In the *context* dimension, also, there was not a single politician who never gave a clear answer, nor was there one politician who always answered questions clearly. Replies depended on the issue discussed, the status of the politician within his or her political group, the politician's aspirations, and perhaps his or her relationships with others.

Receiver Dimension   The coding sheet contained two questions dealing with the *receiver* dimension. The results indicated that 1,023 of the politicians' replies (62.7 percent of the total of 1,631) were addressed to the person who asked the question—i.e. the main interviewer(s) or someone else in the studio. Of the 608 replies (37.3 percent) that were addressed to someone else, 261 (16 percent) were aimed at television viewers; 112 (6.9 percent) at members of the speaker's own party; 104 replies (6.4 percent) were aimed at members of other parties; 68 (4.2 percent) at the government or government bureaucracy; 51 replies (3.1 percent) were addressed to the mass media; and 12 (0.7 percent) were addressed to someone else, such as minority groups, foreigners, or residents of a particular locality. There was not even one case in which it was not clear to whom the message was addressed. That is, according to the criteria established in this study, messages from Japanese politicians were not equivocal in terms of the *receiver* dimension.

Obviously, politicians address their messages during political interviews not only to the individual in the studio who asked a question, but also to audiences outside the studio. As mentioned, to politicians, televised interview represents another important opportunity to disseminate their (and their political groups') ideas, opinions, and stances on variety of issues and policies to the general public and voters. From this viewpoint politicians try to maximize their audience and appeal simultaneously to as many individuals and groups as they can—supporters, voters, other politicians, government officials, as well as to media representatives. In the following exchange between Kan, the leader of the DPJ, and Tahara, Kan addresses an apology to the general public as well as to supporters of his political party:

TAHARA: . . .Well, in the past you collaborated with Mr. Yamamoto Jôji, who [illegally] transferred 20 million yen from one secretary to another secretary. This is a problem. What do you think about it now?

KAN: Um, uh, well, ah, after graduating from the university, [Yamamoto] worked as my secretary for three and a half years. After that, he won a seat on the Tôkyô Metropolitan Assembly, and later became a Diet member. Well, from this viewpoint, by causing this problem [unethical behavior], I, as his senior Diet member, strongly feel responsibility. For this, I have to apologize to the general public. Really, I feel very sorry. (*Sandei Purojekuto*, September 9, 2000)

As leader of the DPJ and a former employer of Yamamoto Jôji, Kan apologizes for the unethical activity of his former secretary, who was later elected as a member of Kan's party. Kan does not give any answer at all to the question he was asked (what he thought about the unethical behavior) because his main concern was to publicly apologize for the misbehavior of one of his comrades.

Interestingly, politicians often appear to be waving "in and out" with their replies during interviews, in the sense that they select audiences for specific remarks, or for portions of their replies. Sometimes they address the interviewer, at other times the general public or an audience in their hometown. They may make an opening remark aimed at potential voters, then direct the next sentence toward government officials, and aim the following statement at their coalition colleagues. During the course of a single interview, politicians will often address replies to a wide range of spectators; they are loathe to miss a chance to make full use of the arena provided by a televised interview to speak to as large audience as they can, regardless of whether their replies constitute answers to the questions posed to them.

Context Dimension   Obtaining specific and complete responses from politicians is one of the main goals of televised political interviews. However, in view of the average score of 3.51 along this dimension, one can say that most replies in this study were not explicit or complete. In fact, only 257 replies (of the 1,631, 15.8 percent) were identified as direct answers to questions. Consider the following extracts from an interviews with Ôgi Chikage, leader of the Conservative party, who gave a clear answer to Tahara's questions:

TAHARA: By the way, you joined Mr Ozawa [Ichirô] in moving to the New Frontier Party [Shinshintô] and then in forming the Liberal Party. I think, Mrs. Ôgi, that you were very much taken care by Mr. Ozawa [yet you left his party and established your own political group]. What did you dislike of Mr. Ozawa?
ÔGI: Well, I did not dislike anything. I still regard Mr. Ozawa highly. (*Sandei Purojekuto*, June 18, 2000)

But in most of their replies, Japanese politicians avoided fully answering questions, or hedged their replies when they did. Rather than directly answer a question, Japanese politicians generally prefer to give a general description of events, to refer to the working style of the government and political parties, or describe historical background that affected a particular process. As mentioned, even though many replies are clear in terms of the content of the message or explicitly reveal the speaker's own opinion, they are most often not direct replies to the questions.

Detailed analysis of the *context* dimension yielded the same results discussed earlier regarding the *sender* and the *content* dimensions; that is, not even one politician equivocated for an entire interview session in terms of the *context* dimension, nor did one politician give direct replies in every case. Many politicians who replied directly to one question equivocated when replying to the next one.

Consider the following example from an interview between Tahara and Doi Takako, the leader of the Social Democratic party:

> TAHARA (referring to the questionable conduct of the ruling parties and govern-
> ment, which were soft on retired government employees, pork barrel public
> works projects, and misuse of public money while at the same time the govern-
> ment cut pension funding, claiming there was not enough money but found
> money to hand over major banks): Are they liars? Are you saying they are liars?
> DOI: Yes! I think they are deceiving. [They are doing it] for election purposes. It
> is obvious.
> TAHARA: Well, let me ask you. Earlier I talked with representatives of the LDP,
> DPJ, and the JCP, and they mentioned about expanding the economics,
> expanding aggressively, initially by three percent. In this election, I think the
> major focal point should be either further support for economic growth by
> restructuring, or greater stabilization of the economy, to address issues related
> to the disadvantaged in society or public services. Which position will the SDP
> take?
> DOI: Which is the position to stand for? Supporting restructuring means
> supporting the position of big corporations, certainly, what will be the position
> of workers in this business? I would like to stand for this [workers'] position.
> (*Sandei Purojekuto*, June 18, 2000)

It is noticeable that Doi replies directly to the first question ("Yes!") in this interview held on the eve of an election. But in her second reply, she says she would like to support the workers without replying to the question about what position her party will take. Perhaps she answered this way to hide the fact that the SDP did not have any clear position on the economy.

Another example comes from an interview between Yoshizaki and Kuroiwa with Yamasaki Taku of the LDP:

> YOSHIZAKI: Mr. Yamazaki, is it true that you often talk with Mr. Katô [Kôichi]
> over the phone?
> YAMASAKI: Yes, we exchange information. Firstly, [we are] close friends, well, I
> also talk frequently with Mr. Koizumi [Junichirô].
> YOSHIZAKI: What do you talk about?
> YAMASAKI: (laughing) Well, Everything . . . various things . . .

KUROIWA: Well, if you talk every evening you must be close friends. Well, regarding YKK [Yamazaki, Katô and Koizumi], as we saw in the video, Mr. Katô did not want to join the Mori administration and that caused conflict. Koizumi supports the government of Prime Minister Mori. Under these circumstances, if one considers the importance of YKK, which way will you go, Mr. Yamazaki? Will you follow Katô? Will you cut your ties with Koizumi?

YAMASAKI: Well, Mr. Koizumi did not join this Cabinet, and this affected our way of thinking. If he had become the Chief Cabinet Secretary, our dialogue would have been much different. Why didn't he join the government? As it were, I have heard that he said if he did [become Chief Cabinet Secretary] he would have implemented structural reforms, financial reforms, as [his] policy, and this would have caused disagreement within the government, and that he did not join [the government] because [he wanted to avoid this]. He said he did not accept [the invitation to join the Cabinet]. This [Koizumi's] opinion and ours is the same, namely, there is a need to huddle together as soon as possible [in order to promote] the structural reforms that will bring financial reforms. The reason he did not join the Cabinet is that the principles of Mori's administration did not change. This [wondering whether Mori's basic philosophy might change] had become his thought. (*Hôdô 2001*, November 5, 2000)

Yamazaki directly addresses the first question, and even volunteers further information about his relationship with Katô (that they are good friends), and the fact that he also speaks often by telephone with Mr. Koizumi. But Yamazaki is not ready to offer any information about the content of these phone conversations ("various things") and completely equivocates—in terms of the *context* dimension—when asked about his support for a colleague. Since he does not want to make any public commitment regarding his support for Katô, he talks instead about why Koizumi did not join the government. Like Ms. Doi, in the previous example, Yamazaki has good reasons for not giving a directly reply. In his case, it is probably important to him to keep good relationship with both colleagues by not stating publicly which one he prefers to support.

It is usually easy to tell if a politician has replied clearly, but "don't know" answers can be problematic. Sometime they represent a genuine lack of knowledge or opinion. But at other times "don't know" may be used to hide a host of other realities: fear of speaking frankly, stalling for time while thoughts are marshaled, or unwillingness to speculate on an outcome. The following exchange between Yoshizaki and Katô Kôichi of the LDP provides an example of an interviewee who answers "I don't know" because he is not willing to commit to a concrete reply:

YOSHIZAKI (referring to Katô's trying to increase support for his ideas within the LDP and on the likelihood of his emerging as a political leader): According to your estimation, when will this (your emerging as a leader) take place?

KATÔ: I don't know. Only God knows. Nevertheless, for me, it is clear that the policy must not be aimed at the short-term, but must be far-sighted. The public has two clear anxieties. One concerns the future of the Japanese economy, and the second is their personal finances. They save money to protect themselves. [The] National pension fund would be incapable if there is so much loans. Money that was entrusted to the national treasury for pensions would be used for the national financial debt of the elder generation. University students are thinking like this, so they ask their mothers to pay their pension fund of 13,300 yen for them. "Oh, it is yours [pension], oh no, this future is uncertain . . . " such a conversation would soon be started. Then I think it is important to destroy their anxieties, and to obtain again the so-called confidence, or reliability. Thus, we [the LDP] should focus on this, and the message from leaders "it is all right" should gain trust. It is not easy, but we should do it strictly. (*Hôdô 2001*, October 29, 2000)

Obviously, Katô has not replied to the When question. He begins his answer by stating that only God knows when he will emerge as the leader of the country. Of course it is impossible for him to specify the date or circumstances when he will take office. If he did so, many of his LDP colleagues would criticize his arrogance or lack of support for the current administration. At the same time, Katô probably did not want to demonstrate too much confidence. So he decided to give a modest reply, and avoided committing himself to a certain time-frame by saying "I don't know." He then turned the topic to the economy. Katô's reply was not a direct reply to the question.

Non-Reply Replies

When coding the *context* dimension, we found many cases in which a reply could be coded neither as a direct response nor as an indirect response to a given question. In other words, interviewees sometimes reacted to questions with utterances that could not be considered replies at all. These included laughing, criticism of the question or of the interviewer, and questions that the interviewee returned to the interviewer in lieu of an answer. All of these were considered as "non-replies."

We identified four types of non-replies that we did not count as equivocation in this study:

1. Intentionally ignoring a question, typically while launching into another discussion;
2. Declining to focus on the question or on the issue under discussion;
3. Denying facts presented in the question and using that as grounds to refuse to answer a question; and,
4. Reflecting a question back to the interviewer(s).

I. Intentionally ignoring a question, typically while launching into another discussion Ignoring a question was one of the most frequently employed methods for avoiding a question. Since the politician is expected to address the question that was asked, and the interviewer awaits a reaction, politicians often changed the subject and launched off into another discussion. Here is an example from an interview between Tahara and Kishi Shigetada with Kan, the leader of the DPJ:

> TAHARA: Well, Mr. Kan, at present, there is a great deal of interest in politics. I visit various places to give public lectures and see this interest, especially among youngsters. Enormous interest.
>
> KISHI: Tremendous! Really the public has changed.
>
> TAHARA: This phenomena is the first time since, ee, the events that followed Ozawa [Ichiro, and his group departure from the LDP] in 1993.
>
> KISHI: Since then, well, the quality is completely different. This time more massive.
>
> TAHARA: More enormous
>
> KISHI: More enormous
>
> TAHARA: Well, finally, Mr. Kan, there is interest [in politics], if there is not a proper response, the public may turn away from politics again. What do you intend to do in this regard?
>
> KAN: Well, I, another important problem now is the recent comment by Nonaka [Hiromu, the LDP's Secretary-General]. That is, the no-confidence vote that he worked very hard to reject. Despite this, the following days . . . (*Sandei Purojekuto*, November 26, 2000)

In this example, Kan was asked how his party plans to maintain or take advantage of the vast public interest in politics. Instead of suggesting concrete measures, Kan completely disregards the question and instead brings up something he calls, "another important problem." Either he has no specific answer to the question, or his party has not yet considered any relevant measures. Or perhaps he really considers the "other important problem" to be important enough to focus on, so he introduces it by completely ignoring the interviewers' question.

Another example of a reply that launched off on another topic, comes from an interview between Tahara and Mori Yoshirô of the LDP:

> TAHARA (Talking about the supplementary budget): Then, if it will be organized, or if it will be unfavorable balance in the rural areas, will you be ready to inject supplementary budget?
>
> MORI: At first, at first, this fiscal year, we have to steadily do as much as possible. Then [we have to handle] the so-called public reserve fund adjusted by the Policy Affairs Research Councils of the three [coalition] parties. (*Sandei Purojekuto*, June 18, 2000)

Mori is asked about injecting supplementary budget [*hosei yosan*] and he answers about completely different issue—the public reserve funds [*kôkyô yobihi*] which will have to be adjusted by the councils of the parties in the coalition. It is very unlikely that he misunderstood the question or that he failed to distinguish between the two terms. Perhaps Mori wanted to avoid discussing the supplementary budget because the matter was still pending and at that point no budget had been proposed in the Diet. Mori may have preferred to discuss public reserve funds in order to avoid the delicate issue of the supplementary budget. But of course we can only speculate as to his true intentions.

2. Declining to focus on the question or on the issue under discussion The following is an example of the second type of non-reply—refusal to focus on the question at hand—from an interview with Tanaka Makiko of the LDP:

> KUROIWA (after showing Tanaka photos of politicians selected through a public survey as potential prime ministers): Well, [politicians such as] Katô [Kôichi] and Mori [Yoshirô] which are seen also within the LDP as the next [members] to lead.
> TANAKA: Yes, they are veterans.
> KUROIWA: [Tell us] one word [about them].
> TANAKA: This [the board of photos] is like a sample of faces.
> KUROIWA: Like a sample of faces. Who is your preference?
> TANAKA: Well, I don't know yet. Umm, uh . . . partly because I know too much, which is perhaps unfortunate.
> KUROIWA: That you know too much is unfortunate.
> TANAKA: Unn. (*Hôdô 2001*, March 12, 2000)

Another example comes from the same interview:

> YOSHIZAKI: . . . I heard that you received an offer [from Ozawa Ichiro] to become the leader of the Liberal Party.
> TANAKA: I forgot [such an offer].
> YOSHIZAKI: What has happened?
> TANAKA: No comment regarding this. No more. Nothing particularly.
> YOSHIZAKI: Aa, yes.
> KUROIWA: That you say "no comment" means you do not deny it.
> TANAKA: I do not affirm it either. (*Hôdô 2001*, March 12, 2000)

It is obvious in the first example that Tanaka does not want to talk about a personnel issue related to her party, i.e. who she prefers as prime minister. In the second example, she does not want to talk at all about the offer she reportedly received from the leader of the Liberal Party. In the first example, she avoids answering by commenting on the style of the photos, and by saying she knows too much about certain politicians. In the second example, she first claims to have forgotten, then resorts to "no comment" to put the issue to rest.

3. Denying facts presented in the question and using that as grounds to refuse to answer a question Below Noda Takeshi of the Liberal

Party offers an example of the third method, denying facts presented in a question:

KUROIWA: (showing a video clip in which Noda was seen in front of a Tôkyô hotel waiting to meet with the prime minister and his aides): . . . This is, a video scoop that we recorded on March 30, at a Tôkyô hotel. As you saw, [LDP] Secretary-General Mori, and Chief Cabinet Secretary Aoki, ee, and you entered [the hotel] and held a meeting. Did you talk about something tangible and new regarding the framework of the coalition?
NODA: Well, is this the same hotel? This, was a coincidence.
KUROIWA: What? You deny it? What did you talk about there? Something about a new policy agreement?
NODA: Well, another person was in charge, well. (*Hôdô 2001*, April 2, 2000)

Noda was shown a video clip that clearly showed himself entering a hotel with two other politicians, but he first pretended that all three might not be at the same hotel, then said it was an incident that they were all at the same hotel, calling it a "near miss." Finally, he said someone else was in charge of a new policy agreement, hinting that he had no reason to be at the hotel to negotiate with other politicians. Noda was obviously embarrassed that the television station was showing his "secret" meeting with other politicians. By denying the facts, Noda avoided answering what the discussion he had with the other leaders was about.

4. Reflecting a question back to the interviewer(s)   Tôkyô Governor Ishihara provides an example of a politician reflecting a question back to the interviewer in an interview about the Tôkyô Metropolitan Assembly's introduction of a new local tax on major banks:

YOSHIZAKI: If the banks oppose your ideas and refuse to pay, what would you do?
ISHIHARA: In that case (laughing), what would happen? (*Hôdô 2001*, February 13)

Or, consider the following extract from an interview between Kuroiwa Yuji and Tanaka of the LDP:

KUROIWA (Calling Tanaka's attention to a board with photos of Diet members which are regarded as potential candidates to become prime minister): What is your opinion about this?
TANAKA: Everybody looks bad, including me . . . ha ha, ha, (laughing) . . . Mr. Takemura (the interviewer-commentator) what is your opinion? (*Hôdô 2001*, March 12, 2000)

Most likely, Ishihara bounced back the question to avoid publicly speculating about the measures he would have to take against recalcitrant banks, since doing so would leave himself open to criticism for being too soft or too tough. In the second case, Mrs. Tanaka, as mentioned before, tries to avoid commenting on personnel issues. In this study, 76 replies (4.7 percent of all replies) were identified as "non-replies."

Conclusion

Televised political interviews are special situations in the sense that they are actually performances that take place in front of an "overhearing" audience of millions. This distinctive social situation affects both interviewers and the politicians who are their interview subjects. Politicians are particularly conscious of the fact that such interviews represent a significant channel for "direct" communication with the general public, or with particular segments of the public. Politicians regard televised interviews as an important channel of political communication and prepare themselves so they can transfer their messages to the public in the most effective way.

This type of communication differs from the private talks that politicians regularly have in their offices with one individual or with small groups. The mood is different, the level of tension is different, and so are the politicians' approaches toward answering questions and presenting their views. In private talks with a limited number of people, politicians tend to reveal their real feelings, to give detailed descriptions of events they took part in, and to frankly predict what will happen in political affairs. In such meetings, they do not necessarily pay much attention to their style of speech or choice of words. But public speech in front of television cameras is different because they naturally must consider how the ideas they express and the words they choose will affect multiple audiences—the general public, their own supporters, fellow politicians, government officials—and the political process.

During televised interviews, politicians must evaluate all their options before addressing the challenging questions that are posed to them. Televised interviews are somewhat like a testing ground where politicians are pressured to quickly decide how to reply in a way that will satisfy the interviewer without causing inconvenience later from the various audiences. Understandably in such circumstances, politicians try to control the situation through their replies and to avoid careless remarks that are likely to invite criticism from colleagues, government officials, or from the electorate. This is why many do not reply immediately but stall for time using devices like "umm," "uh," or "well . . . " as they consider the best way to construct their reply. Often politicians equivocate in their reply.

In this study, only 162 replies (or 9.9 percent of 1,631) by Japanese politicians were coded as full answers, with "full answer" defined as (1) directly answers the question at hand, (2) is clear and expressed in language that is easy to understand, (3) reveals the speaker's own ideas, and (4) addresses the party who asked the question. The fact that less than 10 percent of replies qualified as full answers was astonishing, and the most significant observation of this study. It shows the very high rate of equivocation in answers to questions posed during televised political interviews in Japan. It also raises questions about the goals and the significance of such television programs, given that interviewees do not really answer a great proportion of the questions they are asked. Rather, such programs serve mainly as a stage upon which politicians can present their views on the issues that they perceive as important.

Obviously, Japanese politicians bring to televised interviews, as they do to other public venues, a set of ideas that they would like to transfer to their audience. Transferring these ideas to the public is one of their most important goals. Very often it is obvious that politicians are trying to convey certain opinions through the media regardless of what question they are asked. They talk at length about issues that have little relation to the topic introduced by the interviewer, channeling attention where they want it and diverting attention from other topics. Sometimes politicians seem to misinterpret the meaning of a question, but very often this reflects an intentional equivocation in the *context* dimension. Even if the interviewer, feeling dissatisfied with the reply, should repeat the question in a more pointed form, the interviewee will still focus on the aspects that he or she is prepared to talk about rather than directly answering the question that was asked.

The high rate of equivocation in televised political interviews in Japan contrasts markedly with data available about similar TV shows in Britain. Studies have shown that politicians in the UK reply to about 40 percent of the questions posed to them in televised interviews. Bull (1994) reported that in an analysis of 33 interviews with party political leaders in Britain, 46 percent of the questions received a direct answer. Another study of a completely different set of interviews revealed, for example, that Margaret Thatcher replied to 37 percent of the questions put to her as prime minister during televised interviews conducted during the 1987 general election, while Neil Kinnock (leader of the Labour Opposition, 1983–92), replied to 39 percent during the same period of time (Bull, 2002: 119). Another study of a different set of political interviews (principally with Thatcher and Kinnock) also reported similar results that these politicians gave direct answers to over 39 percent of the questions asked (Harris, 1991).

When comparing Japanese and British data, it must be noted that the British data was concerned only with the *context* dimension, whereas the data from Japan examined equivocation along four dimensions (*sender, clarity, receiver,* and *context*). But even when we look only at *context*-related equivocation in the Japanese sample, barely 15.8 percent of the replies were direct answers to questions. This is still far lower than the rate of full answers from British politicians.

It is also interesting to consider these results relative to reply rates for televised interviews with public figures who are not politicians. Bull reported that Diana, Princess of Wales, replied to 78 percent of the questions put to her. Louise Woodward, the British au pair who was tried for the manslaughter of an infant in her care, replied to 70 percent. And in an interview about her affair with President Clinton, Monica Lewinsky replied to 89 percent of questions posed. The mean reply rate for these three interviews was 79 percent—considerably higher than the mean reply rate of 46 percent for the 33 political interviews reported above (Bull, 2002: 119).

In Japan, reply rates for non-politicians appear to be even higher than in the UK. There were several interviews with non-politicians on the two Japanese programs studied here, during the period covered by the study (January–December 2000). The same coders who examined the interviews with politicians also sampled six interviews with five public figures who were interviewed as experts on social, economic, or educational issues (see Appendix 4.2). The six interviews contained a total of 78 questions, of which the public figures gave full answers to 69 (88.5 percent). Remember that "full answer" used here means not only addressing the question at hand, but doing so in clear, easily understandable language, reflecting the speaker's own views, and directly addressing the interviewer. Only nine of their replies (11.5 percent) failed to meet these criteria.

The fact that reply rates for non-politicians in Japan were higher than those of their British counterparts suggests that equivocation in televised interview by Japanese politicians is not simply a reflection of the often-noted general tendency toward equivocation in Japanese society, which is said to be due to cultural factors. It does indicate that politicians tend to equivocate much more than non-politicians. In light of the empirical evidence provided by the British data, which supports the popular notion that politicians do not reply to a large proportion of questions in political interviews, one could say that *the behavior of Japanese politicians seems to resemble that of other politicians more than it resembles the behavior of other Japanese.*

Why do Politicians Equivocate?

The theory devised by Bavelas et al. (1990) suggests that equivocation by politicians can be understood in the broader context of equivocation as it occurs in daily life; that is, it has to do with the communicative situation rather than with the politicians' personalities. Whether they are politicians or not, people tend to equivocate when they face a communicative conflict—specifically an avoidance–avoidance conflict in which all possible replies to a question have potentially negative consequences but a reply is nevertheless expected. Equivocation in such cases is a response to the individual's communicative situation. Because a high proportion of questions

directed at politicians during interviews present them with a communicative conflict, their responses are highly equivocal.

Elaborating on this notion, Bull and his colleagues (1996) coined the
term "level of threat". The concept of "level of threat" is based on the
proposition that politicians will tend to find "avoidance–avoidance" questions problematic and respond with equivocation. In the sample examined
in my study, not all Japanese politicians were questioned at the same "level
of threat"; some faced tougher questions than others. There was one exceptional interview in which 11 of 22 questions posed to the politician, or 50
percent, were coded as communicative-conflict questions. On the other
hand, in nine interviews (out of the total of 67), not even one such question was asked. The overall ratio of communicative-conflict questions
asked of politicians was 27.7 percent (452 out of 1,631 questions), compared to 11.5 percent (9 out of 78 questions) posed to non-politicians. At
the same time, Japanese politicians, as well as their counterparts in the UK,
also received some extremely sympathetic and supportive questions that
invited them to expound on positive aspects of themselves and their political groups.

We also used the "level of threat" measure to evaluate interviewers in
terms of toughness, and found that certain interviewers tended to ask
tougher questions than others, inducing interviewees to equivocate in their
replies. Tahara Sôichirô emerged as the toughest interviewer. His questions included frequent topical extensions, reformulations and challenges,
and more frequently posed threats to interviewees. Bull and his colleagues
(1996) found that some 87 percent of "avoidance–avoidance" questions—
to which interviewees equivocate in their replies—were couched in a
"yes–no" format. This suggests that politicians found difficulty with these
questions, and were unsure how to tackle them. A high proportion of yes/no
questions would therefore constitute a tough interview, and make a politician appear evasive (in this study, 409 questions were in yes/no format: 110
in *Hôdô 2001* and 299 in *Sandei Purojekuto*).

As a theoretical explanation for equivocation during political interviews,
Bull and his colleagues (1996) proposed the danger of "losing face"; that
is, politicians seek to avoid giving responses that might put them in a bad
light. For example, by equivocating on a controversial issue, the politician
may protect his or her own face by not publicly supporting an opinion that
a large proportion of the electorate finds unacceptable. When a politician
equivocates due to lack of knowledge about a certain public policy, he or
she reduces the risk of losing face by admitting ignorance and thus appearing incompetent or by guessing wrong and looking foolish later. Threats to
face can be seen not only as an important (and rational) force underlying
equivocation, but also as influencing when and why politicians do reply to
questions in political interviews. If, for example, a politician is asked to justify a specific action, failure to offer an appropriate explanation could raise

doubts about the politician's professional competence or about his or her integrity.

"Face management" becomes a particularly delicate matter during political interviews because interviewers can repeatedly ask difficult questions, challenge equivocal responses, and accentuate contradictions in policy matters. The face-threats are intensified by the fact that the interview is transmitted directly to the general public. Maintaining a positive face in interviews is particularly important for politicians because their political survival ultimately depends on the approval of people in their own constituency. A politician's success at face management during political interviews can be seen as a significant indicator of political communication skills. Consider for example the following extract from an interview between Tahara and Kamei Shizuka of the LDP:

TAHARA [talking about the possibility that a general election will take place soon]: Such information comes from executives of the LDP.

KAMEI [irritated]: Well, I am also one of the executives, this, not all [of the executives] said so—even the [LDP] Secretary-General did not say so. And thus, when you present this topic, Mr. Tahara, you should be careful about the language you use.

TAHARA: Don't you recall that the LDP, as a party, has said officially that [the election] will take place either in January or April?

KAMEI: No.

TAHARA: So the executives have their own way of saying things.

KAMEI: Well, there might be people who say things that I don't hear about.

TAHARA: There are people [like that]?

KAMEI: I don't know, I am the only one who doesn't know, and thus you made a mistake when you raised this issue with me. I do not know. (*Sandei Purojekuto*, March 19, 2000)

Here the interviewer threatens Kamei's "face" by insisting that information about an upcoming election came from executives of the LDP. Kamei denies this, but the interviewer again threatens his face by hinting that Kamei is probably pretending not to recall that the party has officially declared the timing of the election. The interviewer threatens again by asking rhetorically if the executives say things just like that. While Kamei is attacked by the interviewer, he keeps trying to presents himself and his party in the best light.

Bull et al. (1996) noted that in the context of political interviews, politicians seek to present the best possible face and support their own face along with that of the political party they represent, and of significant others (such as voters, political colleagues, and allies). At the same time, they have no desire to support the face of negatively valued others, such as political opponents. Bull and his collaborators based their assumptions about face as an explanatory variable for politicians' equivocation on earlier psychological and social psychological studies which claimed that concerns with face are salient in virtually all social encounters. Not only do individuals defend their own face in social interactions, there is also an obligation to defend the face of others. Imai (1981:10), among other Japanese researchers, has suggested that the desire to save face, to avoid embarrassing oneself and others, is a principal reason why Japanese have developed elaborately evasive communication tactics.

The sample examined in this study provided numerous examples of politicians' attempts to support or defend these three "faces" (belonging to self, to one's own political party, and to significant others). Here is an example of how then-LDP Policy Chief Kamei equivocated in order to portray himself in the best light during an interview with Tahara:

> TAHARA: How many years [would it take to reduce phone rates]?
> KAMEI: How many years you say, if I answer this here, it will generate excessive talk, and because I am also [the LDP] Policy Chief I cannot engage in irresponsible talk.
> TAHARA: I am asking [this question] particularly because you are the Policy Chief.
> KAMEI: Well, because of my position I would not say something irresponsible. Mr. Tahara, in about two or three years you will say '[you] did very well' on what I am going to do.
> TAHARA: Two or three years, I understand.
> KAMEI: Well, well, I would not say the target in terms of a number yet I say that there is a need for further improvement. (*Sandei Purojekuto*, March 19, 2000)

Kamei's initial reply suggests that he may not have a concrete idea of how long it will take to reduce telephone rates. In order to avoid embarrassing himself (e.g. by replying that he does not know or by spelling out the time frame but being wrong), he equivocates by claiming that as the LDP's Policy Chief he does not want to make any irresponsible remarks. When the interviewer persists in posing the question, Kamei assures him that he will do a good job and be recognized in "two or three years." To the back-channeling [*aizuchi*] of the interviewer, and perhaps to avoid further questioning in this regard (and probably further threat to his face), Kamei concludes that although he would not specify numbers (of years) he agrees on the need to improve the situation involving the prices of the phone rates.

Next is an example, from the same interview, of Kamei equivocating to protect the face of his party (which runs the government) by not declaring exactly how much the government should reduce prices:

> TAHARA (talking about the high cost of Internet connections in Japan): Wait a minute, Mr. Kamei. As a target, how low would [the government] reduce [the price]? Now ten times [lower], five times, five times, five times, how low would you reduce [the price], what is the [reduction] target?

KAMEI: This is, again, this is, I think it would be appropriate to lower it to the international standard.

TAHARA: Let's make it half [of that], half. . .

KAMEI: In the long run, this . . . , but I think it should be done gradually.

TAHARA: For the time being, for the time being . . .

KAMEI: Therefore, [rates] were reduced [recently], in addition they will be reduced to about half.

TAHARA: Reduce [the price]

KAMEI: Well, it takes some time, it can not be done immediately.

TAHARA: When approximately [this reduction will occur], about how many years [will it take]?

KAMEI: This, this thing [depends on] the situation, situation, what shall I say, I am talking [about this] with NTT [Nippon Telegraph and Telephone Corp.], we [the LDP, the government, and NTT] are talking about this, after all, we should progress with this reform gradually, as we started with it, [we] will continue. (*Sandei Purojekuto*, March 19, 2000)

Finally, here is an extract from an interview that Kamei gave on the same day (although on a different program), in which he equivocates in order to protect the face of another politician, Liberal Party leader Ozawa Ichiro. Because of the likelihood that the Liberal Party would join the LDP and strengthen the coalition at a time when such support was badly needed, Kamei tried to publicly protect the face of his potential coalition partner. He did so despite attempts by both interviewers, Kuroiwa and Yoshizakai, to provoke Kamei into criticizing Ozawa:

KUROIWA (about the likelihood of the LDP and the Liberal Party forming a coalition): As an object, a merger with the Liberal Party would be difficult, wouldn't it?

KAMEI: Well, this is, we [the LDP] say it is possible, but if Ozawa [Ichiro] does not want to do so . . .

YOSHIZAKI: There is a feeling that it is a bit difficult to join together.

KAMEI: As you say it is difficult to merge, if we realize it, however, the coalition of parties will be able to raise its achievements.

KUROIWA: Ozawa [Ichiro] came to your constituency to patronage an official candidate of the Liberal Party [that will run in election against you]. This was extremely meaningful event, already a letter of divorce [to the coalition], isn't it?

KAMEI: Well, there are things like that, there is a candidate [in the constituency] and one is free to come and support [this candidate].

YOSHIZAKI: But in reality you hate [such a thing].

KAMEI: This is not to the extent that I dislike it.

KUROIWA: Is that so?

KAMEI: Well, Ozawa visited also several times the constituency of Nonaka [another leading members of the LDP]. This is a political party against political party, and each political party is different. They are different and [each of them] uses different strategies, and I cannot say to [another political party] leader who has responsibility toward candidates not to do this and that. I am not in a position to do so. I don't care if he wants to do so. This [attitude of Ozawa] and the merging of the Liberal Party with the LDP to strengthen the coalition are completely different dimensions. (*Hôdô 2001*, March 19, 2000)

Although it would obviously be irksome to Kamei to have Ozawa come to his election district and made public speeches in support of his opponent in an election, Kamei declined to reveal his true feelings in front of the television camera because Ozawa and his party might soon join a coalition with Kamei's party. In other words, Kamei tried not to hurt the face of a potential political partner.

As this study reveals, politicians in Japan generally equivocate regarding personnel affairs, leadership tactics and style, controversial policy issues that divide their own political group, matters related to the political agenda, political strategies, and issues related to the formation or maintenance of coalitions. All these topics could be bundled together and categorized according to which of the three "faces" politicians seek to protect through equivocation. Analysis of the sample used in this study revealed that politicians equivocated most often to protect their own face, or that of their party or faction, rather than to support the face of significant others. One reason for this may lie in the nature of the questions they are asked: most questions focused on their own activities or the activities of their own group. Importantly, as discussed above, in a number of cases Japanese politicians employed a variety of tactics for ducking "avoidance–avoidance" conflicts, for example by laughing, repeating the question back to the interviewer, or just moving to another topic.

In conclusion, equivocation can be seen as a response to communicative conflicts, as well as a way of deflecting the face threats that these conflicts present. For a skilled political communicator, equivocation can be a highly effective instrument of self-presentation. As mentioned earlier, certain politicians tended to answer questions more directly than others, used clear and sometimes even harsh language, and revealed their own personal thoughts more often than others. Yet even these politicians equivocated in response to certain questions. One might say that these politicians in particular employ the art of equivocation as an important element of their political skill. They equivocate, using ambiguous or even evasive language, as a strategy for turning difficult situations to their own advantage. In this sense, one might propose that there can be such a thing as "good equivocators" and "poor equivocators" among political communicators in Japan and elsewhere.

Metaphorically Speaking I: Political Processes on the Front and Back of the Stage

This chapter and the following one discuss some ways in which figurative language, especially metaphor, permeates political discourse in Japan.[1] Focusing on language used by news media, politicians, and government bureaucrats, these chapters examine the nature and type of metaphors used to refer to political processes and institutions, and political roles in Japan. Metaphors are essential elements of political rhetoric because they translate complicated political events and situations into more familiar terms that are easier for the general public to comprehend. As such, metaphors play a significant role in providing information as well as perspectives through which the public perceive political activity and issues, and in maintaining and shifting political meanings and behavior (Edelman, 1971; Elwood, 1995; Mio, 1997; Read et al., 1990).

The particular focus of **Chapters 5 and 6** is on metaphors that refer to the "two-layered power structure" of Japanese politics—that is, to the existence of a backstage or true aspect, the *de facto* that is invisible to the public, along with a public or professed version, the *de jure*, which is shown to the public. Each of these sides is characterized by different elements that make up the logic of *Nagatachô*. As the chapters suggest, each of these sides of Japanese politics is characterized by a distinct set of metaphors. Furthermore, the "dual structure" of Japanese politics is a major feature that defines and distinguishes the nature and importance of roles played by KEY PERSONS [*kii pâson*]—decision-makers, politicians, government bureaucrats, and others such as journalists who cover politics for leading news organs—in each "domain" in particular, and in the political system in general. **Chapter 6** in particular focuses on the roles played by various "players" on the visible and invisible sides of politics, and how they are described metaphorically. Political authority, as this chapter details, is often held by people who operate behind the scenes, invisible to the general public, whereas those at the front of the POLITICAL STAGE are often merely figureheads.

The goal of **Chapters 5 and 6** are thus twofold. First, to identify and explain the metaphors used in *Nagatachô*'s two political processes. The first process is based around the idea of VILLAGE POLITICS [*mura seiji*], which suggests that *Nagatachô* is a battlefield where conflicting political groups and their leaders try to strengthen their own CAMP [*jin'ei*] so they can dominate political decisions and activities. Diet members, leaders, and members of the various political parties and party factions are constantly engaged in conflicts, rivalry, and antagonism over positions of power and influence in the Diet, Diet committees, and between and within political groups. The second process is DINNER CLUB POLITICS [*ryôtei seiji*]. *Nagatachô* is where the nation's most important decisions are made, including those related to allocation of the national budget. The image of Dinner Club Politics recognizes that these decisions are reached through negotiations, concessions, and cooperation between members of diverse groups. Lobbyists, government officials, leaders of business associations, Diet members and political party leaders all meet in *Nagatachô* to exchange demands and requests. They conduct lengthy secret negotiations over the content of legislation, Diet procedural questions and the structure of the government until they reach agreements about policy-making and leadership selection. These two processes as they are metaphorically expressed are detailed in **Chapter 5**.

The second goal, which is the focus of the following chapter, is to identify metaphors used to refer to political roles played by various individuals as they participate in the two processes. These individuals include Diet members, Cabinet ministers and their aides, and the prime minister; KING-MAKERS [*kingumeekâ*], SHADOW SHOGUNS [*yami shôgun*] and SCENARIO WRITERS [*senario raitâ*], who influence the course of political action; and members who help in coordinating and mediating functions of members of different groups and activities between members of the same group.

With these goals in mind, **Chapters 5 and 6** examine a representative selection of important metaphors that appear most often in Japanese political rhetoric, indicating also aspects related to the relationships between political culture and figurative language. We begin with discussion on metaphors and their role in politics in general.

Metaphors and Their Role in Politics

The *Oxford English Dictionary* defines metaphor as "the figure of speech in which a name or descriptive term is transferred to some object of different form, but analogous to, that to which it is properly applicable." Metaphor allows people to talk and think about one area of experience (the 'topic,' 'tenor' or 'target domain') in terms of another (the 'vehicle' or 'source domain'). Metaphors thus involve the structure of abstract, complex or unfamiliar target domains in terms of source domains—ideas from different spheres of life—that are more concrete, clear and familiar

(Beer & De Landtsheer, 1999). So metaphor is not simply a figure of speech typical of poetic or highly rhetorical language, but a pervasive and essential feature of all types of language (Lakoff, 1991; Lakoff & Turner, 1989). Metaphors not only embellish a preconstituted reality for rhetorical purposes, but also contribute to the construction and understanding of social reality itself (van Teeffelen, 1994: 384). This notion has special significance in politics, where structuring one domain in terms of another can influence the way large numbers of people perceive sensitive and controversial aspects of their living environment.

As the actual social environment is too complex and changeable to be known directly, individuals are simply not equipped to deal with so much subtlety and variety, and so many changes and associations. To manage this world somewhat efficiently, decision-makers, politicians, and the news media, tend to transfer qualities from another sphere of life, such as nature, sports, health, or work, to political topics. Political issues are more easily explained by using subjects familiar to the audience. Support for policies, for example, is probably less likely to be shaped by conventional understanding of ideology and more likely to be influenced by the policy metaphors that are evoked by particular social issues or policy proposals (Schlesinger & Lau, 2000).

The effects of metaphors in political rhetoric—including their aesthetic and manipulative powers—have been widely discussed. Metaphors can stir emotions, justify action, or bridge the gap between logical (rational) and emotional (irrational) forms of persuasion. The power of metaphors derives from the emotional responses that they can evoke in a variety of political and social contexts (Stone, 1988). When applied consistently and systematically in a particular political context, metaphors can be a powerful tool for changing people's attitudes toward politics, for creating a positive image of political parties and their leaders, for justifying leaders' activities, and for establishing a varied set of relationships between leaders and the general public. Political leaders can use conventional metaphors effectively to present their own views of reality as 'natural' and 'common-sense,' and to reduce the chances that the public will challenge the metaphors involved (Semino & Masci, 1996).

The use of metaphors is affected by various factors such as the political, social, and economic situations at a given time. Health metaphors, for example, frequently appear during recessions as use of the doctor's image fulfills the popular need for a strong political leader who knows what to do (De Landtsheer, 1994). No less important, use of specific metaphors depends on culture, as different societies tend to use different metaphors. As an integral element of the social and political discourse of a given society, metaphors vary in content and intensity, or "strength" (Mooy, 1976: 121). Since metaphors do not exist within a cultural vacuum, they cannot be treated as though they were independent of a social context.

Their various forms and uses are related to specific sets of historical and cultural antecedents. A metaphor that can be frequently used, understood, and generates a certain reaction in one society cannot be used, or at least not as effectively, in another society. In this sense, both the general public and elites in a specific society share a common understanding of the broad meaning of the metaphors used in their society. Knowledge of a society's culture, especially of its language and history, thus facilitates the understanding of what metaphors that society uses in politics, how it uses them, and the meaning and potential effects of these metaphors.

Japan is no exception. Its culture determines the scope, nature and effects of metaphors used, including which metaphors are acceptable or taboo, strong or weak. Those metaphors, in turn, help to mold other aspects of the political culture. For example, many of the metaphors used in Japanese political jargon are based either on traditional customs (e.g. PORTABLE SHRINES carried around during festivals and the sport of *sumô*) or characters or roles from Japan's history—such as samurai aides, MAGISTRATES, or GO-BETWEENS. These terms all frame the context in which people familiar with these traditions and figures understand the functioning of contemporary political figures.

Consider the significance of "war" in Japan. War has a particular meaning in Japan, where the word "war" almost always means World War II. This war symbolizes a dark era in Japanese contemporary history, the outcome of a fascist and authoritarian regime that put Japan on the road to devastation and humiliation followed by starvation and poverty. Most Japanese associate "war" with fascism, death, and the atom bomb. War is something that everyone over a certain age has experienced personally, and something none of them want to experience again. Probably because of this, the word "war" appears less frequently as a metaphor than it does in Western societies in the context of policy issues or measures that a government intends to take to solve important issues. For example, several American presidents used WAR as a metaphor to delineate their stance toward a domestic issue. These included Lyndon Johnson's use of WAR ON POVERTY, Gerald Ford's WAR ON INFLATION, and Ronald Reagan's and George Bush's WAR ON DRUGS to emphasize their determination to seriously and aggressively address issues on the nation agenda until those issues were resolved (e.g. Elwood, 1995; Barry, 1998). Japan has fewer problems related to drugs and poverty than Western societies do, yet it confronts a growing number of other social, economic and environmental problems. Many candidates mention these and other issues in their campaign speeches, as many politicians have done in Diet speeches and deliberations. But one never hears a Japanese politician "declare war" on a specific social or economic problem. Candidates never use the term WAR in regard to environmental problems in their campaign slogans, the government does not "declare war" on unemployment, and the prime minister never "announces war" against immorality among youth, or against deteriorating values.

To further illustrate, following constitutional, geographical, and matters related to its relationships with world powers, metaphors such as HEDGEHOG [*harinezumi*], SHIELD AND SPEAR [*tate to yari*], and UNSINKABLE AIRCRAFT CARRIER [*fuchin kûbo*] were used by different prime ministers in order to make the military buildup of Japan more acceptable to the public. Metaphors were thus effective tools in the hand of the governing elite for the militarization of Japan. The metaphor NUCLEAR ALLERGY [*kaku arerugi*] used by prime minister Satô Eisaki (1964–72) was particularly effective in this respect. The metaphor helped to structure political reality in order to promote and legitimize the government policies regarding both nuclear weapons and nuclear energy, and to disseminate uncertainties among the Japanese concerning their anti-nuclear sentiments (Hook, 1986: 37–40; 67ff).

The discussion now focuses on the two political processes mentioned above and their related metaphors.

Two Political Processes: Conflict and Cooperation

(1) The Politics of Conflict and Rivalry: Village Politics

The first process cited above, VILLAGE POLITICS, refers to the fierce competition and confrontation between and within Japanese political groups over positions of power and prestige. The ever-present, ever-increasing rivalry and antagonism between various groups and their leaders over political influence are depicted in certain distinct metaphors.

Metaphors Representing Village Politics   Japanese political groups— including parties and party factions (especially in the LDP)—are often referred to as VILLAGES [*mura*], (e.g. *Asahi,* July 15, 1986; *Asahi,* December 22, 1986; Itô, 1982: 89). A VILLAGE indicates a group that is separate and distinct from other, similar groups. Each VILLAGE has its own distinct customs, rules, strategies, and secrets *vis-à-vis* rival political groups in the struggle to acquire and hold positions of power. It is a closed, intimate clique whose members have known each other for years, if not for decades. They work closely together, play closely together, and even grieve closely together. The result of all this closeness is a strong sense of cohesiveness and identity with their ultimate goal, i.e. to maintain and increase their membership so they can dominate political decisions and activities. For that purpose, they often join hands with other groups to strengthen their own political CAMP [*jin'ei*]. Below are some metaphors that are often used to describe these VILLAGE-groups and their functions.

General Hospital: Some VILLAGES function as GENERAL HOSPITALS [*sôgô byôin*], (*Asahi*, December 27, 1997). In other words, they have different "departments" that take care of various needs and wants presented by the group's members (i.e. Diet members) and even by "patients" from the outside, including regular citizens, government bureaucrats and young candidates who join the group in search of political office that will help them to get various kinds of "treatment" to their supporters (*Asahi Shimbun Seijibu*, 1992: 183).

VILLAGES may have different ideas and views from each other, but it is usually not their political orientations that set them apart. The LDP is actually an alliance of factions based on personal loyalty to one another [*giri-ninjô*] rather than on ideological views. Each LDP faction is founded on intense ties of mutual obligation, and is characterized by a hierarchical organization based on relationships between paternalistic superiors and their subordinates, and between regular members, whose status depends on the order in which they joined the group. The result is blind obedience and mutual dependence (Mitchell, 1976). These hierarchical relationships are often described using terms like *oyabun* and *kobun* (words for boss and subordinate that suggest a parent–child relationship) or *sempai* and *kôhai* (senior and junior, literally "one who comes before" and "one who comes later"). Juniors show deference to their seniors, provide services whenever seniors require them, demonstrate loyalty and commitment, and support their faction boss in the party presidential election. In turn, seniors are expected to protect and help their juniors. Veteran politicians within the same political group advise those with less political experience on strategies and tactics for getting the support of the electorate, and even travel to their constituencies to speak to local voters on their behalf, thereby helping to build the reputation and name recognition of the junior politicians.

Collar and Sleeves: Each VILLAGE has its own internal hierarchical structure, including positions such as party or faction secretary general, chairperson in charge of policy measures, and spokesperson. In the case of LDP factions, a leader of a faction is called a *ryôshû* (a chief or boss who stands at the top of others or is looked upon as a good model for others) (e.g. *Shûkan Asahi*, December 29, 2000). Literally, *ryôshû* means the COLLAR AND SLEEVES of a shirt, parts that stand out clearly from the main body as a leader naturally does (or should, at least).

General Trading Company: Traditionally, faction leaders provided considerable financial support for the activities of other members of their faction, especially during election campaigns (*Asahi Shimbun Seijibu*, 1992: 161ff). This money has been the main force in maintaining factional solidarity since the LDP's factions were established in the 1950s. The leaders support faction members with money, and the members in turn support their leader in his campaign to be party president. A faction thus often functions as a GENERAL TRADING COMPANY [sôgô shôsha], (Aera, September 10, 1991), which controls incoming funds and distributes it to faction members.

Family and Heirs: Parent–child metaphors are often used to refer to the special relationship of mutual dependency that exists between political party or party faction leaders and their followers. Several promising "children," i.e. young Diet members, have been called PRINCES [purinsu] to indicate that their "parents," i.e. the leaders of their party faction, supported them as a successor. Former Foreign Minister Abe Shintarô was the PRINCE of former Prime Minister (1976–78) Fukuda Takeo's faction (*Asahi*, January 6, 1987), and former LDP Secretary General Katô Kôichi was the PRINCES of the faction led by former Prime Minister Miyazawa Kiichi (*Asahi*, November 9, 1991). (Fuwa Tetsuzô, the leader of JCP, was the PRINCE OF YOYOGI [yoyogi no purinsu] because at the age of 40 he was the youngest member of the central committee and executive committee of his party, which has its headquarters in the Yoyogi district in Tôkyô [Iwami, 1998: 231]).

OZAWA'S CHILDREN [ozawa chirudoren] was the phrase used to refer to people who won their first terms in the Diet as candidates for the New Frontier Party [Shinshintô] that Ozawa Ichirô founded in 1994. The group included a former baseball player, university professor, dentist, government officials, and local politicians who benefited from Ozawa's support and protection (*Asahi*, June 5, 1998; Saikawa, 1999: 301).

Former Prime Minister (1978–1980) Ôhira Masayoshi was called the POLITICALLY ADOPTED CHILD [seijitekina yôshi] of former Prime Minister (1960–64) Ikeda Hayato, who led the faction to which Ôhira belonged (Itô, 1982: 187).

Prime Minister Kaifu Toshiki was perceived as the ADOPTED SON-IN-LAW of the Takeshita faction [takeshita ha no muko yôshi], (*Asahi Shimbun Seijibu*, 1992: 47) to which he in fact did not belong, because of his total reliance on former Prime Minister Takeshita Noboru's support for his administration since Kaifu lacked both a power base of his own and experience with the workings of government.

The parent–child metaphor can even be applied to political organizations. The LDP has sometimes been called the PRODIGAL SON [dôraku musuko] of the financial circles [zaikai] that have supplied the party with financial support since its establishment in 1955 (Masumi, 1988: 353). A politician's support group has often been called the politician's FAMILY. For example, the TANAKA FAMILY [Tanaka famiri] referred to members of *Etsuzankai*—the support organization of former Prime Minister Tanaka Kakuei, its "father" (Masumi, 1988: 248).

Watchdog Reporters and Lantern Stories: VILLAGES guard their own tactics and secrets from rival political groups so closely that leading news media assign a separate WATCHDOG REPORTER [*ban kisha*] to cover each of the LDP factions. This reporter covers the events and personnel affairs of one and only one party faction. The assignment lasts for a year or two, during which time the reporter develops a cozy relationship with the faction leaders and members, and becomes privy to their activities and strategies. The reporter is not supposed to have contact with any members of another faction—otherwise he or she would be suspected of transferring secrets to rivals and would lose the trust of information sources in the faction to which he or she is assigned. WATCHDOG REPORTERS very often take active roles in political competition by providing Diet members with feedback on their strategies, and by advising leaders on what action to take or when and how to react to public opinion. These reporters often accept requests to write *yarase kiji*—literally compulsory articles, which are also euphemistically called LANTERN STORIES [*chôchin kiji*] because they spotlight the activities and achievements of their sources, providing free publicity for the sources (Feldman, 1993a: 131).

Intimate Relationships: VILLAGES sometimes form partnerships among themselves in order to further their own interests. These partnerships can be compared to marriage or romantic relationships between two individuals.

Ozawa Ichirô, then leader of the New Frontier Party, was discussing political groups as if they were sexual partners when he reportedly dismissed the wrath of the Social Democratic Party over an alliance formed by the LDP—its coalition partner at the time—by saying, as noted, "It doesn't matter which WOMAN SOMEONE SLEEPS WITH . . . If the SDP felt jealous of the new alliance, they should have come and joined us."

Ox Walk: Opposition parties often band together to try to force concessions from the ruling party (or ruling coalition). The most popular tactics are various forms of obstruction—such as filibusters, boycotts, and brawls—aimed at paralyzing the legislature or killing a bill. Members of the opposition sometimes block the Diet hall, preventing other members from entering to vote on an issue (for example, a bill to bail out failed housing loan companies in 1996). Or they might express their displeasure with the way the ruling coalition has formulated a certain bill (such as a bill proposed in February 2000 to reduce the number of Diet members in the lower house) by refusing to participate in meetings of the budget committee, the Diet's most important committee. At other times, they may purposely talk or debate at length in order to tie up legislative business.

One of the opposition's famous delaying tactics is the "OX WALK" [*"gyûho senjutsu"*]. When voting by open ballot, every member has to cast a white (for) or blue (against) ballot into a box at the center of the main Diet hall. Opposition party members sometimes delay this process in an attempt to win a time-out by walking extremely slowly to the front of the chamber—sometimes taking half an hour—to cast their vote. Lawmakers participating in an OX WALK meander over to the ballot box so slowly that it can take hours to complete a vote. This tactic was used in 1987 in a successful effort to defeat Prime Minister Nakasone's plan to introduce a 5 percent consumption tax. The tactic was used again in 1988 in an unsuccessful attempt to block the Takeshita Noboru government's tax reform bill, which included a 3 percent version of the consumption tax. In June 1992, when a bill allowing Japanese soldiers to join UN peacekeeping operations came before the upper house of the Diet, members of the SDP and the JCP employed the OX WALK to slow down the vote. The vote took a record 13 hours and eight minutes to complete, although the LDP was trying to rush the bill through the Diet to allow Japanese troops to take part in a UN peacekeeping operation in Cambodia. Another OX WALK took place in August 1999, when the Diet voted on a controversial package of bills allowing investigative authorities to intercept organized crime via telephone, fax, and the Internet. Opposition members, including members of the DPJ, walked at a snail's pace when casting their votes on this bill (*Asahi*, August 13, 1999).

Numerical Power and Wars – *War:* As we see, inter-group interaction in *Nagatachô* is thus like interaction between different VILLAGES. Each clique has its own leadership, its own views on the political process and selection of leaders, and its own preferred ways to handle party problems. Each VILLAGE competes with others to increase its own political power. They choose candidates for election and help them to BATTLE [*tatakau*] against candidates from rival political parties. In order to improve the chances of winning a seat, VILLAGES assist their candidates to get support from as many influential members of the community as possible. Toward that end, candidates engage in CARPET-BOMBING [*jûtan bakugeki*], (*Asahi*, October, 12, 1997), or spreading their names and reputations through influential members all over the constituency, as if spreading a carpet. Because a citizen does not need to reside in a district in order to represent the district in the Diet, there are PARACHUTE CANDIDATES [*rakkasan kôho*] in Japan. Like a parachutist falling from a plane, a PARACHUTE CANDIDATE seems to drop out of the sky to a constituency where he or she may have lived only briefly—or not at all—to become a candidate for political office.

Moving the Mountain: The BATTLE between political groups striving to gain political power is often so fierce and so long that it seems hopeless. After decades of dominating Japanese politics, the LDP lost its majority in the upper house in the election of 1989. The SDP, its main rival for close to

40 years, doubled its presence in the upper house from 22 seats to 46. In light of this significant shift in the Diet makeup, SDP Chair Doi Takako remarked that the socialist force was so powerful that it had done almost the impossible and MOVED A political MOUNTAIN [*yama wa ugoita*], (*Asahi*, July 12, 1995).

Single-Hook Fishing: The competition for numerical strength is an important element of *Nagatachô*'s peculiar "common sense." To increase its political power, each group first concentrates on increasing the number of its members. Having more members gives a VILLAGE greater influence over the political process and decision-making in *Nagatachô*. During the late 1990s, LDP members used SINGLE-HOOK FISHING [*ippon-zuri*] in their effort to restore the LDP's majority in the upper house after they had success with this approach in the lower house toward the end of 1997. SINGLE-HOOK FISHING meant approaching members of other political parties—especially one at a time—and, as if "fishing" them one by one, urge them to join the LDP (*Asahi*, July 2, 1997).

Moreover, the LDP, for example, traditionally allocated Cabinet and top party positions to each faction in accordance with how many members it had. Thus, each LDP VILLAGE strives to increase its membership in order to get Cabinet positions and thereby exert more influence on the course of politics. In their bid to increase their power, various factions have engaged in WARS, that is, struggles over power; in addition, many ambitious members eagerly competed for the chance to take office whenever an administration collapsed. Indeed, WAR and WAR-related metaphors have been used most significantly in Japanese political jargon in relation to the internal struggles of the LDP and its factions.

Army Divisions and Army Corps: During the late 1950s and the 1960s, the LDP's eight factions were called the EIGHT ARMY DIVISIONS [*hakko shidan*], (Masumi, 1988: 346). These factions eventually evolved into the five major factions that have existed since the early 1970s. Each of these factions works like a division of soldiers. Some have grown big enough to be able to exert more influence on political decision-making and selection of leaders. The one that was lead by former Prime Minister Tanaka became known as the TANAKA ARMY CORPS [*Tanaka gundan*]. By the 1980s, the Tanaka group had become the most important dispensing center for influence and patronage within the LDP, and totally controlled the choice of the next prime minister. It also emerged as a powerful actor in public policy formation, dominating Japanese politics until February 1985 when Tanaka was partially paralyzed by a stroke.

Generational Wars: Some of the WARS over leadership positions were GENERATIONAL WARS [*sedai sensô*], (*Asahi*, April 18, 1997) or INTER-GENER-

ATIONAL WARS [*sedai-kan sensô*], (*Asahi*, January 4, 1999). There were WARS between NEW LEADERS [*nyû riidâ*], (*Asahi*, July 1, 1986) and NEO-NEW LEADERS [*neo nyû riidâ*], *(Asahi*, July 16, 1991). "New leaders" were those who were positioned to succeed Prime Ministers Nakasone and Takeshita—they included former LDP Secretary General Abe Shintarô and former Finance Minister Miyazawa Kiichi. "Neo-new leaders" were the politicians who hoped to succeed Prime Minister Kaifu's administration, including Finance Minister Hashimoto Ryûtarô and former Agriculture, Forestry and Fisheries Minister Hata Tsutomu, both of whom served as prime minister in the 1990s.

Forty-Day War: LDP factions were engaged in WARS so constantly and so fiercely that former Prime Minister Ôhira once said the world of politicians is a sea of jealousy, which he had crossed successfully in order to become prime minister. In fact, he won his position after a factional conflict known as the FORTY-DAY WAR [*yon-jû nichi kôsô*], (Masumi, 1988: 310).

Kaku-Fuku War: Power struggles inside the LDP were often symbolized by names of archrivals, such as Ikeda Hayato versus Satô Eisaku, and during the 1970s were dubbed "*Sankaku daifuku,*" referring to the first Chinese character in the family names of four faction leaders—Miki Takeo, Tanaka Kakuei, Ôhira Masayoshi, and Fukuda Takeo, respectively. The longest and most famous WAR within the LDP was the KAKU-FUKU WAR [*Kaku-fuku sensô*], a long and intense rivalry between faction leaders Tanaka Kakuei and Fukuda Takeo. Their mutual antagonism began during the 1960s, when both were busy broadening their political influence and power bases in a bid to succeed Prime Minister Satô (*Aera*, July 24, 1995). After bribing neutral factions of the LDP, Tanaka gained enough support in 1972 to become president of the party, which automatically meant he would be prime minister, since the LDP held a majority of Diet seats. After that, the rivalry between Fukuda and Prime Minister Tanaka entered a new phase and began to escalate even further during the following years.

Awa War: Another famous WAR within the LDP was the AWA WAR, otherwise known as the TOKUSHIMA WAR [*awa sensô* or *tokushima sensô*], referring to the rivalry between former Prime Minister (1974–76) Miki Takeo and former Vice Prime Minister and Chief Cabinet Secretary Gotôda Masaharu, a bureaucrat-turned-politician. Both were from Tokushima Prefecture, on the island of Shikoku in western Japan. During the 1974 upper house election, Miki became furious when Prime Minister Tanaka highhandedly removed incumbent councilor Kujime Kentarô (of the Miki faction) from the LDP slate and had the prefectural party federation sponsor Tanaka confidant Gotôda in Miki's hometown (Masumi, 1988: 237).

Cold War: Since the 1980s there have been several WARS between two or more Diet members competing to succeed faction leaders or prime ministers. Among them were the ONE-SIX WAR [*ichi-roku sensô*], referring to the struggle between Miyazawa Ki*ichi* (*ichi* in Japanese means one) and Tanaka *Roku*suke (*roku* means six) over leadership of the Suzuki (former Ôhira) faction (*Asahi,* October 30, 1991) and the KK WAR [*kk sensô*] that was fought in the beginning of the 1990s between former LDP Secretary General Katô Kôichi and former LDP president Kono Yôhei, who both belonged to the faction led by Miyazawa. Katô described this as a "COLD WAR between generations." Katô represented himself as belonging to a new generation in contrast to the older generation represented by Kono, who was a student of politicians born in the Taishô Era (1910–26) and early Shôwa Era (1926–89) (*Asahi,* May 21, 1991). There was a ONE-DRAGON WAR [*ichi-ryû sensô*] between Ozawa *Ichirô* and Hashimoto Ryûtarô (*ryû* means dragon) over the leadership of former Prime Minister Takeshita's faction, and another ONE-SIX WAR [*ichi-roku sensô*] referring to the rivalry between Ozawa *Ichi*rô and Kajiyama Seiroku. The SIX-DRAGON WAR [*roku-ryû sensô*] was fought between Katô *Mutsu*ki (*mutsu* and *roku* both mean six) and Hashimoto Ryûtarô.

Political Cease-Fires: Constant WARS and power struggles between LDP factions have been a major element of the "common sense of *Nagatachô,*" but sometimes it has been necessary to negotiate POLITICAL CEASE-FIRES [*seiji kyûsen*] between faction leaders in order to accomplish the regular work of the LDP and the Diet (Masumi, 1988: 302). During the years there were numerous calls from various political groups, news media, and political commentators, for the dissolution of the factions, which by extension would mean the elimination of a portion of *Nagatachô* common sense.

Voice of Heaven: Former Prime Minister Kishi Nobusuke called his proposal for dissolving factions in the LDP THE VOICE OF THE HEAVENS [*ten no koe*], (Masumi, 1988: 338), a term often used as a powerful justification for the arguments of someone who wants to settle a contentious issue once and for all. Former Prime Minister Fukuda also jokingly used this phrase after the 1978 LDP presidential election. It had been expected that Fukuda, as the incumbent prime minister, would defeat Ôhira and be reelected. But Fukuda lost to Ôhira, who won the majority of votes cast by rank-and-file party members after an inconclusive first ballot. Before the election, Fukuda was confident of victory and said, "Heaven moves in a sound direction." His surprise at the outcome of the election caused Fukuda to publicly muse, "I think even THE VOICE OF THE HEAVENS can be strange sometimes" ["*Ten no koe mo henna koe mo tama ni wa aru to omou*"], (Masumi, 1988: 307).

Live Ammunition and Supply Lines – *Postmen and Envelopes*: As may be recalled, former Prime Minister Tanaka noted once that "number is power, power is money" ["*kazu wa chikara, chikara wa kane*"], (*Asahi*, December 17, 1993), illustrating that not only numbers (of Diet members) but also money is crucial to maintaining political power. Success in Japanese politics involves money—often a lot of money. It has been estimated that a Diet Member needs 140 million yen per year just to cover daily functions associated with political office (Samejima, 1994: 143–44). In addition, the elaborate and highly structured nature of political campaigning in Japan, a process that actually continues 365 days a year, makes politics a very expensive business. Despite efforts over the years to limit the cost of campaigning by restricting certain campaign methods, and despite the institution of subsidies to deflect campaign costs, the cost of day-to-day political promotion, publicity, entertainment, gifts and other vote-getting activities is still enormous. For example, several times during an election campaign, campaign workers known as POSTMEN [*yûbinya*] go around the constituency delivering envelopes containing 5,000 yen or 10,000 yen bills and asking voters to vote for their candidate. This is called DIRECT SHOOTING [*jika-uchi*]. Each round of such payments, known as ONE ENVELOPE [*kin-ippu*] was 300,000–1,000,000 yen in the 1950s, but shot up to between 600,000 and 2,000,000 yen in the 1960s (Masumi, 1988: 365). Influential members of a district who can get others to vote for a candidate often receive 10 million yen. Such influential individuals are called PILLARS [*hashira*] because they provide essential support that helps the candidate get elected (*Asahi*, October 7, 1979).

Live Ammunition and Bean-Jam Buns: Diet members from different political parties find different sources for the funding they need. Some get it from their party headquarters, while others may rely on the construction industry or another source. As noted above, LDP candidates used to get a considerable amount of their financial support from their faction leader. That money also served to maintain the solidarity of the faction, as members support the party presidential campaign of the leader who has supported them with money. LIVE AMMUNITION [*jitsudan shageki*] was often used to refer to the money that a faction's boss gave to followers (Masumi, 1988: 34, 95). Campaign funds and election expenses were calculated in terms of BULLETS [*jitsudan*], (*Asahi*, September 15, 1993), with one BULLET being equal to 100 million yen. Very often, money used for supporting Diet members' activity was also called BEAN-JAM BUNS [*manjû*], (*Asahi*, May 28, 1993), where one BEAN-JAM BUN is equal to one million yen (*Aera*, October 27, 1992). Political funds were MILITARY SUPPLIES [*heitan*] and the financial circles and other channels through which money reached the various factions within the LDP were called SUPPLY LINES [ryôdô], (Masumi, 1988: 334).

Rice-Cake Money: Faction leaders customarily gave their members cash all year round. The disbursement made at the end of the year, when Japanese are preparing rice cakes traditionally eaten to celebrate the New Year, was called RICE-CAKE MONEY [*mochi-dai*], (*Asahi,* December 18, 1986; Itô, 1982: 28). It consisted of at least three million yen in cash. ICE MONEY [*kori-dai*] was a similar payment distributed during the summer to help, for example, with upcoming campaign expenses (*Asahi,* June 11, 1998), or to stimulate sports and other activities of the support groups of the Diet members within the community during the hot season. Leaders also gave cash for the two traditional seasonal gifts of *Oseibo,* at year-end, and *Ochûgen,* in summer. Because their followers' need for funding is constantly increasing, faction leaders must keep their existing SUPPLY LINES open while continually looking for new sources. Former Prime Minister Kishi, while discussing the amounts of money that each faction leader could bring to a campaign, compared two faction leaders this way: "They may both raise ONE FINGER, but Fukuda's means a million while Tanaka's means a hundred million" (Masumi, 1988: 240).

Whisky as Money: Historically, certain party members received money not only from their own faction's leader but also from leaders of other factions. Those who received money from two faction leaders were called *nikka,* those who received from three factions were *santori,* and those who received money from all the factions' leaders were called *ôurudopâ* (e.g. *Asahi,* August 6, 1989). *Nikka,* Suntory [*santorii*] and Old Paw [*ôrudopâ*] are names of Japanese whiskies. The name *nikka* contains *ni,* which means two in Japanese, *santorii* contains *san,* or three, and *ôrudopâ* contains a Japanese rendering of "all," referring in this case to all the factions.

Whereas the process of VILLAGE politics emphasizes how political groups and their leaders act as rivals as each attempts to increase personal or factional power and influence, the second central aspect of Japanese politics illustrates how political rivals must strive to cooperate in order to solve political, social, and economic problems.

(2) The Politics of Harmony and Cooperation: Dinner Club Politics

DINNER CLUB POLITICS [*ryôtei seiji*] refers to the hidden side of the political process—decision-makers' efforts at achieving enough harmony and cooperation between various political groups to allow them to accomplish specific tasks. This process has often been called a "symbol of *Nagatachô* politics" or "the essence of *Nagatachô*'s common sense" (*Asahi,* August 15, 1993) because it reflects the distinctive way in which policymakers reach decisions about issues that affect the whole nation. Because of the importance of this process in Japanese politics, Dinner Club Politics was considered for years the NATIONAL POLITICAL ADMINISTRATION COMMIT-

TEE [*kokutai seiji iin* or *koku taisaku iin*], (Saikawa, 1999: 17). Dinner Club Politics is in fact an expression of the Japanese "back-room negotiations mentality." In practical terms, Dinner Club Politics means that Diet members and leaders of different VILLAGES—political parties or party factions—meet in fine restaurants (especially those clustered in the *Akasaka* district of central Tôkyô, near the Diet building and the Diet members' offices) to discuss issues of mutual interest. These leaders meet in private, far from the public eye, and conduct secret consultations and "TEA HOUSE" NEGOTIATIONS, otherwise known as "CLOSED-DOOR POLITICS" [*misshitsu seiji*], or "RENDEZVOUS POLITICS" [*machiai seiji*]. This is where they do *nemawashi*, a process whereby prior agreement is obtained through informal negotiation and persuasion before a proposal is formally presented. During these meetings, Diet members and their representatives quietly present to each other their stances on specific issues, express support for—or objections to—the views held by other members on these topics, and try to resolve conflicts of opinions and political tensions behind closed doors while involving all concerned parties in the decision-making process.

In contrast, Diet proceedings are an example of the public side of the political process. In plenary sessions of the Diet, politicians give speeches about important issues and vote to decide procedures to be followed when performing the routine work of both chambers. In fact, though, such votes merely ratify decisions that were already reached in negotiations between party leaders before the session began. Such negotiations, conducted during "RENDEZVOUS POLITICS," are part of the Dinner Club political process. At the fancy restaurant, leaders of political groups bargain, for instance, over how each party will be represented through leadership positions, how long an extraordinary Diet session will last, and where each party's Diet members will be seated. Some bills introduced in the Diet are also pre-negotiated by representatives of various political parties and are jointly endorsed by all of them.

It is at these meetings that politicians decide where to INSERT THE SCALPEL [*mesu wo ireru*], (i.e. who will have to bear the burden of drastic measures aimed at eradicating a specific social, economic or political problem) (e.g. *Asahi*, May 16, 1990). Sometimes it is agreed that the opposition parties will continue to battle the ruling party until the last moment. They will then surrender and allow the ruling party to make a motion to end the "discussion" (actually a stylized question-and-answer period which takes place in Diet's committees) and proceed with a vote.

Tamamushi-iro: Dinner Club meetings often end with an IRIDESCENT AGREEMENT [*tamamushi-iro gôi*], which means an ambiguous accord, or elusively words agreement and settlement reached by politicians and political parties. *Tamamushi-iro* literally means "jewel beetle-colored." The appearance of the beetle's wings changes as the beetle moves, displaying hues ranging from metallic blue to copper, green, and sometimes dark purple, a play of colors producing rainbow effects. In other words, *tamamushi-iro* means something that can't be pinned down, but can be perceived in various ways. It can appear to be all things to all people and, therefore, is satisfactory to all. *Tamamuhi-iro* means thus deliberately vague expressions or ambiguous words that may be interpreted in any way and are satisfactory to all parties concerned. These agreements are usually announced when politicians cannot specify dates for the application or establishment of a certain policy (instead they only state "at the earliest possible date") or when they are forced to make a final decision in the face of a looming deadline but several points have yet to be cleared up (*Asahi*, September 21, 1998). Thus, an agreement is reached for the sake of meeting the deadline, with some issues left open for later settlement. For example, the LDP reached various "agreements" with the Liberal Party during the process of forming a coalition government. A major accord between the two parties was signed in January 1999 with great fanfare, but while it did mention goals and general policies related to national security, Diet deliberations, and reducing the number of ministers, it did not specify when or how these goals were to be implemented (*Asahi*, January 14, 1999).

Slaughterhouse: Dinner Club Politics takes place not only between members of the ruling and opposition parties or members of the ruling coalition, but also between leaders of LDP factions. Over the decades that the LDP dominated Japanese politics, it institutionalized appointment and promotion practices that are based on seniority and factional balance rather than on ability or expertise (Nonaka, 1995: 292). The system has been reinforced by the practice of rotating cabinet ministers and other office holders at very short intervals, in order to make the prestige and perquisites of top government office available to as many members of the ruling party or parties as possible. Dinner Club Politics often involves discussing the appointment of Cabinet members and the distribution of Cabinet seats among different factions. Selection of the LDP president, who many times also serves as prime minister, has usually been done through BACK-ROOM negotiations among the factions. Open election of the party president entails a very complex voting procedure. The procedure is called a SLAUGHTERHOUSE [*tosatsujô*] because it results in humiliation for unsuccessful candidates and causes a great deal of stress and inconvenience to the party and its officials (Itô, 1982: 76, 80). Therefore the LDP has tended to do whatever it could to avoid the SLAUGHTERHOUSE. Through Dinner Club Politics, the LDP's leaders and candidates for the highest position in the party were able to save themselves a great deal of distress. Most recently, this was the method through which Prime Minister Mori was selected to his position in April 2000.

Politics of Harmony: The "logic" behind Dinner Club Politics is based on the notions that Japanese groups place high priority on harmonious relationships among members, and that Japanese society is both conflict-avoiding and consensus-oriented (Feldman, 1999b: 9–10). It is probably the consensual norm of Japanese society as a whole that often forces politicians, including the backstage manipulators who pull the strings behind the BLACK CURTAIN [*kuromaku*], to engage in extensive discussion in order to generate a consensus prior to formal decision-making. This allows to avoid public confrontations between players with conflicting interests. Former Prime Minister Suzuki Zenkô explicitly stated that harmony [*wa*] is one of the most important goals for Japanese to strive for in any social interaction. In a September 22, 1980 television interview, Suzuki likened himself to an ORCHESTRA CONDUCTOR [*shikisha*] whose role is to achieve harmony among the players of his administration. Prime Minister Suzuki, who spoke of the "POLITICS OF HARMONY" [*wa no seiji*], coordinated the activities of party factions, negotiated with opposition parties, resolved differences of opinion and settled intra-factional squabbling (Shiota, 1980). Because of these activities, Prime Minister Suzuki was called SAINT (or BUDDHA) ZENKO [*hotoke no Zenkô*], (Iwami, 1998: 234–35).

The Waiting Politician: Suzuki was not the only political leader who stressed harmony and collaboration in his administration. Almost all of Japan's prime ministers have shown the same attitude. Satô Eisaku, who served the longest term as prime minister in post-World War II Japan (from 1964 to 1972), was called the WAITING POLITICIAN [*machi no seijika*], (e.g. Iwami, 1998: 26), HUMAN AFFAIRS' SATO [*jinji no satô*], and QUICK-EARS SATO [*haya mimi no satô*], (e.g. Saikawa, 1999: 157) in tribute to his extraordinary talent for collecting information and being sensitive to other people's feelings. He would studiously go over information, analyze it and carefully prepare his move, doing and saying nothing that might affect the outcome or hurt others until a consensus was achieved within his party and the nation. Only then would he act. This often resulted in delays of weeks or even months before action was taken on a specific problem. Commenting on Prime Minister Satô's style, famous writer Ryôtarô Shiba noted that "In the postwar era, there was no prime minister who achieved stability like Satô, and there was nobody who was as unattractive as he was. A man like him perfectly suited to serve as a TRAFFIC COP at the crossroads of (political) authority and order" (cited in Iwami, 1998: 78).

Mummy Government: Like former Prime Minister Satô, other prime ministers also postponed decisions to gain time for trying to first secure a consensus opinion. Some of these decisions involved crucial matters that really needed to be addressed immediately. Yet, in the interest of achieving a broad agreement from multiple participants, Japanese administrations have often delayed their responses even to urgent events like natural disasters or social turmoil. The government of Prime Minister Murayama Tomiichi, for example, was termed JAPAN'S MUMMY GOVERNMENT [*nihon no miira seifu*] in 1995 because of its weak and passive response to the great earthquake in Kobe and the *Aum Shinrikyô* cult's sarin gas attack on Tôkyô subways (*Sandae Mainichi*, May 7/14, 1995: 152). The Murayama administration was also called the STAIRWAY LANDING ADMINISTRATION [*odoriba seiken*] because of its passivity and its lack of clear goals, suggesting that it was an inactive, interim administration filling the gap between two "real" administrations (*Mainichi*, July 2, 1995; Saikawa, 1999: 182).

Paddling Like a Duck: Dinner Club Politics can even extend to the international arena when Japan negotiates with representatives of other countries far from the public eye. This was expressed metaphorically by former Prime Minister Fukuda in the early 1970s when he referred to the process of restoring diplomatic relations with China as A DUCK PADDLING IN WATER [*ahiru no mizu kaki*], (*Asahi*, July 6, 1995). He was suggesting that the Japanese government's invisible, below-the-surface efforts were propelling rapprochement with China.

(3) Changes in Dinner Club Politics

From the 1960s through the early 1990s, political Dinner Club meetings were traditionally held at night, at high-priced restaurants around *Nagatachô*. Under the "1955 political system," in which the LDP and SDP dominated the Diet, such meetings were held whenever something needed to be resolved quietly. Usually this was when the ruling party and the opposition parties were at loggerheads and unable to compromise in pubic. In order to reach some kind of agreement, representatives of both parties would meet in private for a frank discussion. This method often resulted in fast and relatively smooth decisions, but Dinner Club Politics was not totally (not publicly, that is) accepted by the news media, political commentators, or the general public. Political analysts and reporters frequently criticized decision-makers, first for meeting at luxury restaurants and secondly for making agreements that were not always supported by the electorate or which were incomprehensible to the public.

Political editorial writers habitually complained that politicians should be more modest in their behavior and that the public was entitled to more details about the political process. Politicians and inside-track political journalists knew all the latest details about contacts that political groups were making behind closed doors, and about the important agreements they concluded, but the public was often left with no information. Moreover, Dinner Club Politics also served as the arena in which political plots were often hatched. To avoid leaks, only politicians known for their discretion were asked to join. They were invited to meetings without advance explanation and instructed to arrive by taxi so as not to leave a flock of black limousines outside, which would attract the attention of news reporters looking for a scoop. The "logic of *Nagatachô*," i.e. what was acceptable to politicians, was not acceptable to the public. What was "common sense" to Diet members (and the close circle of WATCHDOG REPORTERS) was not supported by the public, who want to know in detail how and why a certain political decision was made.

In 1993, the non-LDP administration of former Prime Minister Hosokawa Morihiro honored this public sentiment by announcing that it would negotiate with opposition parties only at official meetings, such as Diet committee meetings. Hosokawa himself declared that he would no longer engage in Dinner Club Politics (*Asahi*, November 3, 1993). Following this declaration, politicians did indeed stop meeting members of opposition parties in restaurants and instead met them in the Diet building. However, Dinner Club Politics has resumed its important role in the political process as the LDP has gradually re-established itself as the ruling party since the mid-1990s, when it forged a series of coalition governments. The formation of coalition governments made inter-party consensus building more important than ever, and has led to even more CLOSED-DOORS negotiations on legislative and policy issues and to expansion of the Japanese decision-making elite to include coalition members as well as opposition leaders and, indirectly, their major support groups.

Conclusion

As mentioned earlier, the "dual structure" of adversary relationships between political leaders and groups on one hand, and the desire to establish harmony and cooperation between those same leaders and groups on the other, is a major feature that affects the nature and importance of roles played by politicians, government officials, and other individuals including journalists—in each "particular domain" and in the Japanese political system in general.

In **Chapter 6** I identify—in terms of metaphors—three groups of "actors" who "play" on or off the Japanese POLITICAL STAGE. The location of each "player" at the front of the stage (site of adversary VILLAGE POLITICS), at the back of the STAGE ready to assist those at the front, or behind the stage (DINNER CLUB POLITICS), reflects the role that specific player plays in the political system.

Metaphorically Speaking II: Political Roles on the Front and Back of the Stage

6

Figuratively, public affairs in Japan always consists of "people who are carried in the palanquin, those who carry the latter, and those who make the braided straw sandals for the palanquin bearers" [*"kago ni noru hito, katsugu hito, sono mata waraji wo tsukuru hito"*], (Iwami, 1995a).

The Japanese Political Stage: The Visible and Invisible Spheres

This chapter specifies three groups or types of "actors" who "play" in the visible and invisible spheres on politics—on or off the Japanese POLITICAL STAGE [*seiji butai*]. The first group performs on stage, in full view of the public. This group includes Diet members who stand at the helm, pledge to bring about political or social reforms, or advocate particular policy issues, along with the prime minister, Cabinet ministers and their aides. These are the people "who are carried in the palanquin."

The second group stays at the back, OFF-STAGE [*butai ura de*], MANEU-VERING BEHIND THE (political) SCENES [*butai ura no torihiki*]. These are the KINGMAKERS [*kingumeekâ*], SHADOW SHOGUNS [*yami shôgun*] and SCENARIO WRITERS [*senario raitâ*]—fixers who influence political activities and the selection of political leaders. These individuals are "those who carry the members in the palanquin."

The last group of actors are those who are on stage only some of the time but are usually unseen by the public. Their role is to provide crucial support to the players who are always out front, helping them to perform adequately and to fulfill their assignments. Some members of the third group are not star players in the political game, yet without their partici-pation the "show" could never go on smoothly. Metaphorically speaking, these individuals are STAGE ASSISTANTS or STAGEHANDS. They are some-times called *kuroko* or *kokui*, referring to puppeteers clothed in black from head to toe in order to remain unobtrusive as they manipulate dolls on stage

130

in *Bunraku*, Japan's traditional puppet theater. They may also be called *kôken-nin*, stage assistants who work in the *Nô* and *Kabuki* styles of traditional drama. Also dressed in black, they help performers change costumes, handle props, and open and close the curtain. On the POLITICAL STAGE, *kuroko* are important first as mediators between members of different groups and between members of the same group. They adjust and coordinate the activities of various groups. In the broad sense, members of this group are "those who make the braided straw sandals for the palanquin bearers."

Each group of players is related to and dependent on the other groups. THE FACES OF THE ADMINISTRATION [*seiken no kao*], (*Aera*, August 10, 1993), in other words, top leaders of the government, political parties, and party factions—including ministers, the three top officials of the LDP, and the prime minister—are selected and supported by off-stage players and in turn, serve the interests of those players. In their daily work they are assisted by *kuroko*, who also receive benefits. The location of each "player" at the front of the stage, at the back ready to assist those up front, or behind the stage, reflects that player's role in the political system. These different "spheres" of activity create a dichotomy between power and authority so that authority and power are not always synonymous (i.e., those with authority do not always have real power or the will to exercise it), and power is not a constant factor (Feldman & Watts, 2000).

(1) The Political Stage: The Front Players

On the visible side of politics, in full view of the public, are those who perform on the POLITICAL STAGE. Among them are those who stand at the helm, or STEERSMEN [*kaji tori*], including the prime minister (who is STEERSMAN of the administration or of the coalition of parties that forms it, e.g. *Aera*, January 25, 1999); the finance minister (STEERSMAN of the economy, e.g. *Aera*, August 10, 1998); and leaders of the ruling parties (STEERSMEN of the country, e.g. *Asahi*, August 2, 1993). The SEA CAPTAIN [*senchô*], (e.g. *Aera*, January 3, 1994) is another metaphor frequently used to refer to the prime minister, often when depicting him in political cartoons (Feldman, 2000).[1]

Together on the stage with these front players are FLAG WAVERS, or CHEER LEADERS [*hata furi-yaku*], including ministers who pledge to do things like create a nursing insurance system (e.g. *Asahi*, September 23, 1996) or to bring about administrative reforms (e.g. *Asahi*, September 20, 1997). Those who perform on stage and are visible to the public are said to play SIGNBOARD ROLES [*kanban-yaku*] for the administration, their political party, or for a particular policy that they advocate. In addition, there are, of course, the "regular" Diet members who do their daily work in *Nagatachô*.

Political Influence and Conspicuousness – *Pipelines and Security Guards:* Perhaps the most important role that Diet members play is that of a PIPELINE [*paipu-yaku*], or a channel that gives voters and supporters access to government bureaucrats and others "in high places" in Tôkyô, so they can benefit from pork-barrel projects (Feldman, 1999a: 33–37). Although in theory they are lawmakers, very few Diet members would qualify as legislators by contemporary international standards. In fact, most Diet members do not see drafting or enacting legislation as their most important work. Instead, Diet members serve as representatives whose activities are primarily intended to benefit their district, or of lobbying groups like agricultural cooperatives, trade unions, or small business associations, which promise support and votes in return for favors. Leading Diet members are often said to act as SECURITY GUARDS or BODYGUARDS [*yôjinbô*], (*Asahi*, June 10, 1997) who guard the interests of special-interest groups by countering the activities of bureaucrats and rival political groups.

The PIPELINE role reflects the nature of Japanese electoral politics, in which both voters and elected officials are notorious for their reliance on pork-barrel distributions. A Diet member's core constituency is made up of supporters who work to get the politician elected and then present him or her with requests. These requests may involve personal needs such as helping to find a job for a supporter's child, helping get a child into the "right" school, or even fixing traffic tickets or averting a tax audit. Other requests address community needs such as improving the quality of the water supply, hospitals, schools or police protection. Such services can usually be rendered most effectively by making government bureaucrats aware of supporters' needs and by allocating public funds, which the Diet members try to influence. To deal effectively with demands from their constituencies, Diet members must have access to people who can get things done. This includes access to all levels of bureaucrats and civil servants involved in fields like construction, transportation, and telecommunications. It includes access to fellow politicians who may be able to help by collaborating on a project or by broadening a Diet member's contacts, and to members of labor unions or other special-interest groups who may be able to provide access to pertinent information or other types of support. The degree to which a Diet member serves as a PIPELINE—i.e. has access to power and the ability to influence spending decisions at the national level—is a measure of political influence that affects his or her image and chances of re-election. In return for playing the PIPELINE role and providing benefits to the district or to individual supporters, the Diet member gets votes that allow him or her to stay in office.

Ministers' Disease: Once a Diet member is in a position of power, he or she is better able to play the PIPELINE role. Therefore, many Diet members are attracted to the prospect of having a Cabinet post and the influence and prestige attendant to such a position. Diet members who are obsessed with such aspirations are said to be afflicted with MINISTERS' DISEASE [*daijinbyô*], (e.g. *Asahi*, February 23, 1994). "Afflicted" Diet members do anything they can to become a member of the Cabinet. In the LDP, Cabinet positions are distributed to reward loyalty to the party and to recognize a politician's influence. In order to ensure that this form of recognition is properly distributed, it is necessary to rotate Cabinet posts frequently. That is why the average term of office for Cabinet members since the 1960s has been less than a year. This excessively frequent rotation of Cabinet posts has prevented most ministers from accumulating the experience they would need to gain real control of their ministry or agency.

First-Grade Diet Members: As in most Japanese institutions, promotions in Japanese politics are based more on seniority than on ability. Thus, newly elected Diet members are treated as though they were the political equivalent of FIRST GRADERS [*ichinen-sei giin*], (e.g. *Asahi*, July 25, 2000). Each time they are re-elected, they move up one grade and get steadily closer to the choice assignments and key political power points. The more experience politicians have as Diet members, the more likely they are to get the choice assignments and influential situations where they can really participate in policy-making. During the 38 years of LDP rule until 1993, and in the years since the party regained its power in 1995, with a few exceptions, LDP Diet members who were re-elected more than three or four times could expect to be named vice-minister or vice-chair of a party or Diet committee. Those who were returned to the Diet five to seven times were likely to be given the chairmanship of a Diet committee, a Cabinet-level position, or the third highest position in the party of vice-secretary general. Very few politicians have been able to sit in the Cabinet before their fifth term in the Diet, representing at least ten years of apprenticeship. Thus the fifth term was usually the crucial point in a Diet member's career. Things have changed however, as explained in the Introduction, after Prime Minister Koizumi assumed office.

Appendix: Until the late 1990s each administration traditionally had around 24 parliamentary vice-ministers [*seimu jikan*], or political appointees who are not members of the Cabinet. They were termed APPENDICES [*môchô*], (Saikawa, 1999: 28) because their role in the administration is as minor as that of the appendix in the human body. The parliamentary vice-ministers' position was largely symbolic, and entailed little real power. They were expected to give inaugural addresses before the Diet but were rarely invited to attend important meetings of their ministry or agency, and remained uninvolved in Diet affairs. As of 1999, as part of plan to transform the administrative structure into one Cabinet office and 12 ministries and agencies in January 2001, vice-ministers were given a more active role in Diet deliberations, particularly during question-answer sessions. In late October, 1999, the Liberal Party's Diet Affairs Committee Chairman Nakanishi Keisuke reportedly told several vice-ministers: "Now your role is almost like that of a LARGE INTESTINE [*daichô*], rather than an APPENDIX" (*Daily Yomiuri*, December 7, 1999).

Eyeball Role: Some vice-ministers and ministers become an EYEBALL (meaning CENTERPIECE, or EYE-CATCHING), [*medama*, meaning "eyeballs"] of an administration, especially a newly formed administration. This may be because their appointments make watchers open their eyes wider in surprise or simply it means that they are eye-catching. This is because they apply themselves to a challenging mission like WAVING THE FLAG of administrative reform (e.g. *Asahi*, September 20, 1997). Or it could be because of their background, perhaps as the offspring of a famous politician or as someone with long experience in public affairs. For example, former Prime Minister Miyazawa, who was invited to join Obuchi's Cabinet in 1998 as finance minister in light of his experience with financial and economic policy and strategies related to revitalization. Or someone might be called an EYEBALL because they were being appointed to the Cabinet at an unusually young age, with an unusually small amount of political experience, or because they are female (Noda Seiko, for example, was a woman who became minister of posts and telecommunications while still in her thirties, after being elected to the Diet only twice). Others who are considered EYEBALLS are private citizens who are invited into a Cabinet due to their expertise in a given policy area; for example, Taichi Sakaiya, who was Director General of the Economic Planning Agency in the administrations of Obuchi and Mori.

The EYEBALL metaphor is applied not only to people, but also to issues that are high on the political agenda and attract a great deal of public attention. Good examples would be the establishment of the nationwide consumption tax, and reduction of pension payments.

Heckling Shogun: Another front-lines conspicuous "actor" is the HECKLING SHOGUN [*yaji shôgun*], a type of Diet member often described as an EYEBALL because of his or her behavior (e.g. *Asahi*, October 5, 1989). HECKLING SHOGUN refers to a Diet member who makes loud interjections or shouts at opponents from his or her seat while someone else is making an official speech in public, either in the Diet, at party meetings, or in front of news reporters. The heckler shouts provocative and sometimes embarrassing things like, "Shut up" [*"damare!"*], "What a nuisance!" [*"urusai!"*], or "Liar!" [*"usotsuki"*], which can eventually interfere with the speech. Former Prime Minister Yoshida Shigeru once commented that "a speech isn't a real speech without heckling" [*"yaji ga nai to enzetsu ni naranai"*]. (But, as noted above, it was heckling that brought down Yoshida's administration. In March 1953, in response to an opposition question during a meeting of the Budget Committee Yoshida shouted, "You damn fool!" ["*bakayarô!*"]. The plenary session of the Diet passed a no-confidence resolution against the prime minister who chose to dissolve the lower house rather than resign.)

Signboard Role   Some players on the political stage take on a SIGNBOARD ROLE [*kanban-yaku*]. They become a symbol of a certain political group or the government as a whole, or they may represent a specific policy issue. A prime minister can be a SIGNBOARD representing the government (e.g. Prime Minister Kaifu, *Asahi*, August 20, 1990). LDP faction leaders—the COLLAR AND SLEEVES of a shirt—also play a SIGNBOARD ROLE. Kan Naoto, of the opposition DPJ (e.g. *Asahi*, December 22, 1999), served as a SIGN-BOARD representing the opposition as a whole.

Shadow or Next Cabinet: SIGNBOARD ROLES are played by members of opposition parties in particular as part of their bid to attract public attention to symbolic activities such as establishing a SHADOW CABINET [*kage no naikaku*], known also as a NEXT CABINET [*nexto kabineto*] or TOMORROW'S CABINET [*asu no naikaku*]. All of these terms refer to a British-style shadow cabinet, but in Japan these activities are less established and less clearly defined. In late 1999, for example, the DPJ established the NEXT CABINET to reflect the party's intention of expanding its presence in the Diet and to demonstrate the party's readiness to seize the reins of power from the ruling tripartite coalition, consisting of the LDP, the Liberal Party, and the New *Kômei* Party. Party leader Hatoyama Yukio was "prime minister" of the NEXT CABINET. He entrusted each of his SHADOW CABINET ministers with two tasks: offer the nation an alternative to the LDP's vision of the future, and draw up policies swiftly (e.g. *Asahi*, October 8, 1999). The DPJ's SHADOW CABINET also had a "chief cabinet secretary" and 13 other "ministers" with responsibility for areas such as foreign affairs, security, and fiscal policy. This CABINET lacked manpower, with only about 10 policy research officials and a few secretaries, and its funding for policy research was far from adequate.

Finishing the Game: In addition to ministers and opposition leaders, the Speaker of the lower house is another figure in a SIGNBOARD role, as a symbol of the Diet and authority. The Speaker is responsible for maintaining order in the chamber and for ordering the business of the day, and has broad powers including the right to limit debate and assign committees. He or she often works to settle political disputes and helps rival political groups negotiate in order to keep the Diet functioning smoothly. This is called the REFEREE role. The Speaker is often said to have FINISHED THE GAME [*seijika no agari*], (Iwami, 1998: 150), in the sense that there is no other position beyond this on the political promotion ladder. In the mid-1990s, the position of lower house Speaker was offered to Obuchi Keizô while he was vice president of the LDP. Knowing he could not get a higher position if he accepted this role, Obuchi rejected the offer and went on to become prime minister a few years later, in 1998 (Iwami, 1998: 150).

Sumô Wrestlers: The "Big Three" of the LDP also play a SIGNBOARD ROLE. They are the Secretary General, Chair of the Executive Council, and Chair of the Policy Affairs Research Council, the highest posts in the LDP after the President.[2] They are called *san'yaku,* a term also used to refer to sumo wrestlers in the three highest ranks below Grand Champion [*yokozuna*]: *ôzeki* (second rank), *sekiwake* (third), and *komusubi* (fourth). According to this analogy, the prime minister would be a Grand Champion. At least one prime minister—Tanaka Kakuei—was in fact known as Grand Champion (Iwami, 1998: 68). The LDP's *san'yaku* are engaged most actively in controlling personnel affairs, policies, and finances for Japan's strongest political party.

Magistrate and Bridge: The LDP's Secretary General, second only to the party president in responsibilities and importance, is often called *daikan*, referring to the chief magistrate who executed orders for a feudal lord in the Edo period (1603–1868). He administered the domains that were directly controlled by the shogun, or military ruler of Japan. He was also in charge of collecting land taxes and supervising local police. The Secretary General also serves in a BRIDGE ROLE [*hashi watashi-yaku*], (e.g. *Asahi*, December 26, 1999), mediating within the party and especially coordinating the activities of the different factions. He also coordinates the activities of the LDP with those of other political groups, including coalition partners and opposition parties.

Portable Shrines Most conspicuous at the front of the POLITICAL STAGE is the prime minister. In the news media's rhetoric, a large number of metaphors like SEA CAPTAIN and STEERSMAN associate the national political leader with strength, decisiveness, command, and determination. Yet, by international standards, the Japanese prime minister is remarkably weak and passive or reactive. Japanese prime ministers do not usually have clear policy goals or agendas to advocate. They only apply their energy to issues that happen to be salient at a given time. They rarely take initiative to instigate change in the way Japan operates, and are not directly involved in determining the content of change. Nor are they directly involved in setting a political agenda or determining the details of policy changes and legislation. Unlike their counterparts in Western societies, Japanese prime ministers have been relatively weak when it comes to taking responsibility for defense and foreign policy issues. Instead, they try to coordinate broad policy programs or resolve conflicts at crucial times (Feldman, 1999a: 13–16).

Far from being strong and assertive, these "leaders" emphasize collective movement and attach much importance to group dynamics and consensus decisions. Political leaders in the West are expected to demonstrate their own personal style, determination and dominance as they achieve political objectives; leadership is thus usually linked to an individual's proven abilities, successful performance, and other personal attributes. But in Japan, the prime minister (and other leaders) function more like managers. They are expected to monitor relations among all members of their group, to be sensitive to the feelings of subordinates, to defer to their followers' preferences and wishes, to cool emotional conflicts, and to elicit widespread support for achieving common goals. The mark of a good leader in Japan is the ability to build consensus rather than to make decisions or wield authority (Feldman & Kawakami, 1989). This difference is conspicuous even to foreign observers like Henry Kissinger, who noted that "a Japanese prime minister is a custodian of the national consensus, not the creator of it" (Kissinger, 1985).

Disposable Prime Ministers: Only two men held the position of prime minister from 1960 to 1972. Ikeda Hayato was elected LDP president—and thus prime minister—three times between 1960 and 1964, and Satô Eisaku was elected four times between 1964 and 1972. But the Japanese prime minister's term of office began to shrink after that, when voting behavior became erratic due to an increasing array of problems requiring political attention and an increase in vocal criticism of politicians and the political system. From 1972 (when Tanaka Kakuei became prime minister) until November 1982 (start of the Nakasone Yasuhiro administration), each prime minister served only one term (a full term was three years in 1970–76, and was reduced to two years after that). During this period, there were five prime ministers who served an average of about two years each: Tanaka Kakuei (1972–74), Miki Takeo (1974–76), Fukuda Takeo (1976–78), Ôhira Masayoshi (1978–80), and Suzuki Zenkô (1980–82). Nakasone Yasuhiro then served as prime minister for five years (1982–87), but after his exceptionally long term of office, the average term of office shrunk to under two years: Takeshita Noboru served a year and seven months (from November 1987 to June 1989), Uno Sôsuke only 69 days (from June 1989 to August 1989), Kaifu Toshiki served 818 days (August 1989–November 1991), Miyazawa Kiichi 644 days (November 1991–August 1993), Hosokawa Morihiro 263 days (August 1993–April 1994), Hata Tsutomu 64 days (April 1994–June 1994), Murayama Tomiichi 557 days (June 1994–January 1996). Prime minister Hashimoto Ryûtarô lasted a relatively long 932 days (January 1996 through July 1998), Prime Minister Obuchi Keizô served less than two years (July

1998–April 2000), and Prime Minister Mori Yoshirô served a year (April 2000–April 2001). Prime ministers changed so frequently that former Prime Minister Takeshita called them "DISPOSABLE" [*tsukai-sute*], adding that "singers keep their popularity for one year, and prime ministers are disposable after two" ["*kashu ichinen, sôri ninen no tsukaisute*"], (Saikawa, 1999: 13).

Karaoke Politics: Because of the way prime ministers and Cabinet ministers are chosen, Japanese politics is often called KARAOKE POLITICS [*karaoke seiji*]. This applies to how leaders are chosen in Japanese society in general, as well. On a *karaoke* stage, singers come and go one after another, while their songs and rhythms remain the same, selected from a limited, rarely changed menu. By the same token, in KARAOKE DEMOCRACY [*karaoke minshushugi*], prime ministers (along with other political "leaders" who lack their own clear policy goals or agenda) come and go one after another, while the selection of issues and policies remains unchanged (Inoguchi, 1995).

Closing the Curtain: A Japanese prime minister is often portrayed as the symbol or representative of an era, and with his resignation or death, he is said to CLOSE THE CURTAIN [*maku hiki*] on that era. Prime Minister Miyazawa, for example, closed the curtain on the long era, lasting close to 40 years, in which the conservative camp dominated politics and government in Japan (*Asahi*, July 4, 1993). He was the last in a line of LDP prime ministers that was unbroken for 38 years until he PASSED THE BATON [*sekinin tenka*] to Prime Minister Hosokawa, founder of the short-lived Japan New Party. The death of Prime Minister Kishi (in August 1987, two years before the end of the Shôwa Era), symbolized the CLOSING OF THE CURTAIN on a momentous Shôwa period of Japan's history.

Portable Shrine: Because of their function, the Japanese prime minister is sometimes seen as a PORTABLE SHRINE [*mikoshi*], a decorative object carried along by a large group which pretends that it has power, like the miniature shrines carried on long poles across the shoulders of many bearers during traditional Japanese festivals. In other words, the prime minister serves as a mere symbol whereas the people who hold him up share the real power. That means, the supposed center of power (the POLITICAL STAGE) serves only to legitimate, while those behind it actually control who will act on the stage, how decisions will be made, and what course public affairs will take—for better or for worse. In the words of one Diet member, "No matter how splendid a PORTABLE SHRINE may be, if those who carry it are bad, they will pull it in the wrong direction. By the same token, even if the PORTABLE SHRINE is not so splendid, it will be all right as long as it is carried by excellent people. That's how politics works" (Tanaka 1995: 53).

The Missing Leader   *Black Curtain:* This "dual structure" characterizes postwar Japanese politics, with a figurehead prime minister who is "lugged around" by other politicians. So the prime minister represents authority and bears the greatest political responsibility. He is the symbol of the country as he visits various places around the nation, attends international gatherings and meets with world leaders. Sometimes he flits about so busily, he is called a DRAGONFLY TURNING BACKWARD SOMERSAULTS [*tombo-gaeri*], dashing from one place to another and immediately returning back home. For example, the prime minister might attend a summit meeting in the US, then go straight to London for the Japan Week opening ceremony, and immediately afterwards visit his hometown, then stop in another prefecture to check on a specific industry before returning to his residence in Tôkyô. In February 1999, Prime Minister Obuchi flew to and stayed for only seven hours in Jordan to attend the funeral of King Hussein before TURNING BACKWARD to Japan (e.g. *Asahi*, February 10, 1999). Likewise, in March 2001, Prime Minister Mori attended the reception for members the International Olympic Committee in Ôsaka, Japan, and after finishing his brief greetings returned immediately back to *Nagatachô*, Tôkyô (*Asahi*, March 1, 2001).

At the same time, however, backstage manipulators pull the strings behind the BLACK CURTAIN [*kuromaku*] and actually control the political scene. The prime minister himself is powerless, and rarely demonstrates determination or ability to lead the nation. The degree of power exercised by prime ministers over the years has ranged from weak to only moderately effective. Only a handful of postwar prime ministers have shown any signs of what Westerners would call leadership of the magnitude displayed by distinctive personalities like Winston Churchill or John F. Kennedy, who knew how to guide public opinion and could tell which policies would receive public support.

One-Man Prime Minister: In the years after World War II, former Prime Minister Yoshida Shigeru, who held office in 1946 and 1947 and again from 1948 to 1954, demonstrated a comparatively Western style of leadership. He led Japan forcefully as it made its transition from occupied-nation status toward independent nation in the late 1940s and early 1950s, and earned the nickname ONE-MAN [*wan-man*] Prime Minister. The same characteristic of forceful leadership that made Yoshida so successful also made him widely detested among his peers in postwar Japanese politics (Kioi, 1967).

Computerized Bulldozer: Tanaka Kakuei was another exception to the norm of the powerless prime minister. When he became prime minister in 1972 (through 1974) he was given various affectionate nicknames including *saishô* (PRIME MINISTER OF COMMON ORIGINS) and *ima-taikô* ("modern *taikô:*" *taikô* was a popular name for Toyotomi Hideyoshi, the warlord of humble origins who completed the unification of Japan in 1590). Tanaka was also called the COMPUTERIZED BULLDOZER [*konpyûteraizudo burudohzâ*] of Japanese politics. He was a quick-thinking political genius of sorts who described his own style as "the politics of deciding and doing" ["*ketsudan to jikkô*"]. He normalized relations with China and tried to "remodel the Japanese archipelago" in the early 1970s. Tanaka possessed tremendous stamina and administrative ability, and was able to manipulate bureaucrats to accommodate his own needs (Masumi, 1988: 21, 157).

Unsinkable Aircraft Carrier: Another decisive Japanese leader was former Prime Minister Nakasone Yasuhiro, who served from 1982 to 1987. Nakasone seemed to be more like a Western leader, crisp and resolute, taking a major and active part in Japanese policy-making. His political style was a product of his emphatic and hawkish views, his notion that Japan and the Japanese people are somehow unique, and his belief that Japan must play a greater role in world affairs. Nakasone favored cutting income taxes, trimming government bureaucracy and paring the nation's swelling budget deficit. He also advocated the privatization of many government-run companies, administrative reform, and opening markets in order to reduce economic conflict with the USA. Nakasone made all his Cabinet ministers promise to find a way to carry out reforms, and clearly stated that he would dismiss bureaucrats who tried to block government policies—a promise that he kept. Nakasone also called for stronger defense forces and stronger security and economic ties with the USA and the rest of the West. In January 1983, after discussing defense issues with US President Ronald Reagan, Nakasone called Japan an "UNSINKABLE AIRCRAFT CARRIER" ["*fuchin kûbo*"] that could prevent penetration of Soviet Backfire bombers into Japanese airspace.

More Nicknames for Prime Ministers and Their Cabinets *Ball-of Flames Cabinet:* In an attempt to display strong determination and commitment to administrative reform when he formed his second cabinet in November 1996, former Prime Minister Hashimoto said, "I will accomplish this even if I GO DOWN IN FLAMES" (meaning "even if it destroys me") ["*hidaruma ni natte mo yaru;*" *hidaruma* means literally "a ball of flames") (*Asahi*, November 8, 1996). The mass media then dubbed Hashimoto's new cabinet the "BALL-OF-FLAMES CABINET" ["*hidaruma seiken*"]. Unfortunately, Hashimoto resigned from office without achieving the reforms he had promised.

Many Japanese prime ministers have been assigned metaphorical nicknames that reflected their personal characteristics and behavior patterns—including their lack of decisiveness in leading the nation.

POLITICAL ROLES ON THE FRONT AND BACK OF THE STAGE

Prime Minister Yoshida was nicknamed "one-man" for his autocratic ways. Prime Minister Satô was called, in addition to the WAITING POLITICIAN as mentioned above, HUMAN AFFAIRS' SATO, and QUICK-EARS SATO due to his talent for collecting information and picking up other people's feelings. As noted above, Prime Minister Suzuki was also called SAINT (or BUDDHA) ZENKO because of his emphasis on avoiding conflict and keeping harmony and peace in his administration. Prime Minister Ôhira was called A DULL BULL [dongyû], (Asahi, October 22, 1984). Prime Minister Fukuda was called the KOMON OF THE Shôwa ERA [shôwa no kômon-sama], (Asahi, July 4, 1997) referring to Tokugawa Mitsukuni, a seventeenth-century lord popularly known as Mito Kômon, who was famous for his effective and benevolent rule. Mitsukuni's popular image was that of a wise, ideal feudal ruler who, even after retirement, traveled over the country teaching and guiding the people, just as many people viewed Prime Minister Fukuda in the Shôwa era.

Due to his ability to adjust and mediate opinions and activities within the ruling LDP and among bureaucrats and politicians, Prime Minister Takeshita was playing the ROLE OF MEDIATOR [chôsei-yaku] and was viewed as COORDINATION DEVICE [chôsei sôchi], (Mainichi, May 11, 1999). Prime Minister Uno was called AN INSTANT WATER BOILER because he was prone to angry outbursts when he didn't like a reporter's question. Former Prime Minister Hosokawa was called the FEUDAL LORD PRIME MINISTER [tonosama shushô] because his ancestors were feudal lords. When Hosokawa first established his administration in 1993, it was called CASTLE OF GLASS [garasu no shiro], to indicate its fragility (Takemura, 1994: 26).

Shôwa Ghost and Giant: Former Prime Minister Kishi was called the SHÔWA GHOST [shôwa no yôkai], (Aera, January 23, 1995) because he "came back to (political) life" after "dying" (serving a prison term for his role in World War II) during the Shôwa Era, and because he later survived several scandals without being convicted. He re-entered the political scene and assumed leadership positions as of the 1950s, whereas most of his colleagues were either executed for war crimes or died of old age. Kishi was also dubbed the SHÔWA GIANT [shôwa no kyôkai], (Asahi, August 8, 1987), indicating that he remained in politics throughout the Shôwa Era: before, during and after the World War II.

Balkan Politician: Due to his strategic maneuvering and his tendency to change his policies and actions to fit shifting circumstances, Prime Minister Miki was called a BALKAN POLITICIAN [barukan seijika], (Masumi, 1988: 264).[3] In 1976, there was a movement within the LDP to remove Miki from his position—DUMP MIKI [miki oroshi]—because of how he handled the Lockheed scandal and the issue of party modernization (Masumi, 1988: 288ff). In February 1976, Shiina Etsuzaburô, then Vice

President of the LDP, commented to reporters: "Miki is a SMALL-TIME SHOPKEEPER. I cannot have him in charge of a BIG SHOP like the LDP" (Masumi, 1988: 286).

Weathervane: Prime Minister Nakasone was called a WEATHERVANE [*kazamidori*], (*Aera*, December 30, 1996) because of his political opportunism and "flexibility," especially during the 1960s. Nakasone was regarded as having no firm opinions or principles of his own, but was seen as shifting with the political winds. Nakasone defended his "flexibility" as being an appropriate quality for Japan to express in the international community. He claimed that the weathercock, with its fixed legs and very flexible body that allows it to sense the direction of the wind, was a good model for how Japan should express its good sense and good judgment (e.g. *Asahi*, October 1, 1997). Like Prime Minister Kishi, who was called the SHOWA GHOST, Nakasone was called HEISEI GHOST [*heisei no yôkai*], (Saikawa, 1999: 275), because he remained active in politics after the Heisei Era began (in 1989), despite his old age and long years of involvement (He retired from politics in 2003).

Mediocre Man and *Cold Pizza:* When Obuchi Keizô, Koizumi Junichirô, and former LDP Secretary General Kajiyama Seiroku ran for the LDP presidency in July 1998, Tanaka Makiko nicknamed the three "MEDICORE MAN" (*bonjin*), "ECCENTRIC MAN" (*henjin*), and "ARMY MAN" (*gunjin*) respectively. And these nicknames have been widely used since then. Right after Prime Minister Obuchi was elected LDP president, the *New York Times* described him as "colorless and malleable" and quoted a financial analyst who said he had "all the pizzazz of COLD PIZZA." This expression was used to contrast Obuchi with his predecessor, Hashimoto, who was regarded as more dynamic. Soon the local media picked up the phrase and dubbed Obuchi the "COLD PIZZA [*sameta pittsa*] Prime Minister." Later, the media referred to him as an ORDINARY PERSON [*bonjin*] to indicate that Obuchi did not have any special characteristics to distinguish him from other Japanese (e.g. Kobayashi, 1998). Obuchi has often been called also A DULL BULL (*dongyû*, like Prime Minister Ôhira), (*Asahi*, September 4, 1998), and, because of his poor use of language, "poor vocabulary" (*bokyahin*) (*Asahi*, May 15, 2000), and the VACUUM PRIME MINISTER [*shinkû shushô*], (e.g. *Asahi*, December 26, 1998) because he was seen as devoid of his own opinions and ideas and had nothing substantial in himself so he could absorb anything. Prime Minister Nakasone called Obuchi VACUUM PRIME MINISTER saying Obuchi "May not have a charisma yet can accept every possible policy" (*Asahi*, July 7, 1999). Obuchi's administration was called BLACK HOLE ADMINISTRATION [*burakku hôru seiken*] because it "swallowed" every issue it dealt with (Saikawa, 1999: 360).

Japan's Boss: Obuchi's successor, Mori Yoshirô, also failed to demonstrate much determination to make changes. His attitude was summarized by Kamei Shizuka, then LDP Policy Research Council Chairman, in a June, 2000 television interview: "Mori is Japan's BOSS. Japan does not need a leader like Napoleon. A Japanese prime minister is like the chairman of a meeting. He himself has no authority. It is enough if he makes the bureaucrats work properly" (cited in *Asahi*, June 4, 2000).

So the traits that most Japanese prime ministers have in common are a lack of vision, a lack of strongly held or expressed original ideas and personal opinions, and the job of acting at the front of the POLITICAL STAGE while being manipulated by others who act elsewhere.[4]

(2) Off the Political Stage

The individuals who actually held power over the years have been called by different names, the most common of which is KINGMAKER [*kingumeekâ*]. A KINGMAKER refers to a strong person who is not always publicly active on the political scene, but carries enough clout behind the scenes to influence the decisions of a prime minister. This includes heavy influence over the choice of candidates for pivotal posts in the political world, including ministers and the three leading officials of the LDP (*Asahi*, August 7, 1987).

Shadow Shôgun and Kingmakers: Tanaka Kakuei played the role of KING-MAKER after he stepped down as prime minister. Tanaka acted like an AUTOCRATIC COMPANY PRESIDENT [*wan-man shachô*], (Itô, 1982: 69) or SHADOW SHOGUN [*yami shôgun*, literally, "underground" or "dark" shogun], (*Asahi*, March 12, 1990; Masumi, 1988: 279ff). He was the power broker whose SHADOW ["*kaku-ei*," a play with the Chinese characters of his first name], (*Asahi*, November 1, 1984) affected the course of Japanese politics and leadership selection. Tanaka himself said in 1976 that since there seemed to be no one else around who was qualified to play the role of SHADOW SHOGUN, he was "the only choice, and I am going to be SHADOW SHOGUN for the time being" (Itô, 1982: 189). For about 15 years, Tanaka made most of Japan's important political decisions. For many of those years, he operated BEHIND CLOSED DOORS, even long after he had been indicted in the Lockheed bribery scandal and ousted from office and from the LDP. Endowed with the authority to hand-pick a prime minister, he wielded the decisive say in the formation of three subsequent Cabinets formed by supporters of his—Ôhira, Suzuki and Nakasone. Tanaka was so firmly established at the center of Japanese politics that it was possible to explain any political phenomenon as being Tanaka's influential power or wish [*yuikaku shikan*], (*Asahi Shimbun Seijibu*, 1992: 1; Saikawa, 1999: 29) His reign ended only when he was physically incapacitated.

Former LDP Vice President Kanemaru ("Don") Shin took over Tanaka's role in the late 1980s, and acted as KINGMAKER or GODFATHER [*goddofazzâ*], instructing the cabinets of Uno, Kaifu, and Miyazawa. Kanemaru was instrumental to the functioning of these cabinets, with help from former Prime Minster Takeshita and later from former LDP Secretary General Ozawa Ichirô. Ozawa was known as a MAN OF TROUBLED TIMES [*ranse no otoko*], (Saikawa, 1999: 31), because he tended to play conspicuous role in times of crisis, or AX MAN [*nata no otoko*], (*Aera*, March 6, 1990), because of his tendency to quickly dispense with an issue in one swipe rather than working it out slowly and cautiously.

Rotating the Stage: Kanemaru, Takeshita, and Ozawa maneuvered behind the political scenes in endless BACK-ROOM DEALINGS [*butai ura no torihiki*]. They played a significant role in the selection of prime ministers, Cabinet ministers, and others assigned to a variety of leading positions in the government and the ruling party (Schlesinger, 1999: 157ff). They used their power and influence to ROTATE THE (political) STAGE [*butai mawashi-yaku*], (*Asahi*, August 7, 1991; Saikawa, 1999: 34), deciding who would stand at the helm of the country at a given time. Sometimes they looked for a person to play what they called a RELIEF ROLE [*ririfu-yaku*], (from relief pitching in baseball), meaning someone to serve as prime minister for a short time until another, more capable person could be found. This was the case after Prime Minister Takeshita resigned following the Recruit scandal, when Kanemaru proposed that former Prime Minister Fukuda step in temporarily as prime minister, and this was also what happened after Prime Minister Kaifu resigned (*Asahi Shimbun Seijibu*, 1992: 56, 97).

Planner Role: The same three Diet members also played the role of PLANNERS [*shikake-nin*], (e.g. *Aera*, December 7, 1998), "helping" the new administration and its leaders coordinate activities. They displayed superb skills in BACK-ROOM negotiations with opposition leaders over key political issues, and successfully manipulated party affairs. One way they did this was by installing relatively unqualified and inefficient party leaders, assuring that those leaders would be fully dependent on the KINGMAKERS. For example, Watanuki Tamisuke was not in the leading cadre of the LDP or even of the faction he belonged to when he was tapped by Kanemaru's crew to be the party's Secretary General. Because of his lack of experience and skill, he had to consult frequently with Kanemaru or Ozawa on matters related to his daily work. People made fun of Watanuki's habit of frequently visiting Kanemaru or Ozawa, calling it GOING TO WORSHIP AT Kanemaru's—or Ozawa's—SHRINE [*Kanemaru môde* or *Ozawa môde*], or GOING TO ARMY HEADQUARTERS [*daihonei iki*], (*Asahi Shimbun Seijibu*, 1992: 156).

Scenario Writers: Kanemaru, Takeshita and Ozawa were also called SCENARIO WRITERS [*shinariyo raitâ*], (e.g. Saikawa, 1999: 84), since they determined the role each Diet member would play on the POLITICAL STAGE. They selected what issues would be put on the agendas of the LDP and the Diet, including the timing and order in which those issues would be addressed, and played a decisive role in the various administrations they created, affecting decision-making processes within both the ruling party (or coalition of parties) and the entire government. The terms "KANEMARU WHISPER" or "KANEMARU MURMUR" [*kanemaru sasayaki* or *kanemaru tsubukaki*], "KANEMARU SOLILOQUY" [*kanemaru hitorigoto*] and "TAKESHITA CALENDAR" [*takeshita karendâ*] were used to describe the way Kanemaru and Takeshita planned political events, including the timing of Cabinet reshuffles and when to hold the next election, the selection of people to fill specific leadership positions, and determining the next scenario to unfold in *Nagatachô* (e.g. Iwami, 1995b).

Private Tutor: Takeshita's influence was so strong that the administration of Prime Minister Kaifu (and later Prime Minister Miyazawa) was described as the MARIONETTE ADMINISTRATION [*ayatsuri ningyô seiken*], (*Asahi Shimbun Seijibu*, 1992: 15). Kaifu lacked experience with the work-ings of government and had no power base of his own, so he had to rely exclusively on Takeshita's support and guidance to the extent that he was perceived as a SON-IN-LAW of the Takeshita faction [*takeshita ha no muko yôshi*], (*Asahi Shimbun Seijibu*, 1992: 47). Kaifu's aides referred to Takeshita as the prime minister's PRIVATE TUTOR [*katei kyôshi*], (*Asahi Shimbun Seijibu*, 1992: 48). Later, when Ozawa's power increased and the "dual structure" of power became more visible, some Diet members noted that "the administration's face belongs to Kaifu, but the real power belongs to Ozawa" [*"kao wa kaifu jikken wa ozawa"*], (e.g. Koike, 1995: 29).

Tractor Role: Ozawa was instrumental in causing the LDP's fall from power in the 1993 election, by playing the important TRACTOR ROLE [*kenin-yaku*]. Ozawa, then co-leader of the Renewal Party [*Shinseitô*], strongly pushed for a change of administration (*Asahi*, September 9, 1994) by persuading Hosokawa, head of the minor JNP, to seek the prime minister's post. After Hosokawa won, Ozawa dictated important decisions to Hosokawa just before he was to unveil them (Schlesinger, 1999: 273). This close relationship between Ozawa and Hosokawa was regarded by the news media and Diet members as a TIME BOMB [*jigen bakudan*] that could explode at any time and cause a political catastrophe (Hamada, 1994: 91).

This type of "dual structure" continued also during the administrations of Hashimoto and Obuchi, with former Prime Minister Takeshita pulling the strings until his death.

(3) The Political Stage: The Back Players

Stage Assistants or Stagehands: The third group of players on the political stage are the *kuroko* or the *kôken-nin*—the STAGE ASSISTANTS or STAGE-HANDS. Among them are former prime ministers, the Vice Chief Cabinet Secretary (*Asahi*, September 8, 1998), leading members of the LDP, and the cadres of the party factions [*kanbu*], the most politically adroit individuals [*jitsuryoku-sha*] of the parties (e.g. *Asahi*, February 25, 1999). The latter are sometimes called *bugyô*, or SAMURAI MAGISTRATES (e.g. *Asahi*, November 16, 1999). *Bugyô* was the official title of the samurai family that administered under a shogun. The *bugyô* took charge of finances, supervised regional governors and citizens, and were responsible for the administration of temples and shrines. *Bugyô* work for many years to solidify their political group and gather people who are capable of governing the nation. Very often this cadre consists of only a handful—often five to seven—leading members of a faction. These are called the FIVE SAMURAI MAGISTRATES [*go-bugyô*] or SEVEN SAMURAI MAGISTRATES [*nana-bugyô*], depending on the number (*go* means five and *nana* means seven) (*Asahi*, January 14, 1991). The group is composed of the closest aides of the various faction leaders.

STAGEHANDS may not work at the front of the political stage, but they are often called up from the back of the stage to support players at the front, including the prime minister. Their help in "greasing the wheels" of the political machine is essential to keeping it running smoothly. In practice, these players are those who most often take part in the second process we observe in *Nagatachô*, that of Dinner Club Politics. STAGEHANDS serve to support the administration—the government, the Cabinet, and in particular the prime minister, and to assist the leaders of political parties and factions.

Prime Minister's Wife: The Chief Cabinet Secretary is the most conspicuous STAGEHAND. Politicians and political commentators often refer to the Chief Cabinet Secretary's role as that of the PRIME MINISTER'S WIFE [*nyôbô-yaku*], (for example, *Aera*, February 28, 1994). The Chief Cabinet Secretary is the prime minister's right-hand person—his most trusted aide who is expected, like a devoted wife, to do everything possible to smooth the way for the prime minister to implement his plans. The job includes acting as a liaison between government ministries and agencies, and negotiating with the opposition over proposed legislation. The Chief Cabinet Secretary must also be prepared to coordinate politics among Cabinet members and be well versed in Diet affairs. As the top spokesperson of the Cabinet, he or she briefs news reporters twice a day and answers questions on all kinds of issues, domestic and international. With these requirements in mind, and because of the power and influence they have, the Chief

Cabinet Secretaries have been termed "top cabinet managers," or "Cabinet signboards." Many past prime ministers have served as Chief Cabinet Secretary before assuming the position of the national leader.

Because the Chief Cabinet Secretary is expected to play a crucial and supportive role *vis-à-vis* the prime minister, it is only natural to see them as husband and wife. But not all Chief Cabinet Secretaries have always been "faithful" to their "husbands." Some have been described as rivals who often opposed the prime minister's decisions. Takemura Masayoshi was one of these. He played ministerial roles in several administrations and served as Chief Cabinet Secretary under Prime Minister Hosokawa. Because of his attitude toward the administration, he was called a BALKAN POLITICIAN, like Prime Minister Miki. Several other Chief Cabinet Secretaries were viewed as "influential wives" who tried to manipulate their boss, the prime minister, while others were regarded as "best friends," such as Gotôda Masaharu, who was Nakasone's Chief Cabinet Secretary and helped Nakasone a great deal in managing government and party affairs. He was also called RAZOR GOTODA [*kamisori gotôda*] due to his intellectual sharpness (*Aera*, May 25, 1993).

Kajiyama Seiroku, who was Chief Cabinet Secretary for Prime Minister Hashimoto, referred to his role in a speech on November 2, 1996, following the general election. He said, "I also intend to work as a VICE-SHOGUN of Japan" (Iwami, 1998: 146). Kajiyama was referring to Tokugawa Mitsukuni, known as Mito Kômon, who was from Ibaraki Prefecture, the district from which Kajiyama was elected. Kajiyama was apparently trying to say that he would work like Mitsukuni, who, as mentioned above, was known as a wise and benevolent feudal ruler. At the same time, Kajiyama probably intended to convey the idea that he is committed to devote himself to work and to serving his "master," the prime minister. Like Mitsukuni in his time, Kajiyama as Chief Cabinet Secretary did not have a formal authoritative position, but had actual power.

Founding Fathers: Other STAGEHANDS who support the work of the prime minister are called FOUNDING FATHERS [*genrô*], (*Genrô* means literally, "the original elders"). Historically, *genrô* was the unofficial designation given to the "founding fathers" of the modern state of Japan who survived into the middle of the Meiji era (1868–1912). Although they held no constitutional or other official position, they acted as advisers to the emperor and exerted considerable influence on government decisions, participating in Cabinet meetings and conferences in the presence of the emperor. Their role was particularly important in connection with the appointment of prime ministers, since their recommendations to the emperor were in practice decisive (Hackett, 1973). FOUNDING FATHERS refers to "tribal elder" Diet members who are behind "the pick of their activity" in the front of the political stage.

These include former prime ministers, former leaders of political factions, and former officials of the LDP or other political parties who quietly manage party and personnel affairs (*Asahi*, April 19, 1995; *Asahi*, March 28, 1996a).

Instructors: Veteran politicians are often called upon to share their experience, especially when a new prime minister assumes office. When a new national leader tackles a series of assignments and challenges that he has never experienced, especially in the few first weeks of office, it is crucial for him and the nation as a whole to have access to the guidance and support of people who have experienced this type of work. At such times, experienced politicians are called on to play the role of STAGEHAND [*kôken-yaku*] or INSTRUCTOR [*shinan-yaku*] to the new administration, and to offer advice, feedback, and suggestions. For example, former Prime Minister Nakasone played INSTRUCTOR to Prime Minister Takeshita, who succeeded him in office (*Asahi*, May 19, 1989); Komoto Toshio, a veteran politician and a faction leader, played this role in the new administration of Prime Minister Kaifu (*Asahi*, September 3, 1989); and former Prime Minister Hashimoto—along with former Prime Minister Takeshita—served as INSTRUCTOR to his successor, Prime Minister Obuchi (*Asahi*, August 16, 1998).

Watcher Role: LDP faction members also function as important STAGE-HANDS. Two of their significant roles, sometimes also played by the Chief Cabinet Secretary, are aimed at supporting party and faction leaders—and thus the party itself—without necessarily directly supporting the prime minister. The first role is that of CUSTODIAN of public morals, or WATCHER [*metsuke-yaku*], (e.g. *Asahi*, May 14, 1990) (*Metsuke-yaku* was originally a superintendent officer in the feudal age who was charged with ensuring that rules were abided by under the Tokugawa shogunate). People who fill this role are concerned with the regular, daily activities surrounding the leader, whether they are watching the leader of a faction or the prime minister himself, who is usually also leader of an LDP faction. Their task is to see that all goes well and no troubles arise, that communication is maintained between the leader and regular members, and that there is no disturbance in the flow of money.

This latter role of watching over the money is known as KEEPER OF THE SAFE [*kinko-ban*], (e.g. *Aera*, March 23, 1993). It includes taking care of the finances of the leader and the faction as a whole. Individual Diet members also have a secretary who serves as SAFE-KEEPER. Diet members are allowed three secretaries whose salaries come from the national budget, and one of these is usually the SAFE-KEEPER who manages finances for the Diet member.

Chief Clerk Role: The second role played by cadre members and the Chief Cabinet Secretary is that of CHIEF CLERK [*bantô-yaku* or *ôbantô*], (e.g. *Asahi*, February 21, 1995). In this capacity, the Chief Cabinet Secretary or close aides to faction leaders (or sometimes even committee chairs who have strong contacts with members of various political groups, Kishima, 1991: 34), play the GO-BETWEEN ROLE [*nakôdo-yaku*], (*nakôdo* is a go-between who arranges a marriage by negotiating between the families of a prospective bride and groom). GO-BETWEENS mediate between political groups, playing the COORDINATOR ROLE [*chôsei-yaku*] or ADJUST [*chôsei-yaku*] activities to smoothing differences among groups in order to maintain the momentum of political action. They often conduct *hanashiai*, talks among power brokers held behind closed doors. In these meetings, the Chief Cabinet Secretary and faction leaders' close aides who represent their bosses, meet other players in the political game in order to present their views to each other and coordinate activities. When for some reason the cadre of a certain political party or faction cannot meet to exchange opinions or cannot find a way to collaborate, news reporters—especially the WATCHDOG REPORTERS who cover LDP factions—are often called upon to help mediate.

Night Attacks: Reporters have often assumed the important role of GO-BETWEEN in *Nagatachô* negotiations, transferring information between rival political groups and helping to smooth decision-making. In order to gather and transfer political information, reporters conduct NIGHT ATTACKS [*yo-uchi*] or NIGHT ROUNDS [*yo-mawari*] on political leaders' homes. They meet a politician in his or her living room after working hours, and may provide the Diet member with essential information. Reporters may then move to the house of another politician (or ask a fellow reporter) to inform the Diet member of a rival's opinion, often paving the ground for mutual understanding and settlement of disputes (Feldman, 1993a: 90–93).

Referee Role: Sometimes, despite tremendous effort, it remains difficult to achieve consensus between rivals or to resolve issues that are underpinned by complex personal conflicts. On such occasions, a STAGEHAND may serve as REFEREE [*gyôji*], (*gyôji*, originally, a sumo referee). This person has to get things in order. Sometimes the REFEREE is the Speaker of the lower house, who tries to arrange meetings between members of different groups, notably the ruling and opposition parties, in order to resolve a deadlock and keep the Diet functioning. This was the case in April 1976, following the disclosure of the Lockheed Scandal when the intervention of the Speaker of the lower house, Maeo Shigesaburô, was needed. Maeo said, "although I may be the REFEREE, that doesn't mean I can do nothing" (Iwami, 1998: 180), indicating that he should not just wait and see what would happen, but should take an active role in resolving the situation.

The vice president of the LDP may serve as REFEREE and "coordinate" candidates for small constituencies in districts were two or more people would like to run in a particular election (*Asahi*, November 3, 1995). The Executive Chairman of the LDP or some other member of the cadre often "coordinates" opinions about reform of the electoral system (*Asahi*, June 10, 1993) or about issues such as whether the Self-Defense Forces should be allowed to participate in UN Peacekeeping operations (PKO) (*Asahi*, April 24, 1992).

As mentioned, LDP members have generally preferred to avoid the process of electing a party president, and instead tend to choose a new president through negotiations among faction leaders. When talks among power brokers do not proceed smoothly and there does not appear to be one candidate who can gain the full support of all members, members may decide to ask someone to assist by "judging" the issue (*Asahi*, July 13, 1998). In December 1974, after the Tanaka Cabinet resigned amid allegations of improper financial dealings, there was fierce competition among Ôhira Masayoshi, Fukuda Takeo, Miki Takeo, and Nakasone Yasuhiro for the post-Tanaka leadership. Each one wanted to be party president and prime minister. Several factions that had confidence in their power advocated holding an election among party members. Other, smaller factions demanded that the next party president be appointed through talks held BEHIND CLOSED DOORS. They threatened to boycott any party convention called for the purpose of pushing through an election. At this stage, then LDP Vice President Shiina Etsusaburô was asked to serve as REFEREE to determine who would be the next prime minister. Eventually, Shiina boldly bypassed the strongest factions and the "logic of numbers" and proposed Miki, who belonged to a minor faction, as a compromise candidate. This "verdict" was accepted and Miki indeed became the next prime minister. Along the way, Ôhira complained to Shiina: "The ghost called *hanashiai* (negotiation) is on the prowl. Once we were in the [sumo] ring, we noticed the referee was wearing a wrestler's loincloth. It seems that Shiina [the referee] is also interested in the position [of prime minister]" (Iwami, 1998: 52).

Machiavellians: To reiterate, the roles played by the Chief Cabinet Secretary and faction cadres are crucial to maintaining the functions of the party and the Cabinet. These STAGEHANDS mediate between political groups and leaders in their attempt to achieve cooperation and collaboration among all participants in the political game. STAGEHANDS are viewed as *newaza-shi*, or MACHIAVELLIANS who use skills like talking and persuasion rather than power to get things done (e.g. *Asahi*, March 28, 1996b). They must be patient, but in the end take final and decisive action. *Newaza* means basic judo techniques, and Kanemaru Shin, who had a high rank in judo and was accomplished at "throwing" his rivals, was often called a *newaza-shi*.

Conclusions

Although **Chapters 5 and 6** are limited in their scope, focusing only on certain aspects of political processes and roles in Japan, they reveal a wide range of metaphors related to these features, and the richness of these metaphors. These metaphors were associated, among others, with the human body (e.g. Appendix, Eyeball Role), sports (e.g. Sumô Wrestlers, Referee Role), family relations (e.g. Ozawa's Children, Prime Minister's Wife), health (e.g. General Hospital, Ministers' Disease), food (e.g. Rice-Cake Money, Cold Pizza), nature (e.g. Moving the Mountain), and animals (e.g. Ox Walk). Not only ornaments, stylistic devices that embellish rhetoric and written text, but these metaphors also reflect, and help to perceive and interpret, the working of the political system.

Consider a metaphor such as POLITICAL STAGE. This metaphor provides the Japanese public (and the news media) with a framework, or "map," for locating the main political players and explaining their roles in the political system: there are those who act on the POLITICAL STAGE in view of the public; influential members who act off the POLITICAL STAGE, behind the scenes, out of view, deciding who to put on stage and what to put on the political agenda; and the STAGEHANDS, who work on stage but discreetly, helping members of the first group to function as party members and as members of the administration. When used adequately, POLITICAL STAGE, as a metaphor, makes it easier to the Japanese public to understand (and to the media to explain) not only political dynamics and decision-making processes, but also the relationships between political groups and politicians, and the roles of certain politicians (or government officials) in creating and effecting political situations and the public agenda.

Metaphors are thus important tool of reasoning which also impact the way individuals understand politics, and the way they construct their images of politicians and events. Another mode of figurative language that is also important in this regard is political cartooning, the theme of **Chapter 7**.

Lampooned Prime Ministers: The Implicit Meaning of Editorial Cartoons in Japanese Dailies

1

Another important feature related to the function communication plays in politics is the non-oratorical discourse that is usually synonymous with editorial cartooning (or political cartooning; the terms "political cartoon" and "editorial cartoon" are here used interchangeably). In detailing selected aspects of editorial cartoons in two Japanese national dailies, several lines of inquiry are investigated, including the cartoons' tone, content, and the way they depicted nine recent prime ministers. The chapter examines in particular the role dominance of prime ministers and semantic dimensions of prime-minister depictions; it identifies and measures categories of humor employed; and details the cartoon depictions of the political process as part of the discourse that take part in Japanese polity.

"Political cartoon" is defined here as a representational or symbolic drawing that makes a satirical, witty, or humorous point about a political subject. It typically takes the form of a stand-alone, non-sequential panel that makes an independent statement or observation about political events or social policy. As a form of persuasive communication, political cartoons visually symbolize, satirize or caricature some topic, action or person. They provide visual images of ideas or issues that might otherwise only be thought of in terms of verbal abstractions. By stimulating thought about issues and ideologies, and stimulating laughter at the foibles of political leaders and candidates, editorial cartoons can help to educate the public about political leaders and the political process, guide readers' thinking about the issues of the day, inspire changes in sensibility and, like other forms of political media, set political agenda through the cartoonist's choice of what to depict (Bormann, Koester, & Bennett, 1978; Edwards, 1997; Gamson & Stuart, 1992; Langeveld, 1981).

The subjects addressed by political cartoons are also treated in political news stories and editorials. Both types of media inform readers and interpret political affairs for them. But cartoons are distinguished by their use of the power of pictures: their graphic imagery can convey messages that would be unacceptable if spelled out in words (Seymour-Ure, 1986: 170). The concentrated information contained in cartoon drawings facilitates comprehension better than most photographs (Ryan & Schwartz, 1956). And, unlike their verbal counterparts, ideographs can be made to speak to the members of a culture in a variety of ways, including addition, omission, or distortion of component elements (Edwards & Winkler, 1977).

It is often argued that visual representations can effectively shape people's understanding of political reality, and can influence the beliefs and behavior of the public and politicians—sometimes even more powerfully than verbal messages. Gombrich (1982: 138–40), for example, asserts that while language is superior to pictures alone at conveying information and formulating arguments, the visual image is "supreme" in its ability to arouse emotions. This notion is particularly significant in a society that uses a written language like Japanese, in which meaning is visually conveyed largely through ideographs rather than phonetic symbols. Japanese would therefore presumably find the use of graphics to convey information more compatible than would a society that uses an abstract alphabetic script (Beniger & Westney, 1981). Indeed, the Japanese seem especially adept at instantly grasping the large amount of information presented in images such as photographs or cartoons, and are able to perceive and distinguish between minute imagistic nuances (Schodt, 1986: 18–25). Japanese newspapers, for example, place particular emphasis on the visual aspects of page layout in order to allow readers to rapidly absorb large amounts of information by simply scanning headlines, which usually consist of short strings of Chinese ideographs with highly concentrated message content.

Political cartoons thus play two important roles: *first*, they reveal the essence of a situation, person or issue, and portray and reflect political reality in relation to the roles political leaders play and the different styles of political leadership that exist in a particular country (Edwards, 1997). While analyzing the content and nature of editorial cartoons, I shall also explore the extent to which these cartoons reflect characteristics related to the roles, functions, and leadership style of the Japanese prime minister. And *second*, editorial cartoons affect the public's attitudes toward the political process; they can influence perceptions of a prime minister's qualities and working style as well as shaping deep-seated attitudes toward the political system as a whole. Aspects related to the possible influence of political cartoons on public's attitudes and perceptions toward national politics are also discussed.

Japanese Leadership

Japanese politics has often been characterized by the lack of a strong, charismatic, visible, and articulate leader capable of motivating the common people. Leaders in Japan are described as "political brokers" or "legitimizers" rather than as "originators" (Feldman, 1999a: 13–16). They tend to monitor relations among members of their group, display sensitivity and defer to supporters' preferences and wishes rather than defining and articulating their own goals, and eliciting widespread support while leading followers toward attaining a common goal (Feldman & Kawakami, 1989).

The prime minister is a case in point. Although the Japanese prime minister is the nation's chief executive, most of the postwar prime ministers have been viewed as weak and passive or reactive people who have no clear policy goals or agenda to advocate. As discussed in **Chapter 6**, they generally do not take the initiative to effect change and are rarely directly involved in determining the precise direction of change. One reason the Japanese prime minister is weak is that he rarely demonstrates determination or ability to lead, and thus is often regarded as a "portable shrine" [*mikoshi*], i.e. a figurehead carried around by fellow group members. His group of shrine bearers includes "kingmakers," "godfathers," and "shadow shoguns." They are the ones who really lead the country by allocating power, making decisions and taking care of policies.

Another reason the prime minister lacks the political authority to guide the state, govern the people, or politically dominate the institutions of government lies in the constitutional structure of the government. Compared to the democracies of most other industrialized nations, the Japanese prime minister has less real power to establish new priorities for the nation or to implement important measures, and is relatively free of policy-making responsibilities (Feldman, 1999a: 16).

The purpose here is to detail the manner in which these traits of the national political leader, the prime minister, have been depicted in an important form of political communication—political cartooning in two national daily newspapers—the *Yomiuri* (with a circulation of 14.5 million for both morning and evening editions combined together) and the *Asahi* (12.9 million) since the 1980s. Both dailies distribute their newspapers nationwide; the *Yomiuri* represents a relatively conservative editorial orientation, while the *Asahi* is relatively progressive. Throughout the past decade, both papers have published editorial cartoons [*fûshi manga*] every day in a prominent place on their political pages. These cartoons depict political figures and situations on both the domestic and international scenes. The focus is on the way the two dailies portray Japan's national political leader.

Analysis focuses on the cartoons that appeared during the first three months after the inauguration of nine prime ministers. Many people believe that reporters traditionally give new ministers a honeymoon [*goshûgihyô*, literally, "congratulatory gift"] each time a new Cabinet is formed after an election (Feldman, 1993b). In other words, there is said to be a grace period of two or three months during which reporters voluntarily refrain from criticizing the Cabinet, and instead lend support in the form of favorable reporting that gives the new administration time to get established. Thus we shall observe the way the two national dailies portrayed prime ministers during their first months in office, and analyze the extent to which the content and orientation of editorial cartoons changed as new administrations got under way.

Methodology

Political cartooning in Japanese newspapers was examined by means of content analysis of editorial cartoons that appeared regularly on the political pages of the *Yomiuri* and the *Asahi* during the first three months of the terms of nine of the past eleven prime ministers: Suzuki Zenkô (inaugurated July 17, 1980); Nakasone Yasuhiro (November 27, 1982); Takeshita Noboru (November 6, 1987); Kaifu Toshiki (August 8, 1989); Miyazawa Kiichi (November 5, 1991); Hosokawa Morihiro (August 5, 1993); Murayama Tomiichi (June 30, 1994); Hashimoto Ryûtarô (January 11, 1996); and Obuchi Keizô (July 31, 1998). Two prime ministers, Uno Sôsuke and Hata Tsutomu, were excluded from the study because they only remained in office for 69 days (June 2 to August 8, 1989) and 64 days (April 28 to June 30, 1994), respectively.

Earlier data that was analyzed and discussed elsewhere served as the basis for the design of the present study (Feldman, 1993c; Feldman, 1995). Coding sheets were used to compile information about the way in which the prime minister in office at the time appeared in each cartoon. Content was first characterized as being mainly oriented to either domestic or foreign/international issues. Next, dominance was measured by considering whether the prime minister was shown alone or with other people. If he was shown with others, attention was given to the role that the prime minister played in the cartoon: was he the main figure or subordinate to others? Was he drawn as bigger, equal to, or smaller than other figures?

In addition, the cartoon-version prime ministers were analyzed according to the types and degrees of exaggeration or deformity with which they were drawn. Illustrations of prime ministers were measured along ten dimensions, such as Strong, Sociable, Decisive, or Active (the full list appears in figure 7.6). To observe how prime ministers appeared in the cartoons, a seven-interval semantic differential scale was constructed for each of the ten items, ranging from "very much" to "not at all."

In order to explore the nature of the cartoons, three categories of humor were selected: aggression, superiority, and incongruity (for details see Berlyne, 1969; Sheppard, 1977). Aggression-related themes included hostility, violence, or threats; superiority (incompetence) themes illustrated individuals as inept, bungling, or unable to comprehend their own situation; incongruity was characterized by the juxtaposition of incompatible elements. Each cartoon was coded if it belonged to one of the above categories. The effectiveness of these types of humor was then evaluated using a 5-point scale where 1 is very funny and 5 is not funny at all.

Finally, the cartoons were examined in terms of how they depict the political process. This was done by completing the phrase "Politics is. . ." using one of the following six endings:[1]

(1) ". . . a competition": Cartoons in this category show confrontation, fighting, rivalry, or strategic planning. People are either shown racing toward a goal (as in a marathon) or striving against each other (as in a boxing match). Sports contests are the most common metaphors, but not a few cartoons also portray people in political settings such as the Diet or international summit meetings.

One example (*Asahi*, September 28, 1980, figure 7.1) shows then-Prime Minister Suzuki as a pitcher in a baseball game. The batter represents opposition parties facing a prime minister who is not yet ready to "throw the ball," or take on the opposition. The prime minister is standing on the pitcher's mound, but his mitt is on the ground and he shouts "Time out!" while he scans a primer on diplomacy and textbooks on defense, administrative reform, and taxation policy. The catcher (bottom center) is Miyazawa Kiichi, one of Suzuki's closest aids (and later a prime minister himself). Miyazawa appears to be very pressured or embarrassed as he tries to pacify the impatient umpire. The caption says "A rookie reliever steps in for the first time," pointing to Suzuki's lack of leadership experience when he took over as prime minister following the sudden death of Ôhira Masayoshi. Another example (*Asahi*, September 3, 1994): Prime Minister Murayama is depicted as a sumo wrestler up against local branches of his own Socialist Party on the eve of the party's general meeting.

(2) ". . . a gamble": These cartoons show situations in which it is hard to predict the outcome. The people involved appear to be at risk of losing something, or of getting hurt physically or emotionally. They have two or more options, from which they actively and voluntarily choose one course of action. Typical situations have the prime minister driving a car, captaining a ship, or walking in the desert.

One example (*Asahi*, December 5, 1982, figure 7.2) illustrates Prime Minister Nakasone trying to command a boat through a huge storm accompanied by high waves. The clouds above represent Japan's fiscal problems; the big wave on the right represents the administrative reforms that Nakasone promised to implement; the threatening shark stands for

Figure 7.1 Yamada Shin, *Asahi*, September 28, 1980
Reprinted with special permission of the cartoonist and the *Asahi*

trade friction; the wave on the left represents personnel problems within the administration of the prime minister, and the rock represents the trial of former Prime Minister Tanaka for taking bribes from US manufacturer Lockheed Aircraft Corp (the trial cast a shadow on the Nakasone administration because of his close relationship with Tanaka, and because of "kingmaker" Tanaka's major role in installing Nakasone as prime minister). The caption is a message from the terrified sailor shown behind Nakasone (representing the Japanese people) who begs, "Captain, we already know you are eloquent, so please just steer the ship!" The message is that it was high time for Nakasone to commit to a course of action and produce some practical results after having made many fine speeches and promises before assuming the prime minister's office.

Another cartoon (*Yomiuri*, July 5, 1994, figure 7.3) shows Prime Minister Murayama flying the airplane of Japanese diplomacy toward the upcoming summit of the Group of Seven nations in Italy. The other leaders who will take part in the summit are labeled as having long and solid experience in dealing with each other. They are covered in clouds, suggesting that the nervous Murayama—whose airplane bears the beginner's mark that Japanese drivers must display for a year after first getting their license—cannot see them clearly. The caption is, "Flown by a makeshift pilot . . ."

(3) " . . . a show": Cartoons in this category show politicians performing publicly in order to entertain (as by ballet dancing or stripping), rather than to deceive, as described below. This category sometimes includes illustrations of people acting as puppets manipulated by others.

One caricature (*Yomiuri*, January 25, 1996) shows Prime Minister Hashimoto as a street performer struggling with all his might to balance a globe and airplane on one foot (representing the importance accorded to the Japan–US Security Pact) along with a stack of small objects on a rod in his mouth (representing shrinkage of US military bases in response to protests from Okinawa residents). From a balcony in the background, the Governor of Okinawa—a leader of the drive to reduce the American military presence—observes the prime minister's performance.

(4) "... a serious, earnest profession": These cartoons show people who are dedicated to politics as a profession, to serious political activity, policy making, and to negotiations with other politicians and groups of citizens. They appear to be interested in seriously discussing and really solving problems that affect the public, such as issues related to social welfare or taxes.

One example (*Asahi*, September 5, 1993, Figure 7.4) shows Prime

Figure 7.2 Yamada Shin, *Asahi*, December 5,1980
Reprinted with special permission of the cartoonist and the *Asahi*

Figure 7.3 Fukiyama Ro, *Yomiuri*, July 5, 1994
Reprinted with special permission of the cartoonist and the *Yomiuri*

Minister Hosokawa looking worriedly out into cloudy night skies (symbolizing economic recession). A clear-skies charm [teru-teru bozu][2] labeled "income tax cuts" is hung from the Diet building. The caption says, "Is it just a superstition, or does it really work—that's the question." Another cartoon (Asahi, July 25) presents Prime Minister Murayama as a dedicated student, dripping sweat as he struggles with homework problems involving the Constitution, taxes, and his party's upcoming general meeting.

(5) "... a dangerous business": Cartoons in this category depict people who appear to be powerless to control the outcome of various dangerous situations. They differ from the "gamble" situations described above in that the participants cannot choose their own options. These include drawings of falling stones, typhoons, and driving a truck with failing brakes on a mountainside.

In one caricature (Asahi, September 7, 1980), Prime Minister Suzuki is shown in the eye of a typhoon above Japan, looking powerless and wondering what to do. The typhoon was created by a minority group of very vocal Diet members who advocate changing the Japanese Constitution. Peeping from both sides of the cartoon are leaders of foreign countries who are concerned about the outcome. The caption states: "Abnormal weather patterns. . . now there is even a clockwise-spinning typhoon!?" The idea of a typhoon that winds toward the right (as opposed to a regular typhoon, which moves toward the left) alludes to the pressure being placed on the prime minister by right-wing legislators. In another illustration (Asahi, August 24, 1998, figure 7.5), Prime Minister Obuchi is seen as a truck that symbolizes the ruling Liberal Democratic Party. One of its wheels is rolling away, representing several LDP members who established a "research group" and were exploring the possibility of leaving the party. The caption reads, "The Liberal Democratic Party's screws are starting to come loose."

Last, (6) "... deception": People in these cartoons are seen as trying to cheat, trick, misrepresent facts, or conceal their true feelings and thoughts. They smile when they are actually suffering, or promise to do important jobs that they have no intention of doing.

An example is a cartoon (Yomiuri, March 6, 1996) showing Prime Minister Hashimoto trying to spoon-feed the public a bitter medicine, representing a plan to use 685 billion yen of taxpayers' money to liquidate failed housing loan companies, while pretending it is something sweet.

The prime minister was coded only once in each cartoon. A well-trained graduate student worked closely with the author on the coding. Any questions that arose during the coding were discussed and resolved immediately.

Figure 7.4 Yamada Shin, *Asahi*, September 5, 1993
Reprinted with special permission of the cartoonist and the *Asahi*

Figure 7.5 Kojima Ko, *Asahi*, August 24, 1998
Reprinted with special permission of the cartoonist and the *Asahi*

Results and Discussion

Subject Matter of the Cartoons

A total of 1,533 political cartoons appeared in the two newspapers during the study period. Acting prime ministers were depicted in 743 of these cartoons. In other words, approximately 48.4 percent of the cartoons that appeared in the political pages of the *Yomiuri* and the *Asahi* portrayed the national leader. This high proportion reflects the prime minister's position at the center of national government news coverage. The large amount of coverage is not necessarily related to the prime minister's real political power, however, or to his ability to establish national priorities or to solve important problems. Rather, it is related to the fact that politics is personal in Japan, so newsgathering efforts, as discussed in **Chapters 1 and 2**, focus on people, and most intensely on a few top figures including the prime minister.

Instead of focusing on policy, the wisdom of various options, or moral and ideological issues, politics is seen in terms of personal and partisan strategic power games, including intrigues within and between party factions. Outcomes are of interest because they show the shifting fortunes of key power brokers and help readers keep track of winners and losers. Political events are presented as the actions of certain political leaders: they result from what people in key positions do and think. The political climate in Japan is thus reflected best in stories that tell why and how party and faction leaders, "kingmakers" and other political power brokers—and particularly the prime minister—create and manipulate events (Feldman, 1993a: 103). Thus, to a large degree, editorial cartoons mirror the content of political articles by frequently portraying the prime minister.

In these cartoons, the prime minister's figure represents several distinct forces. At times he stands for political power, the government, or the ultimate policy-maker. At other times he symbolizes the ruling party or the leadership of the ruling coalition of parties. Frequently he represents all Japanese people or the "regular" Japanese, the person on the street. Alternatively, his figure may appear as an icon of the traditional, conservative values of Japanese society.

The most common style of humor in editorial cartoons depicting the prime minister was the juxtaposition of incompatible or incongruous elements. Sometimes the prime minister was shown in unusual forms such as a fish, bird, or snake with a human head; his face might be on the slope of an active volcano; or he might be a complex building or have other people on his shoulders. When evaluating the various types of humor on the 5-point scale (1 = very funny; 5 = not funny at all), caricatures containing an aggressive element averaged 3.24; those with superiority/incompetence themes rated 2.21; and incongruity scored 1.94. Not only did incongruity-related cartoons appear most often, they were also the funniest.

Table 7.1 Means and SD of Funniness by Type of Humor of Editorial Cartoons

	Aggression			Superiority			Incongruity		
	Mean	SD		Mean	SD		Mean	SD	
First Month	3.3	1.82	(51)	2.31	1.60	(63)	2.09	1.58	(52)
Second Month	3.28	1.76	(47)	2.27	1.57	(51)	1.92	1.50	(38)
Third Month	3.14	1.74	(63)	2.09	1.52	(66)	1.82	1.41	(53)
Total	3.24	1.77	(161)	2.21	1.56	(180)	1.94	1.49	(143)

Based on 5-point scale ranging from 1 – very funny to 5 – not funny at all.

Note Figures in parentheses indicate the number of editorial cartoons in which a certain type of humor appeared in the period examined.

It is interesting to observe how often these three types of humor are used relative to the length of time each prime ministers had been in office. Table 7.1 shows clearly that all three types (aggression, incompetence, and incongruity) became funnier as time passed. In other words, the longer a prime minister was in office, the funnier the cartoons became. This trend held true for all the prime ministers, without exception. There was a growing tendency to depict the national leader in funnier fighting situations—engaged in football collisions, down for the count in boxing matches, at war—struggling in increasingly humorous situations against typhoons or dragons, being hurt by falling objects or trying to command a boat in the midst of a stormy ocean.

Portraying the Political Process

Table 7.2 shows the various ways in which cartoons portrayed politics. The breakdown of the six categories explained above revealed the following: politics was illustrated most often as a competition, battle, or a race. This contest theme dominated 178 editorial cartoons (24 percent of the total). People were shown in different types of struggles and arguments. Equally importantly, they were shown working on strategies to realize various targets, sometimes thinking only of their own personal interests. Prime ministers were frequently shown contesting leaders of opposition parties, leaders and officials of their own parties, groups of citizens and even world leaders, in their bid to achieve political ends. In several cartoons they challenged rivals in an attempt to maintain their status or to save face.

Table 7.2 Portraying Politics in the Editorial Cartoons of the Dailies along the Examined Period ("Politics is . . .")

Month	A competition	A gamble	A show	A serious profession	A dangerous business	Deception	Total
First month	59 (21.0)	41 (14.6)	33 (11.7)	38 (13.5)	69 (24.6)	41 (14.6)	281 (100.0)
Second month	49 (25.5)	23 (12.0)	22 (11.5)	31 (16.1)	41 (21.4)	26 (13.5)	192 (100.0)
Third month	70 (25.9)	29 (10.7)	32 (11.9)	53 (19.6)	38 (14.1)	48 (17.8)	270 (100.0)
Total	178 (24.0)	93 (12.5)	87 (11.7)	122 (16.4)	148 (19.9)	115 (15.5)	743 (100.0)

Note Figures in parentheses indicate the percentage of editorial cartoons illustrating politics in a certain way relative to the total number of cartoons in each month.

The next most frequently observed category (148 cartoons or 19.9 percent) was cartoons that illustrate politics as a dangerous business. This was followed by cartoons in which politics was depicted as a serious, earnest profession (122; 16.4 percent), as a deception (115; 15.5 percent), a gamble (93; 12.5 percent), and lastly as a performance (87; 11.7 percent).

So taking the first two categories together, a large number of the editorial cartoons (326, or over 43 percent) portrayed politics as competitive and unsafe. In this arena, people are constantly quarreling—with foes and partners alike. They fight to realize policies as well as to protect their own reputation; they scheme and try to manipulate others. At the same time, they risk being hurt by falling objects, run over by cars, or drenched by a huge storm.

The ways in which the political world is portrayed become more significant when observed along the study's three-month time-line. Table 7.2 reveals that as time went by, a higher percentage of the cartoons showed politics as a competition (from 21 percent in the first month to 26 percent in the third). There were increases in the proportions of cartoons presenting politics as an earnest endeavor (from 13.5 percent to 19.6 percent), and as a con game (from 14.6 percent to 17.8 percent). In other words, as time passed and each new administration became more established, the prime minister and his administration were increasingly depicted as trying to seriously tackle political and social issues; but at the same time they were increasingly shown in confrontations or engaged in deceit.

On the other hand, there were decreases in the percentages of cartoons illustrating politics as dangerous (from 24.6 percent in the first month to 14.1 percent in the third) or as a gamble (from 14.6 percent to 10.7 percent). Although the prime minister and other leaders were seen as trying to tackle issues, they were also seen as less inclined to take risks or initiate public policies, and thus less likely to expose themselves to unpredictable outcomes. Typically, they were seen as being more concerned with keeping the status quo, avoiding the public eye while implementing unpopular economic measures, or in generating social plans.

If cartoons do reflect political reality as claimed, one can surmise that Japanese administrations tend to refrain from acting decisively and determinedly on important issues—whether domestic or foreign—in order to avoid failure and possible criticism from opposition parties and the news media. Instead, they tend to lean on bureaucrats for handling delicate issues, or try to negotiate with opposing groups behind closed doors, far from the public eye, in order to achieve "safe" consensus decisions.

Differences between the Two Dailies

The two newspapers carried approximately the same number of cartoons showing a prime minister's figure or face. The *Asahi* had 370 (49.8 percent of its total number of political cartoons) and the *Yomiuri* had 373 cartoons (50.2 percent). It is significant that cartoons depicting the prime minister appeared on almost the same days in both papers.

The two dailies did not differ markedly in their treatment of the national political leader, providing further proof of the high degree of uniformity that exists among Japanese dailies; all are nearly identical in their coverage of events, selection of news, make-up and formats because they use the same newsgathering methods, rely on a limited number of information sources, and conform to various unwritten codes. Consequently, there is a great deal of uniformity among all Japanese newspapers in the amount of emphasis they give to a particular news item (McCargo, 1996). Since editorial cartoons reflect the political stories and editorials appearing in national dailies, they naturally tend to illustrate identical issues from very similar perspectives, thus contributing even further to the "harmony" of the Japanese media.

Both papers showed a clear tendency to feature the prime minister in the context of domestic issues more frequently than in relation to foreign affairs. There were 523 cartoons (70.4 percent) that featured the prime minister dealing with issues related to political parties, party factions and the government bureaucracy; in 220 cartoons (29.6 percent) the prime minister appeared in the context of international matters such as relations with the US or Europe, UN-related activities or defense issues. Of the total of 523 cartoons focused on domestic issues, 251 (48 percent) were in the *Yomiuri* and 272 (52 percent) were in the *Asahi*. Of cartoons illustrating subject matter related to foreign affairs, the *Yomiuri* ran 122 cartoons (55.5 percent) and the *Asahi* ran 98 (44.5 percent).

Although there are many similarities between the two dailies, they differed in how they portrayed public affairs as a whole. As table 7.3 indicates, the *Asahi* tended to have more cartoons portraying politics as competition (54.5 percent of the cartoons in this category appeared in the *Asahi*), as dangerous (55.7 percent) and especially as deceitful (60 percent). In contrast, the *Yomiuri*'s cartoons were dominated more by gamble-related themes, politics as a performing art, and politics as an earnest business.

If these editorial caricatures do indeed reflect the content of political stories in the two newspapers, one can conclude that the *Asahi* tends to emphasize the rivalry between political groups, scrutinize the conduct of politicians, and "warn" the public of possible deception, while the *Yomiuri* focuses more on the political process and politicians' activities. These tendencies may be related to the conservative editorial orientation of the *Yomiuri* and the progressive inclination of the *Asahi*.

Table 7.3 Portraying Politics in the Editorial Cartoons of the Two Dailies ("Politics is . . . ")

Newspaper	A competition	A gamble	A show	A serious profession	A dangerous business	Deception	Total
Asahi	96 (54.5)	40 (42.6)	33 (37.5)	49 (40.5)	83 (55.7)	69 (60.0)	370 (49.8)
Yomiuri	80 (45.5)	54 (57.4)	55 (62.5)	72 (59.5)	66 (44.3)	46 (40.0)	373 (51.2)
Total	176 (100.0)	94 (100.0)	88 (100.0)	121 (100.0)	149 (100.0)	115 (100.0)	743 (100.0)

Note Figures in parentheses indicate the percentage of editorial cartoons which appeared in a newspaper relative to the total number of cartoons portraying politics in a certain way.

Portraying the National Leader

How did the editorial cartoons treat and evaluate the national leader over time? The breakdown of the number and percentages of cartoons illustrating the nine prime ministers during their first three months in office is presented in table 7.4, which reveals, first, a gradual increase in the total number of cartoons showing successive prime ministers. Prime Minister Suzuki was featured in 34 editorial cartoons during his first three months in office, whereas the five most recent prime ministers (Miyazawa, Hosokawa, Murayama, Hashimoto, and Obuchi) were shown in at least two and a half times as many. This trend is related to the fact that in recent years the prime minister has become an increasingly important source of news and object of media attention.

Table 7.4 Number and Proportion of Editorial Cartoons Illustrating the Nine Prime Ministers by Month in Office

Prime Minister	First Month	Second Month	Third Month	Total
Suzuki Zenko	12 (35.3)	7 (20.6)	15 (44.1)	34
Nakasone Yasuhiro	19 (38.8)	14 (28.6)	16 (32.6)	49
Takeshita Noboru	26 (31.0)	22 (26.2)	36 (42.8)	84
Kaifu Toshiki	24 (33.8)	20 (28.2)	27 (38.0)	71
Miyazawa Kiichi	39 (34.5)	29 (25.7)	45 (39.8)	113
Hosokawa Morihiro	40 (40.0)	21 (21.0)	39 (39.0)	100
Murayama Tomiichi	47 (42.7)	31 (28.2)	32 (29.1)	110
Hashimoto Ryutaro	35 (36.5)	27 (28.1)	34 (35.4)	96
Obuchi Keizo	39 (45.3)	21 (24.4)	25 (30.2)	86
Total	281 (37.8)	192 (25.8)	270 (36.3)	743

Note Figures in parentheses indicate the percentage of editorial cartoons illustrating a certain prime minister relative to this prime minister's total number of cartoons.

Table 7.4 also shows that the number of cartoons showing a prime minister varied from month to month; there was no constant rate of increase or decrease in number that persisted throughout the period examined. Combining all the prime ministers, there were 281 cartoons in the first month, 192 in the second and 270 in the third. The number of cartoons depicting each prime minister did decrease in the second month compared to the first month, then increase in the third month compared to the second, for every prime minister without exception. For each prime minister, 30 to 45 percent of the total number of cartoons appeared during the first and third months; while 20 to 28 percent appeared in the second month.

This tendency is of great importance and deserves special attention. It is related to the nature of coverage the newspapers give a new administration and its prime minister. Examination of the newspapers' editorials reveals that during the second month after the inauguration of a new administration, there is a considerable decrease in the number of pieces that refer to the prime minister. This trend starts about a month after each administration is formed. During the first three weeks from the day the prime minister takes office, there are many stories and editorials about the selection of the prime minister. Stories and editorials feature leading politicians involved in the process, initial talks that the new prime minister conducts with opposition leaders and heads of economic organizations, and, particularly, the views the prime minister holds on various issues: his plans, ideas, and promises regarding new policies.

Typically, an exceptionally large portion of political coverage during this period is related to foreign/international affairs. This is because the prime minister usually travels abroad during his first month in office to meet with leaders of other nations, primarily the US president and leaders of other G-7 nations, to introduce himself and discuss mutual concerns. Editorials and political stories focus on these talks and the relationships that are established. This coverage gives the impression that the prime minister is an international figure who can talk with world leaders on equal terms and will represent Japan abroad with honor. Coupled with the prime minister's pledges on new policies, this type of coverage attracts much public attention and strengthens public confidence that change will come with the new administration. Overall, such coverage creates an optimistic atmosphere, inspires hope for better, more effective and more pragmatic leadership, and generates support for the new administration.

After the first three weeks, however, there is a sudden shift in political coverage, reflected in a decrease in the number of stories related to the prime minister and the new administration. The prime minister suddenly "fades" from newspaper headlines. There are fewer reports on the national political leader's activities and on the government's activities. Instead, the political pages contain many feature stories and theses written by opinion leaders and scholars about how the government should react to issues such as the economic situation and world affairs. Newspapers give detailed reports on the results of their own public opinion polls that gage support for the new administration. During this period there are many interviews with and profiles of government leaders and top bureaucrats. This is the "honeymoon season," during which reporters voluntarily refrain from criticizing—indeed from even reporting on—the Cabinet and the prime minister, giving the new administration time to get established.

The tendency to run fewer stories on the prime minister's performance and work begins to change at the beginning of the third month. Once the administration has more or less settled in and begun tackling controversial and/or pressing problems, the press pays more attention to such issues as new taxes, revising the education system, and environmental protection.

As discussed later, this results in the expression of more negative views toward the prime minister.

Analysis also disclosed that the Japanese prime minister seldom appeared alone in the editorial cartoons. Among the 743 cartoons, prime ministers were drawn alone in only 92 cases (12.4 percent). In 651 cartoons (87.6 percent), he appeared with other people. Among these people were world leaders such as the leaders of G-7 nations (132 cartoons); leaders in his own political party, especially leaders of Liberal Democratic Party factions (164); leaders of opposition parties (136); Cabinet ministers (86), and "regular Japanese" such as farmers, housewives, or children (102).

It is worth noting that many of the cartoons that included "regular Japanese" depicted them as generally disinterested in the political process, confused by politicians' actions, unable to make decisions, or expressing apathy or cynicism toward the political process. For example, they were drawn as bored observers at a baseball game or separated from a table where politicians made decisions.

The fact that the prime ministers usually appeared with other people facilitated comparison of their relative role and size in the cartoons, as well as their relative power, sincerity, warmth, problem-solving ability and attitudes toward colleagues and the general public. When appearing with other figures, the prime minister was the main figure in 577 cartoons (out of 651, 88.6 percent) and played a secondary role in 74 cartoons (11.4 percent). He was bigger than the other figures in the same cartoon in 158 cases (24.4 percent), smaller in 175 cases (26.8 percent) and about the same size in 318 (48.8 percent).

As the main figure in one cartoon, a prime minister was depicted as the driver of a truck. He tries to brake, but the truck is running away down a steep slope, out of his control. In another he was a baseball player who reached home base just as the game (symbolizing recent elections) was ending. He was shown as a patient suffering from a headache (decreased public support) while a leading figure in his party was arrested on bribery-related charges.

The prime minister was portrayed in a variety of forms and fashions. He was often drawn as a "regular" person (361 cases, 48.6 percent); as a sportsman (mainly a sumo wrestler or baseball player) in 88 cases (11.8 percent); as a driver (of truck, bus or train), captain (of ship or airplane), cook, fireman, doctor, or sick person in 34 cases (4.6 percent). In 21 cases (2.8 percent), the prime minister appeared as an animal (fox, bird) or inanimate object such as a safe or a statue.

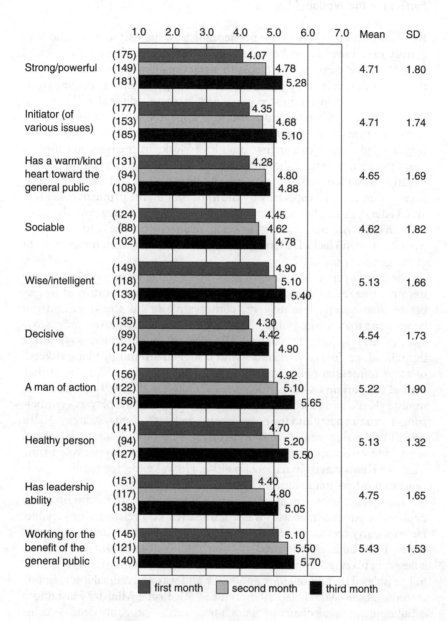

Figure 7.6 Means and SD Evaluations of the Nine Prime Ministers for each of the Ten Items

Evaluating the National Leader

By using various forms of the prime ministers, the cartoons were able to convey messages that evoke and stimulate certain emotions. Like political anecdotes, the cartoons were able to attract readers' attention and affect their attitudes, creating or shaping specific impressions or images. How, then, was the prime minister perceived in these editorials? Figure 7.6 reveals how the different prime ministers appeared in the cartoons.

The analysis clearly reveals that the prime ministers were shown in a negative light during their first month of work. In their second month, every prime minister, without exception, was illustrated in an even more negative way than in the first month. As time passed and the administrations got under way, especially by the third month, the prime minister was attacked more harshly with the weapon of ridicule. His image was the same in both national newspapers: a weak, relatively unwise and indecisive person, one who lacks leadership ability and does not work for the benefit of the general public.

The mean average in figure 7.6 (in which a higher score indicates a more negative image) suggests that the prime minister was portrayed as less bright than others, less diligent, conservative in his thinking, and not benevolent toward the public. The chief executive appeared unhealthy-looking and lacking in energy. He was often illustrated as a mere figurehead, or "portable shrine," who is lugged around by "kingmakers" or other influential politicians who manipulate him by pulling his strings behind the curtains. One cartoon (*Asahi*, October 28, 1989) shows Prime minister Kaifu as a baseball team's manager. While all the players (symbolizing the ruling party and the government) gather to discuss strategy, Kaifu sits off to the side, remote and uninvolved. The caption says: "Wait until we decide on an appropriate strategy," hinting at the puppet role Prime Minister Kaifu played in national politics. He was expected to follow decisions that others made for him.

The typical cartoon image of a prime minister after two months in office depicted a passive man who was cold-hearted and relatively unsociable. He was ugly, feeble, unhealthy, made disastrous errors, and was always worried and defeated. He tried in vain to climb steep mountains, traverse a desert in blazing summer, or cross a street in a typhoon with an umbrella full of holes. He did not enjoy good luck and was a perennial loser. In one cartoon (*Asahi*, March 19, 1996, figure 7.7), Prime Minister Hashimoto is falling from an airplane; he faces a tragic end—probably death—as his parachute is tangled up with that of Ichiro Ozawa, the leader of the biggest opposition party.

The longer a prime minister was in office, the more frequently he was depicted with a distorted face, tired eyes, wrinkles, or as a person who tries to slip away from hard work. Compared to other figures in the same

空転——もつれたパラシュート

小島　功

Figure 7.7　Kojima Ko, *Asahi*, March 19, 1998
Reprinted with special permission of the cartoonist and the *Asahi*

cartoon, the prime minister was thinner, older, had weaker, shakier legs, was more fearful and less confident. He looked so miserable that he inspired sympathy.

Conclusions

The aim of this chapter was twofold, in view of two important roles that political cartoons play as a form of political communication. One aim was to explore the extent to which the cartoons reflected the roles, functions, and leadership styles of Japanese prime ministers. The other was to evaluate what influence the cartoons might have had on the public's attitudes toward and perceptions of political leadership and by extension, national politics as a whole.

The study suggests that editorial cartoons mirror political reality and portray the prime minister "as he is"; a relatively indecisive leader who lacks determination and usually sits on the fence, trusting others (power-brokers, bureaucrats, and party officials) to make important decisions and do the work for him. Like other leaders in Japan, the prime minister is portrayed like a traditional business manager who attaches much importance to smoothing group dynamics and achieving a consensus of opinion. He "leads" by steering clear of ideological conflicts while placing much importance on behind-the-scenes politicking and secret negotiations between political groups.

In the cartoons that portray him, as in reality, the national leader invests much of his energy in making deals behind closed doors in order to maintain harmonious relations with individuals and groups. He is passive in regard to policy issues and administrative problems, and reactive to topics brought up by others. In this sense, political cartoons serve as clear reflections of Japanese political leaders and Japanese political culture.

But editorial cartoons do more than merely echo the activities and leadership style of the prime minister. They also contain a satiric "bite" that becomes more severe over time as the administration of a new prime minister gets underway. The prime minister is always portrayed as having gradually less power, less confidence and less morality as his term progresses. This concept is related to the second question about the effectiveness of editorial cartoons.

In the last few years, the Japanese public has become particularly disaffected with politics and politicians. Distrust of politicians and the political system has gradually increased. This has been accompanied by a growing sense of political apathy and a sense of decreasing political efficacy. Voter turnout has markedly declined, party support has slipped, and independent candidates have won many seats on both the national and the local levels. There is increasing dissatisfaction with current leaders and a widespread desire for "change." The public's expectations of their leaders have noticeably diminished. While there is evidence indicating that the news media—particularly in their political stories and editorials—have played a significant role in effecting these shifts in public attitude toward leaders and the political process, so far not one study has tried to explore the specific influence of editorial cartoons in this regard.

Nevertheless, it can be assumed that political cartoons play a prominent role in shaping the public's images of the political process. Their impact may not be independent, but probably complements that of political articles and editorials (and broadcast media's coverage of politics). Most readers, presumably, do not look solely at political cartoons that appear in the middle of the political page without at least glancing at the political stories on that page. But because of the graphic depiction they contain, political cartoons add a special and perhaps powerful perspective to the information presented in the neighboring political stories. These cartoons often help to organize the data presented verbally in political articles and editorials, and facilitate the understanding of events and the often-complex balances of power that exist among political leaders and groups.

Editorial cartoons contribute greatly to strengthening existing negative attitudes toward politicians, by frequently illustrating the prime minister as weak, confused in his decisions (the few that he actually makes), manipulated by others and lacking confidence in his work. Constant—and more significantly—increasing ridicule of the chief executive, the symbol of political authority, and indeed of political leadership and decision-making in general, enables political cartoons to further shape perceptions of politics and politicians in a way that increases disaffection with the way politics operates, and increases distrust and apathy toward politicians and the political system as a whole.

8 ▶ Continuing the Conversation: Slogans, Names, and Moods

Earlier chapters covered various aspects of Japanese political discourse that have the potential to affect the political attitudes and behavior of the general public, political decision-makers, and government officials. Needless to say, there are other aspects that were not addressed although doing so would have provided a broader outlook and opportunities to include additional data related to the multifaceted language used in Japanese politics. For the preceding discussion, I selected the aspects that I consider to be most important in order to underline the significant roles that communication processes in general, and language in particular, play in public affairs in Japan. This chapter reviews some of the findings presented in this book and positions them within the broad context of political communication. I will also suggest topics that I feel deserve to be examined in future studies on political discourse in Japan.

Making Sense of Politics

As mentioned in the Introduction, from a broad viewpoint, the literature of contemporary political behavior is increasingly becoming a literature of communication. Citizens communicate their needs and desires to politicians, government officials, and others involved in public policy matters, and decision-makers, in turn, inform the public of their activities and intentions. Open, democratic societies must have informed citizens who feel motivated to take an active part in public affairs. In order for citizens to adequately evaluate the various options that they are asked to choose from, they must first gain some understanding of the complicated and messy business of politics. Among other things, they must be aware of new developments in public policy and political issues, know about emerging candidates, and have a grasp of the course of political and social events.

It is mostly through political messages and words that politicians, political activists, policy analysts, reporters and editors try to influence the way citizens make sense of politics. They endeavor to simplify the political world for the general public, explain policy positions, suggest ways in which a policy or candidate might advance or harm a citizen's interests, and affect the standards by which citizens evaluate specific policies and issues. All of these actors engage in word-based campaigns aimed at getting individuals to understand political process, to perceive and interpret situations in specific ways, to apply certain standards or criteria when evaluating options, and to frame the political milieu.

In a democratic society, it is expected that the news media in particular will disseminate and interpret information that the public needs in order to be able to participate in the political realm in a healthy way. The quality of information that the public receives—whether through newspaper articles or editorials, television news programs, political talk shows, or television debates, etc.—ultimately determines the quality of the public's political attitudes and behavior. The media also exert significant influence over the degree of priority that the public assigns to policy concerns: high-volume coverage of an issue makes the issue appear to be more significant in the public mind. Media messages can affect or "prime" the criteria that individuals use in making political evaluations, their thoughts about "important issues," and their preferences.

Classical models consider the political elite, the media, and citizens as interrelated components in the democratic process. Political information is an important parameter in this regard: as long as reliable information is available to the public, democratic society can prevail. On the other hand, open society is weakened when the public loses trust in the reliability of information presented by journalists, for example when the public believes there is an excessively symbiotic relationship between journalists and the political elite. In Japan, criticism of the media has focused especially on the *kisha* club system, a collection of informal rules and customs (discussed in **Chapters 1 and 2**) aimed mainly at maintaining smooth and congenial relationships with information sources. This system forces reporters to conform to various practices that prevent them from easily obtaining exclusive information and compels them to cooperate with colleagues who are all looking for the same details on political events and processes.

The fact is that if a reporter refuses to observe the *kisha* club system's unwritten rules, that reporter will not be able to complete his or her assignments. Scholars and media personalities often complain that the *kisha* club rules work against the ideals of free expression and free competition among media organizations, and that they are detrimental to the ethics of reporters. They say that because of this system, beat reporters end up relying on handouts and updates fed to them by influential Diet members and government bureaucrats, so that the reporters serve merely as "messengers" who passively transmit information. Information sources, especially high echelon Diet members, "encourage" reporters to cover the specific issues that they want to see high on the public agenda, and as a result investigative and critical political journalism is viewed as lying beyond the responsibility of the national media (Feldman, 1993a; Tase, 1994). According to this view, the rhetoric of the major news media in Japan reflects to a large degree the expectations and wishes of members of the political elite.

Rhetorical Style of Politicians

In this book, I have discussed in detail various rhetorical modes used by Japanese politicians during briefings to news reporters, Diet deliberations, public speeches, and television interviews. Politicians' speech styles generally fit into one of two categories: *honne*—the honest and informal, or *tatemae*—the formal and ceremonial. Things that are said in private, behind closed doors, are not always said in public venues such as large gatherings of supporters or live television interviews.

Another feature of politicians' talk is the use of direct appeals and indirect appeals. Direct appeals are most often made to fellow politicians when negotiating legislative bills, and to supporters throughout election campaigns. During the November 2003 lower house election campaign, for example, Japan's major parties appealed to voters through "manifestoes," or packages of promises that included numerical targets or other specific goals, and a timetable for achieving the promises. It was the first time in the history of Japanese politics that the term "manifestoes" was used. The news media and the public saw the manifestos as an improvement over previous election pledges and platforms, which were generally abstract jumbles of vague promises apparently aimed at pleasing everyone. In the 2003 election, the various parties offered pledges that actually differed from each other in their stance toward specific issues such as the privatization of highway corporations, national security, and the dispatch of Self-Defense Forces to Iraq.

One of the challenges of making a direct appeal in front of a large audience or a group of reporters is the risk of saying something that may later be criticized as an "indiscreet remark" or a "slip of the tongue." As discussed earlier, not a few politicians have been condemned for making careless remarks in public. An even worse fate for a politician is to be blamed for lying in public, whether by withholding facts that they are aware of, providing false information, or by making promises that they fail to keep.

A famous example of this occurred during the 1986 Diet campaign, when Prime Minister Nakasone said, "I will not introduce the kind of so-called 'large scale indirect tax' that the public is opposed to. Do I look like someone who is telling a lie?" ["*Kokumin ga hantai suru yô na ôgata kansetsu-zei to shô suru mono wa yarani. Kono watakushi ga uso wo tsuite iru kao ni miemasu ka?"*]. Yet, after the LDP's landslide victory in the election, the government's Advisory Tax Commission began considering the implementation of new taxes, and at the end of 1986, the ruling party proposed a new 5 percent indirect tax to be called a "sales tax" [*uriage-zei*]. In response to the outrage expressed not only by opposition parties but also by farmers and other staunch LDP supporters, Nakasone insisted that the proposed sales tax could not be called a large-scale indirect tax because some items such as food and medical services would be exempt. (A national sales tax was in fact implemented in 1988. It started as a 3 percent tax, with no exemptions even for basic necessities such as food, rent or medical services; In 1996, it was raised to 5 percent.) As many people saw the tax as a violation of Nakasone's campaign promises, the public branded the prime minister as a "liar" [*usotsuki*], and this mistrust caused the LDP to suffer major setbacks in gubernatorial and local assembly elections, and in the next upper house by-election.

Another prime minister who was branded as a liar was Miyazawa. In the wake of a series of scandals including the *Recruit* and *Tôkyô Sagawa Kyûbin* flaps, public demands for political reform intensified until Miyazawa responded by pledging to "fully commit" himself to promoting reform. During a television interview in May 1993, he promised, "I will implement political reforms during the current Diet session. I have never lied before" [*"Seiji kaikaku wa kon kokkai de yarimasu. Watakushi wa, katsute 'uso' wo tsuita koto wa gozaimasen"*]. However, getting the LDP to reach a consensus regarding political reform proved to be too difficult for Miyazawa. His pledge was termed a "public lie" [*uso hatsugen*], and his failure to deliver on his promise caused the largest LDP faction to split apart, allowing the opposition to successfully call for a vote of no-confidence and dissolve the lower house, ending 38 consecutive years of political domination by the LDP.

Nevertheless, a decade later, in January 2003, Prime Minister Koizumi dared to tell the lower house Budget Committee that it was "not a major problem if I am unable to stick to promises" made two years previous. Following this remark, Koizumi's public support declined significantly as he was criticized for breaking three key campaign promises: to pay an official visit to Yasukuni Shrine each year on August 15, to limit issuance of new government bonds, and to cap government protection of savings deposits as originally scheduled.

Another type of direct appeal or feature of political communication that warrants examination is the mysterious quirks of memory to which politicians can be prone. Some Diet members and a number of government officials have learned that it can be more convenient to "forget" certain events rather than try to deny or explain them, in order to avoid being publicly criticized for their words or actions or being accused of lying. In 1988, Prime Minister Takeshita was the chief target of criticism when it was discovered that he and many other politicians accepted pre-listed shares in a real estate subsidiary of *Recruit Co.* At first he denied having taken any donations from the company, but during parliamentary interrogation by members of the JCP, Takeshita grew increasingly uncomfortable, sometimes turning red and trembling. In response to one question, he said, "I can tell you what I know, but I can't tell you what I don't remember." In mid-April 1989, Takeshita promised that he had disclosed the full extent of his relationship with *Recruit*, claiming, "I do not remember details of my [earlier] statement, but I probably did not have a clear recollection."

More than a decade later, in May 2001, during a debate in the lower house Budget Committee, Finance Minister Shiokawa Masajûrô was questioned by a member of the JCP regarding comments he made during a television interview (on Kume Hiroshi's popular show, "News Station") in January that year about the use of government classified funds when he was Chief Cabinet Secretary in 1989. The JCP member said that Shiokawa had remarked that such funds were used for "taming" opposition parties under Prime Minister Uno Sôsuke. When asked whether his remarks about the funds were true, Shiokawa repeatedly said: "I do not remember" ["*Oboete inai*"] and "I cannot recall" ["*Omoidasenai*"]. He further noted, in a press conference that "I forgot what I said, but I was surprised when I saw the videotape [of the television news program]. I don't know what I was thinking . . . [*Nani wo itta ka wasureta ga, bideo wo mite bikkuri shita. Nani wo omotte itta no ka . . .* "], (*Mainichi*, May 17, 2001).

Among the indirect appeals used by Diet members are metaphors and symbols. These can be as important as direct appeals. I have already discussed ways in which political jargon has incorporated particular metaphors from such fields as war, medicine, sports, nature, food, money, and the human body. Metaphors and other figurative language are used by politicians, news reporters, and government officials alike, and play an important role in the public sphere by helping citizens to make sense of political events and practices as well as by contributing to the structuring of social and political reality. In addition to communicating information and perspectives that guide individuals' understanding of political issues, roles, processes, and relationships, metaphors also evoke strong emotional responses. This emotional aspect of political language was not examined in this book, but I believe it deserves special attention in future research on political communication in Japan.

Another facet of political language that was not examined but which I think should definitely be analyzed in the future, is nonverbal political rhetoric in Japan. This would include gestures, facial expressions, and other displays of happiness, anger, fear, etc. Examples are smiling, eye contact, touching, body language, and sometimes silence, for example when an embarrassed politician declines to answer a difficult question during a television interview. Nonverbal dimensions of rhetoric have been known to play a central role in relations between leaders and followers (e.g. in the context of persuasion), but researchers have largely ignored them. Before the age of television, politicians' nonverbal cues were rarely seen by anyone who was not physically present when the politician spoke. However, now that the general public has frequent opportunities to see close-up images of political leaders participating in press conferences, campaign debates, and live interviews, non-verbal expressive behavior has become a more important form of political communication. Since nonverbal cues are very important to human social interactions in general, we can assume that they likewise have important effects on the way voters establish or change their attitudes toward politicians, political issues, and the forming of judgments related to politics in general. Thus it is important to examine how viewers respond emotionally to expressive displays by Japanese Diet members in the context of political discourse that they witness via television (and perhaps even homepages display in the internet).

As a final point about indirect appeals, it is important to remember to watch the explicit and implicit rhetoric of the news media along with that of the politicians, as both play important roles in the political process. Japanese journalists face the same challenges as journalists anywhere else as they select the content to include in newspapers and broadcasts: ideally, they seek to keep the public well-informed both by providing objective coverage that passively mirrors reality, and by exercising their watchdog function, i.e. through active reporting that exposes deviations from what is presented as the surface reality. Journalists and commentators feel pressure to produce material—that is, to select words—that please both their audiences and their information sources. This aspect of political journalism has been discussed to a certain extent in this book, and in detail elsewhere (e.g. Feldman, 1993a).

Political Language and the Creation of "Mood"

One interesting aspect of Japanese political language that was not discussed in detail is the use of words, metaphors, and slogans to create *"mûdo,"* meaning mood or atmosphere. The prime minister and other high-echelon Diet members, as well as government officials and the news media, often try to produce (often successfully) a certain feeling such as optimism, loyalty, cooperation, encouragement, or community spirit, in order to spur or guide action related to specific public issues or the political agenda.

Selection of Words

The primary tool for building a mood is the selection and use of certain words. Consider, for example, the word *heiwa* (peace). Kawano (1999) argues that prime ministers in post-World War II Japan have frequently used the Japanese word *heiwa* in their policy speeches in the Diet in order to invite sympathy and support from the public.

Likewise, the word *dômei* ("alliance") has been used to spark support and understanding *vis-à-vis* Japan's close relationship with the US. Prime Minister Ôhira made up his mind in 1979 to become the first prime minister in Japan to use the term *dômei* to describe Japan-US relations despite his concern that the term might stir up nationalism because it suggests that the participants in the alliance are of equal rank. Japan was—and still is—highly polarized over issues related to defense and alliance with the US, and two years later the news media and the public chastised Prime Minister Suzuki for using the same word in a communiqué that he issued after official talks with President Ronald Reagan in May 1981. Suzuki's Foreign Minister, Itô Masayoshi, resigned to protest the prime minister's refusal to admit that there was a military intent in the "alliance" referred to in the communiqué.

Another example of creating a certain mood is regarding the use of euphemisms and vague expressions instead of direct, or blunt expressions. Hook (1986) suggested that the Ministry of Education's censuring of politically sensitive expressions from textbooks is an example of using euphemisms to structure reality for political purposes. High school social studies textbooks introduced during the 1980s used the word "advance" [*shinshutsu*] into China to describe what the rest of the world saw as Japan's "aggression" [*shinryaku*] during the 1930s. The choice of the euphemistic expression "advance" over the more honest and direct term "aggression" in school textbooks is highly significant for two reasons. First, textbooks play a central role in the formation of political attitudes among youngsters. And second, language is an important means of legitimizing particular interpretations of history in the minds of Japanese school children. The expression that is chosen affects which aspects of reality are revealed or concealed, and this in turn affects attitudes and understanding.

This applies to other vocabulary related to World War II. Some Japanese call the war itself the World War II [*dainiji sekai taisen*], while others call it the Greater East Asia War (*daitoa sensô*) or the Pacific War [*taiheiyô sensô*]. Critics say that for the past 50 years, the Japanese government has tried to play down Japan's defeat in World War II. Consequently, newspapers have used the word *shûsen* ("end of the war") more frequently than *haisen* ("defeat in the war"). For example, the *Asahi*'s data base reveals that from January 1, 1994, through December 31, 1999, the word *shûsen*—along with the Pacific War [*taiheiyô sensô*]—appeared in newspapers' stories 656 times, while the word *haisen* appeared 551 times in the same period. Similarly, the Allied Occupation Forces were called *shinchûgun* ("stationed forces") more often than *senryôgun* ("occupation forces"). Government officials and the media have purposely chosen specific terms to guide the national psyche toward a desired mood.

Cabinets and their Political Slogans

"Sound bites" are another tool that Diet members often use to generate a particular mood. Some sound bites become slogans that represent a given administration. At other times, the prime minister or a member of his administration may create a pithy slogan used for generating an atmosphere that is positive, sympathetic, and supportive toward the administration. As shown by the examples below, these rallying phrases reflect the tone of the times as well as the administration's hopes and concerns.

Japanese administrations have a long history of using catch phrases to spread specific ideas among the public. But it was Ikeda Hayato who started the tradition of including a slogan that sums up the underlying philosophy of a new prime minister's administration in his first policy speech before the Diet. Prime Minister Ikeda inaugurated this practice in 1960 with his use of "Income Doubling Plan" ["*shotoku baizô keikaku*"] to describe policies focused on actively promoting economic growth and nudging the economy toward international openness. The Ikeda administration also emphasized engaging opposition parties in dialog as expressed in a second slogan: "Tolerance and Patience" ["*kan'yô to nintai*"].

Prime Minister Satô Eisaku's Cabinet came up with the slogan "Tolerance and Harmony" ["*kan'yô to chôwa*"] and pursued policies geared toward furthering "respect for human dignity" and "social development" ["*ningen sonchô to shakai kaihatsu*"], by protecting the public from illnesses related to pollution and environmental destruction. This was followed by Tanaka Kakuei's Cabinet, whose slogan was "Decision and Execution" ["*ketsudan to jikkô*"] which meant dealing effectively both with problems associated with rapid economic growth and with the normalization of China–Japan diplomatic relations. Prime Minister Miki Takeo used "Dialogue and Cooperation" ["*taiwa to kyôchô*"] as the slogan of his newly formed "Clean Cabinet" ["*kuriin naikaku*"]. Fukuda Takeo's Cabinet adopted the phrase "Cooperation and Solidarity" ["*kyôchô to rentai*"] as its basic political philosophy, to highlight the need to overcome intra-party turmoil. Ôhira Masayoshi's Cabinet took up the slogan "Trust and Consensus" ["*shinrai to gôi*"] to express its political goals, while Prime Minister Suzuki Zenkô's slogan was "Politics of Harmony" ["*wa no seiji*"]. Prime Minister Nakasone 's slogans were "Final Settlement of Postwar

Politics" ["*sengo seiji no sôkessan*"] and "Internationalization of Japan" ["*kokusai kokka nippon*"].

Prime Minister Takeshita introduced the slogan, "Rejuvenation of Rural Communities," or "Reviving our Hometowns" ["*furusato sôsei*"]. Under his *furusato* program, each city, town, and village in the nation received 100 million yen in government funds to support independent projects planned at the grassroots level. Uno's slogan was "The Reform-advancing Cabinet" ["*kaikaku zenshin naikaku*"], which purported to create a slim government. Prime Minister Kaifu Toshiki expressed his desire to foster a "fair and compassionate society" ["*kôsei de kokoro yutakana shakai*"] under the banner of "Politics of Dialog and Reform" ["*taiwa to kaikaku no seiji*"]. Prime Minister Miyazawa's slogan was "A Lifestyle Superpower" ["*seikatsu taikoku*"]. In the following administration, Prime Minister Hosokawa Morihiro announced that his cabinet would be "an administration of political reform" ["*seiji kaikaku seiken*"] with the slogan "Responsible Change" ["*sekinin aru kaikaku*"] representing his administration's commitment to ending cozy ties between politicians, bureaucrats, and special interest groups. In his first policy speech in the Diet after being elected prime minister in May 1994, Hata Tsutomu reiterated his promise of "Reforms and Cooperation" ["*kaikaku to kyôchô*"] and "Plain-Language Politics" ["*futsu no kotoba no tsujiru seiji*"]. In July 1994 Prime Minister Murayama Tomiichi proclaimed his slogan to be "A Government that Cares About People" ["*hito ni yasashi seiji*"], and Hashimoto Ryutarô, in his first policy speech as prime minister in January 1996, cited the goals of his cabinet as "Renovation and Creativity" ["*kaikaku to sôzô*"] and proposed reforms designed to revolutionize Japan's postwar political administrative system. Prime Minister Obuchi Keizô declared in his first policy speech that his cabinet would be dedicated to "Economic Revitalization" ["*keizai saisei, keizai shinsei*"] while Prime Minister Mori's slogan was "IT ["Information Technology"] Revolution" ["*ai'tii kakumei*"]. Most recently, in his first policy speech in the Diet after being elected prime minister in April 2001, Prime Minister Koizumi Junichirô coined the slogan "Structural Reform Without Regard for Sacred Cows" ["*sei'iki naki kôzô kaikaku*"].

As mentioned above, these slogans reflect the concerns that dominated the nation's thoughts at a given time. Whether or not each administration actually delivered the virtues expressed in its slogan is another question. The important point here is that prime ministers and other senior politicians use slogans, that is language, as a means of boosting the public's support for their Cabinet.

Political Groups and their Names

The naming of political groups or issues is also used to encourage a certain climate of opinion that influences attitudes and behavior. The name of an object often affects people's images, attitudes, and behavior toward it. Politicians are extremely sensitive to how things are named, because names can affect the prism through which the public views and judges things. Below are a few examples of naming political parties and groups, and naming of taxes.

During the last 15 years or so, since Japan's economy entered a recession in reaction to the hyperinflation that marked the "bubble economy" of the late 1980s, the nation has been engulfed in a whirlwind of change, including repeated re-shufflings of the political deck. Again and again newcomers have emerged on the political stage: some new political groups with new names, and some old political groups repackaged with new names. During this period, the political roster of Japan contained parties, factions, and "study groups" whose names contained words like Democracy, Liberal, and Reform, or with names hinting at new beginnings, bright futures, and harmony. Especially since the advent of a new age of Japanese coalition politics in August 1994, ruling and opposition parties alike (with the exception of the Japan Communist Party) adopted new names for the parties themselves or for party factions. As in the case of slogans, little attention was paid to the connection between a political group's name and the goals that it aimed for or eventually really achieved. Nobody checked the extent to which groups with "democracy" or "liberal" in their names were actually practicing those concepts in their daily activities. What mattered was the image that was projected as each group vied to call attention to its existence.

To illustrate: after the July 1993 lower house election, the Liberal Democratic Party that had governed Japan alone for 38 years was replaced by a coalition government. The coalition consisted of parties whose names included words like New, Democratic, Clean, United, and Reform: Japan New Party [*Nihon Shintô*], Social Democratic Party of Japan [*Nihon Shakaitô*], Clean Government Party [*Kômeitô*], Democratic Socialist Party [*Minshatô*], New Harbinger Party [*Shintô Sakigake*], Renewal Party [*Shinseitô*], United Socialist Democratic Party [*Shaminren*], and the Democratic Reform Party [*Minkairen*]. In December 1994, the Renewal Party merged with the Democratic Socialist Party, Japan New Party, Clean Government Party, and five other parties or groups to form the New Frontier Party [*Shinshintô*]. In January 1996, after the Social Democratic Party of Japan suffered the worst setback in its history in the July 1995 upper house election, it changed—not its policies or philosophy—but its name, to Social Democratic Party [*Shakai Minshutô*, or *Shamintô* for short].

The trend toward political realignment and the adoption of fresh names continued in September 1996 with the establishment of the Democratic Party of Japan [*Minshutô*] by secessionists from the New Harbinger Party, New Frontier Party, and Social Democratic Party. At the end of 1997, the

New Frontier Party split into six groups: Liberal Party [*Jiyûtô*], New Peace Party [*Shintô Heiwa*, consisting mainly of the former Clean Government Party], New Fraternity Party [*Shintô Yûai*], Voice of the People [*Kokumin no koe*], Club of Dawn [*Reimei Kurabu*], and Reform Club [*Kaikaku Kurabu*].

In January 1998, three splinter groups from the disbanded New Frontier Party [*Shintô Yûai, Kokumin no Koe*, and From Five [*Furomu Faibu*], along with three other opposition parties—*Minshutô*, the Sun [*Taiyô*] Party, and the Democratic Reform Party—formed a parliamentary alliance nicknamed *Minyûren* (an abbreviation of *Minshu Yûai, Taiyô* and *Kokumin Rengô*). In April, the new Democratic Party of Japan [*Minshutô*] was launched, combining four parties—the former *Minshutô*, New Fraternity Party, Democratic Reform Party, and Good Governance Party [*Minseitô*]. In November, the New Peace [*Shintô Heiwa*] and the *Kômei* group merged under the name Clean Government Party [*Kômeitô*]. In December 2002 several disgruntled members of the Democratic Party of Japan members defected and merged with the Conservative Party [*Hoshu*], forming the New Conservative Party [*Hoshu Shintô*], and the Liberals joined the Democratic Party of Japan. Following the 2003 election, the New Conservative Party disbanded itself and joined the Liberal Democratic Party.

It is true that various Diet members have established political groups with the sincere desire to express specific ideas or pursue concrete political goals such as clean politics, disarmament, or peace, but the primary motivation of politicians when selecting a name for a new or existing group is to suggest the image that they believe will have the most appeal to the public.

The practice of frequently changing names in order to promote a new image has affected party factions as well as the parties themselves. An example is *Keiseikai* [*keisei* meaning conduct of state affairs and *kai* meaning association or group), which was inaugurated in July 1987 by LDP members who supported Takeshita Noboru as party president. The group split in two due to strife triggered by the exposure in August 1992 of illegal political donations funneled to former LDP Vice President Kanemaru Shin, who was *Keiseikai*'s chairman at the time. One of the resulting groups, headed by Hata Tsutomu and Ozawa Ichirô, bolted from the LDP and formed the Renewal Party, while leadership of the other group was given to then-Chief Cabinet Secretary Obuchi Keizô. This group remained in the LDP and retained the name *Keiseikai* until April 1994, when it changed its name to Heisei Political Study Society (abbreviated as *Heiseikai*). The group decided to get rid of the old name and its associations with bribery scandals like the *Recruit* and *Tôkyô Sagawa Kyûbin* affairs and "start afresh" with a new name chosen by ballot by the entire group (as opposed to the traditional method of having the elders decide among themselves behind closed doors).

Politicians are also careful when selecting names—and by extension images that can affect attitudes and behavior—for new policies and taxes. Decision-makers try particularly hard to select a name for a proposed tax that will provide the greatest chance of convincing the public of its importance and relevance, and thereby winning public acceptance.

In October 1979, shortly before a lower house election, Prime Minister Ôhira announced the introduction of a five-percent "general consumption tax" [ippan shôhi-zei]. The result was a miserable defeat for the LDP, which won fewer than half of the contested seats. The tax was not actually introduced at that time. Seven years later, as mentioned above, ahead of a general election in July 1986, Nakasone claimed that he had no intention of introducing a "large-scale indirect tax" [ôgata kansetsu-zei]. Yet after the election the government began considering a "New Indirect Tax" [shin-gata kansetsu-zei], which was nothing other than a large-scale indirect tax with a new name. At the end of 1986, 5 percent "New Indirect Tax" was proposed under the name of "sales tax" [uriage-zei]. Because of this extremely unpopular tax, and perhaps because of its unpopular name, the LDP suffered major setbacks in gubernatorial and local assemblies elections, and in the upper house by-election. Prime Minister Takeshita took note of the unpopularity of the "sales tax," and in July 1988, his administration proposed a 3 percent "consumption tax" [shôhi-zei]. By the end of 1988, the "consumption tax" bill was finally pushed through the Diet.

"The Consumption Tax Dissolution" [Shôhi-zei kaisan] was the nickname given to Prime Minister Kaifu's dissolution of the lower house on January 24, 1990. In a bid to repeat the victory they had scored the previous year, the opposition parties once again made the unpopular 3 percent consumption tax a major campaign issue. The LDP came through the election with a stable majority in the lower house, but began to think about changing the name of the consumption tax to "National Welfare Tax" (kokumin fukushi-zei). In the end, the name remained as it was.

In April 1992, in an attempt to change the public image toward this tax, Prime Minister Miyazawa was advised to try changing the name to "environment tax" [kankyô-zei]. In February 1994 Prime Minister Hosokawa announced a plan to have a 7 percent "National Welfare Tax" [kokumin fukushi-zei] replace the 3 percent "Consumption Tax." He thought that adding concepts like "national" and "welfare" boost the tax's image and invite support from the public, but even his partners in the coalition government opposed the plan, and five days later Hosokawa announced the end of the idea. In April 1997, under Prime Minister Hashimoto, the "Consumption Tax" was raised to 5 percent. As a result, the LDP lost the upper house election of July 1998 and Hashimoto had to resign.

This kind of anecdotal evidence suggests that names of political groups and policies, slogans, etc. are probably important for creating a certain mood and manipulating public images and behaviors. The extent to which such word choices affect the political process and influence political behavior is worthy of future research.

Aspects of Political Humor

Political humor is another important aspect of political language that has not received much research attention in Japan. In addition to the editorial cartoons discussed earlier in this book, political humor consists of jokes, comedy, satire, or caricatures that overtly make fun of the power structure, including the political system and institutions themselves as well as political leaders and other decision-makers. It draws upon the semantics and pragmatics of political language, contextual information, and the political culture of a given society. Political humor can sometimes help individuals vent their frustrations with political institutions or policies.

As I have indicated elsewhere (Feldman, 2000), one finds significantly fewer expressions of political humor in Japan than in many Western societies. Moreover, the Japanese seem to prefer laughing at anecdotes and purportedly true episodes related to politics and politicians, rather than making fanciful jokes about their governing institutions and individuals. One well-known anecdote has Prime Minister Yoshida Shigeru looking particularly robust. When asked, "Prime Minister, what have you eaten?" Yoshida answered, "I ate a human being." This famous story became a joke in Japan because his choice of words—"*hito wo kutta*" (literally, "I ate a human being")—sounds arrogant. Few Japanese would speak that way, but it was very typical of that particular prime minister. Like many other anecdotes, this story loses a great deal in translation.

Prime Minister Yoshida was not the only politician whose remarks made Japanese laugh. Former Justice Minister Hatano Akira once said, "To seek such virtues as honesty or cleanliness in [Japanese] politicians is like asking for fish at a vegetable shop" ["*Seijika ni shôjiki ya seiketsu nado to iu tokumoku wo motomeru no wa, yaoya de sakana wo kure to iu noni hitoshii*"], (*Asahi*, November 9, 2002).

Sakurauchi Yoshio served as Foreign Minister for one year from November 1981. Hopefully it was humor that he was aiming for when he stunned US reporters during a March 1982 visit to the US by saying, "My name is Cherry" ("Sakura" means cherry). When asked, "What do you think of Japan–US economic friction?" he answered, "Cherry blossoms will eventually bloom on Japan–US relations." During that visit he shouted loudly, "*America banzai*!" ("Long Live America!"). Whenever he met with Washington officials, he introduced himself by saying, "I am Japanese Yul Brynner," while pointing at his bald head.

Former Prime Minister Kaifu tried hard to win concessions and even to change policies in response to aggressive US moves related to trade, earning him personal praise from President George Bush. Political observers in Japan complained that Kaifu would not do anything without first consulting with President Bush. They started calling the telephone in Kaifu's residence a "Bush-phone" instead of a "push-phone" (Japanese for a push-button telephone).

In a similar vein, the Japanese media talked about the "Buchi-phone"—again a mutation of "push phone"—used by Prime Minister Obuchi in late 1999. Obuchi reportedly rang people who did not expect to hear from him, and opened the conversation by saying something like, "Hello, this is Obuchi Keizô, I mean the prime minister." Almost no one believed it was really him, but Obuchi went ahead and chatted about social issues.

There are fundamental reasons why political jokes and satire are not as widespread in Japan as they are in Western societies. Political humor lies hidden deep within a society's psyche, drawing on common experiences, images and stereotypes from that society and its culture. It also reflects general attitudes that citizens have toward political authority, institutions, and the political system as a whole.

In societies where domestic and foreign affairs are of major concern to citizens and interest groups, and the psychological involvement of individuals in politics is relatively high, jokes can serve as a means of relaxation from political tension, routine life and social and economic insecurities, as well as providing opportunities to attack political authority. This is not the case in Japan, however, where politics is not generally perceived to be as important or central as it is in other societies. Public opinion surveys have shown a gradual decline in public interest in domestic policies and a low level of general concern with international affairs. The Japanese often describe themselves as having "A first-rate economy with third-rate politics" [*keizai ichiryû seiji sanryû*]—reflecting both the greater importance that Japanese attach to economics relative to politics, and the psychological distance they feel from politics.

The dearth of political humor in Japan can also be attributed to the fact that politicians, along with other authority figures such as medical doctors, lawyers and teachers, are granted an unusually large measure of social prestige. They are generally addressed respectfully as "*sensei*," the same title used for medical doctors and professors. In Japan, one rarely sees the level of suspicion, criticism, or hostility toward public figures that one finds displayed in Western countries, regardless of what negative feelings Japanese may feel toward them. Japanese attitudes toward civil authority and workplace superiors resemble attitudes directed only toward God in the West (Feldman & Watts, 2000).

There is a saying in Japan: "A monkey remains a monkey even if it falls from the tree, but a Diet member who loses his seat becomes a mere human being" ["*Saru wa ki kara ochitemo saru daga, kokkai giin wa senkyo ni ochireba tada no hito da*"]. Nevertheless, no one would tell jokes even about a legislator who failed to be re-elected. Rather, people would continue to demonstrate respect, calling the person *"sensei"* despite the loss of political position.

Although humorous expression is not as widespread in Japan as it is in Western societies, Japanese do not totally lack a sense of humor. They do exchange jokes, albeit not nearly as frequently as Westerners do, and they do have means for publicly expressing humor and political criticism. One such means is *senryû*.

Senryû, or satirical verse, are humorous poems consisting of 17 syllables in 3 lines. *Senryû* deal primarily with everyday people in everyday situations. Anyone can compose *senryû*, and the national newspapers publish *senryû* composed by readers almost every day. *Senryû*'s literary value lies in the light, witty realism of its expression and penetrating, intuitive observations of human foibles and events that are generally overlooked by poets in other genres. At its best, *senryû* contains keen insights into social mores and daily life, sometimes expressed as excellent satire, but some *senryû* writers take a harsh view of humanity, and their work has the flavor of mere sarcasm or scandal-mongering (Kôdansha Encyclopedia of Japan, 1983; Spellman, 1997).

Here are some examples of *senryû* from the *Yomiuri*: *"Tenmei no sôri ga tsuzuku chôju-koku"* (The Japanese live long, but life as prime minister is short). This juxtaposes two facts: Japanese have the highest life expectancy in the world, and in the five-year period from 1989 to 1996, eight prime ministers assumed office (cited in Spellman, 1997: 12)."*Heisei no kodomo ichi-hime han-tarô"* (The average Heisei family: first a girl, then half a boy). This is a twist on an old axiom proposing that it is ideal for a young couple to have a girl first, followed by two boys. It makes fun of the fact that the average family had 1.57 children in the Heisei era that began in 1989 (cited in Spellman, 1997: 42). And, *"Kôyaku ga ichiban ukeru shigatsu baka"* (April Fool's Day is when politicians' public promises are best received) (cited in Spellman, 1997: 17).

During the 2003 lower house election campaign, the following two verses of *senryû* appeared in *Asahi*, November 9, 2003: 30: *"Manifesuto yori mo tenki de kawaru hyô"* (Voting is affected more by the weather than by manifestoes). In other words, cold and rainy weather have more power to affect voter turnout than any promises that politicians might have made. *"Hajimete no skoshi ki ni naru mago no hyô"* (This is the first time that I worry a bit about how my grandchild will vote). And one more from the *Mainichi* on November 4, 2003: 2: *"Iryô-hi ga agari, byôki no heru nippon"* (Medical costs rise in Japan, and illnesses decrease). Once citizens were obliged to pay a greater percentage of the cost of doctor visits, they stopped seeing the doctor so often.

Another unusual medium for political humor in Japan during the upper house election campaign in June 2001 was television advertising produced by the political parties themselves. Apparently trying to win the hearts of voters through humor rather than by emphasizing policy issues, their television commercials showed their leaders in improbable and amusing situations. In the JCP's commercial, party chair Shii Kazuo tightened his belt to an impossible degree, in a visual pun on a Japanese phrase that literally means "belt-tightening" but refers metaphorically to renewing one's determination. In the advertisement for New *Kōmei* Party, its leader Kanzaki Takenori, dressed as a samurai-era hero in an historic setting, shouts at a corrupt official who receives a bribe, "*So wa ikanzaki!*" (You won't get away with that!). The phrase is a play on Kanzaki's name.

The Liberal Party featured its leader Ozawa Ichiro wrestling with a huge robot that bore the words "The Old Regime." Ozawa defeats the robot and promptly shouts "Renew Japan!" The Social Democratic Party, which opposes amending the Constitution to allow more participation in international military operations, portrayed its leader, Doi Takako, as the owner of a small store who cries out "I won't let you change it!" The New Conservative Party featured its leader, Ôgi Chikage, dressed as a doctor who parades around the Diet and promises a miracle cure that will produce "a healthy Japan."

Despite the lack of attention they have received to date, I think political humor and satire in Japan are important enough to warrant examination in future studies of political language in this country, along with the other topics proposed here. Such study will enhance our understanding of the dynamics of political decision-making processes at the local and the national levels, which in turn will help us to understand the modes of public policy formation, political behavior, and verbal and non-verbal communication that underpin the causes and effects of the "logic" and the "wisdom" of Japanese politics.

Appendices

Appendix 4.1
The Sample of 67 Interviews with Politicians Examined in this Study

(Figures in parenthesis indicate the television programs and the number of times a politician appeared in this program. H—*Hôdô 2001*; S—*Sandei Projekuto*).

Prime Ministers: Obuchi Keizô (S 1); Mori Yoshirô (H 1, S 1).

Secretary Generals of the LDP: Mori Yoshiro (H 1, S 1); Nonaka Hiromu (H 2, S 2); Koga Makoto (H 1, S 1).

Secretary General of the New Conservative Party: Noda Takeshi (H 1, S 1).

Secretary General of the New *Kômei* Party: Fuyushiba Tetsuzô (S 1).

Leaders of political parties: Doi Takako of SDP (S 1), Fuwa Tetsuzô of JCP (S 1); Shii Kazuo of JCP (H 2); Hatoyama Yukio of DPJ (H 2, S 5); Kan Naoto of DPJ (H 6, S 3); Kanzaki Takenori of the New *Kômei* Party (H 1, S 1); Ozawa Ichirô of the Liberal Party (H 1, S 3).

LDP's factions leaders: Katô Kôichi (H 3, S 2); Yamazaki Taku (H 1).

Ministers: Nukaga Fukushirô (H 1); Ôgi Chikage (H 2, S 2).

Chief Cabinet Secretary; Nakagawa Hidenao (S 1).

Other Diet members: Kamei Shizuka (H 1, S 1); Suzuki Muneo (S 1); Omi Kôji (H 1); Kumagai Hiroshi (H 1); Tanaka Makiko (H 1).

Prefectural Governors: Ishihara Shintarô of Tôkyô (H 4, S 3); Kitagawa Masayasu of Mie (S 1); Tanaka Yasuo of Nagano (S 1).

Appendix 4.2
The Sample of Six Interviews with Non-Politicians Examined in this Study

(Figures in parenthesis indicate the television programs and the number of times an individual appeared in this program. H—*Hôdô 2001*; S—*Sandei Projekuto*).

Former public prosecutor: Tsuchimoto Takeshi (H 1)

Writer and the Director General of the Economic Planning Agency: Sakaiya Taichi (H 1, S 1).

President of the Dai-Ichi Kangyô Bank and Chairperson of the Association of Japan Banks: Sugita Rikiyuki (S 1).

Professor, Tôkyô University: Tsukio Yoshio (S 1).

President of the Sumitomo Bank and Chairperson of the Association of Japan Banks: Nishikawa Yoshifumi (S 1).

Notes

1 *The* **Nagatachô** *Beat: Writing with Wolves*

1   Each commercial broadcaster is affiliated with one of the five national news-papers. The broadcasters are Nippon Television Network (NTV), affiliated with the *Yomiuri*; Tôkyô Broadcasting System (TBS), affiliated with the *Mainichi*; Fuji TV (Fuji Television Network) affiliated with the *Sankei*; TV Asahi (Asahi Broadcasting Co.) affiliated with the *Asahi*; and TV Tôkyô, affil-iated with the *Nihon Keizai*.

2   As of 2003, New *Kômei* Party had 22 members in the upper house and 31 in the lower house. Its total of 54 Diet members made it the nation's third largest political party.

2 *Beat Reporting and the Search for Information*

1   The first time the Japanese media chartered a commercial aircraft in order to accompany a prime minister on an overseas trip was in September 2002, when 90 members of the media flew to Pyongyang, North Korea, during Prime Minister Koizumi's visit.

3 *Two Sides of the Political Coin: Façade and Substance in Political Talk*

1   The following discussion draws on Feldman, 1998.

5 *Metaphorically Speaking II:* **Political Roles on the Front and Back of the Stage**

1   Metaphors appear in these chapters in capital letters.

6 *Metaphorically Speaking II:* **Political Roles on the Front and Back of the Stage**

1   Metaphors related to the sea appear often in the speeches of political leaders. For example, in September 1993, in his first Diet speech as prime minister, Hosokawa said the "GOVERNMENT IS A SAIL, THE PEOPLE ARE WINDS, THE COUNTRY IS THE SHIP, AND THE TIMES ARE THE SEA" ["*Seifu wa hô de ari, kokumin wa kaze, kokka wa fune, jidai wa umi de ari*"]. Saikawa, 1999: 72. In a speech Prime Minister Hashimoto delivered to the Diet after establishing his administration in 1996 he referred to the admin-istration as "A SHIP" [*fune*], to the beginning of the administration as "SAILING OF A SHIP" [*funade*], and to the confronting opinions and oppo-sition to his administration as "WINDS" [*kaze*] and "CONTRARY

WINDS" [*gyakufû*]. He said that "THE SHIP LEFT AGAINST CONTRARY WINDS, YET WITH EVERYBODY'S POWER I HOPE TO TURN IT INTO A FAVORABLE WIND" [*"Gyakufû no naka deno funade da ga, minasan no chikara de gyakufû wo junpû ni shite hoshi"*], meaning that his administration started with a large opposition yet he hoped to overcome this opposition. *Mainichi*, September 13, 1997.

2   The post of Secretary-General [*kanji-chô*] is the second most powerful in the LDP, after the presidency [*sôsai*]. Working in conjunction with the party president (who is often also the prime minister), the Secretary-General has decision-making authority regarding: (1) political funding within the LDP; (2) appointment of cabinet members and party directors; (3) ratification of the LDP's official candidates for elections; and, (4) formulation of domestic and international policies, the national budget, and other matters. The Chair of the Executive Council [*sômukai-chô*] is in charge of the party's basic policies, and the responsibility of the Chairperson of the party Policy Affairs Research Council [*seimuchôsa-kaichô*] is to review all matters related to policy affairs that are formulated by the bureaucracy.

3   Miki's wife, Mutsuko, was called POLITICAL GODMOTHER [*seikai no goddomazzâ*]. Iwami, 1998: 175.

4   Some leading Diet members besides the prime minister are also given nicknames. Hori Shigeru, who served as Speaker of the lower house and in other posts, was called a RACOON DOG [*tanuki*] by his colleagues (Iwami, 1998: 32). In Japanese fairy tales, raccoon dogs often deceive people. Asanuma Inejirô, the chairman of the Socialist Party who was assassinated by ultra nationalist in November 1960, was nicknamed a HUMAN LOCOMOTIVE [*ningen kikansha*], because he moved from one place to another like a locomotive that endlessly moves from one station to another. His home was likened to a station—in which he spend just a few minutes before rushing off to his next destination (Iwami, 1998: 223). Likewise, the former Minister of Health and Welfare in Prime Minister Hashimoto's cabinet and later the leader of DPJ, Kan Naoto, was called NERVOUS KAN [*ira-kan*] because of his well-known impatience and irritation (Saikawa, 1999: 328). Last, the jolly-looking grandfather Shiokawa Masajûrô, while serving as the Finance Minister in Prime Minister Koizumi's Cabinet, was extremely popular among young people who refer to him affectionately as "GRANDPA-SHIO [*shio-jii*], (he was the oldest, 80 year old, among the 17 ministers in the Cabinet).

7 Lampooned Prime Ministers: The Implicit Meaning of Editorial Cartoons in Japanese Dailies

1   These endings were developed in a pilot study conducted by the author and are partly based on Medhurst & Desousa, 1981: 222.

2   A *teru-teru bozu* is a paper doll hung outside at night by children who want the next day to be fair. If the weather is fair the next day, the doll is traditionally thrown into the nearest river.

Bibliography

In the case of dailies *Asahi*, *Yomiuri*, and *Mainichi*, all references are from the morning edition unless noted differently.

Akasaka, T. (1986). *Nakasone shitsugen mondai no yukue* [The whereabouts of prime minister Nakasone's slip of tongue]. *Bungei Shunjû*, 11, 162–66.

Akasu, K. & Asao, K. (1993). Sociolinguistic factors influencing communication in Japan and the United States. In W. B. Gudykunst (ed.), *Communication in Japan and the United States* (pp. 88–121). Albany: State University of New York Press.

Asahi Shimbun Seijibu (ed.) (1992). *Takeshitaha shihai* [The dominance of the Takeshita faction]. Tôkyô: Asahi Shimbunsha.

Barry, H. (1998). Functions of recent US presidential slogans. In O. Feldman & C. De Landtsheer (eds.), *Politically speaking: A worldwide examination of language used in the public sphere* (pp. 161–69). Westport, Conn.: Praeger.

Bavelas, J. B., Black, A., Bryson, L., & Mullett, J. (1988). Political equivocation: A situational explanation. *Journal of Language and Social Psychology*, 7, 137–45.

Bavelas, J. B., Black, A., Chovil, N., & Mullett, J. (1990). *Equivocal communication*. Newbury Park, CA: Sage.

Beer, F. A. & De Landtsheer, C. (1999). Metaphorical meaning and political power. A paper presented at the annual meeting of the International Society of Political Psychology. Amsterdam, The Netherlands.

Beniger, J. R. & Westney, D. E. (1981). Japanese and US media: Graphics as a reflection of newspapers' social role. *Journal of Communication*, 31, 14–27.

Berlyne, D. E. (1969). Laughter, humor, and play. In G. Lindzey & E. Aronson (eds.), *Handbook of social psychology*, vol. 3 (pp. 795–852). Reading, MA: Addison-Wesley.

Bormann, E. G., Koester, J., & Bennett, J. (1978). Political cartoons and salient rhetorical fantasies: An empirical analysis of the '76 presidential campaign. *Communication Monographs*, 45, 317–29.

Bull, P. E. (1994). On identifying questions, replies and non-replies in political interviews. *Journal of Language and Social Psychology*, 13, 115–31.

—— (2002). *Communication under the microscope: The theory and practice of micro-analysis*. Hove: Routledge.

Bull, P. E., Elliot, J., Palmer, D, & Walker, L. (1996). Why politicians are three-faced: The face model of political interviews. *British Journal of Social Psychology*, 35, 267–84.

Bull, P. E. & Mayer, K. (1993). How not to answer questions in political interviews. *Political Psychology*, 14, 651–66.

De Landtsheer, C. (1994). The language of prosperity and crisis: A case study in political semantics. *Politics and the Individual*, 4, 63–85.

De Landtsheer, C., & Feldman, O. (eds.) (2000). *Beyond public speech and symbols: Explorations in the rhetoric of politicians and the media.* Westport, Conn.: Praeger.

Edelman, M. (1971). *Politics as symbolic action: Mass arousal and quiescence.* New York, NY: Academic.

Edwards, J. L. (1997). *Political cartoons in the 1988 presidential campaign: Image, metaphor, and narrative.* New York, NY: Garland.

Edwards, J. L., & Winkler, C. K. (1997). Representative form and the visual ideograph: The Iwo Jima image in editorial cartoons. *Quarterly Journal of Speech*, 83, 289–310.

Elwood, W. N. (1995). Declaring war on the home front: Metaphor, presidents, and the war on drugs. *Metaphor and Symbolic Activity*, 10, 93–114.

Feldman, O. (1993a). *Politics and the news media in Japan.* Ann Arbor, MI: University of Michigan Press.

—— (1993b). Political Alienation and Cynicism in Contemporary Japan. *Tsukuba Journal of Sociology*, 18, 1–58.

—— (1993c). *Seijimanga ni miru 'nihon no shushô'* [How the Japanese prime minister is depicted in the editorial cartoons]. *Ushio*, 12, 120–27.

—— (1995). Political reality and editorial cartoons in Japan: How the national-dailies illustrate the Japanese prime minister. *Journalism and Mass Communication Quarterly*, 72, 571–80.

—— (1998). The Political Language of Japan: Decoding What Politicians Mean from What They Say. In O. Feldman & C. De Landtsheer (eds.), *Politically Speaking: A Worldwide Examination of Language Used in the Public Sphere* (pp. 43–55). Westpoart, Conn.: Praeger.

—— (1999a). *The Japanese political personality.* London: Macmillan.

—— (1999b). Introduction to political psychology in Japan. In O. Feldman (ed.), *Political psychology in Japan* (pp. 1–23). New York, NY: Nova Science.

—— (2000). Non-oratorical discourse and political humor in Japan: Editorial cartoons, satire, and attitudes toward authority. In C. De Landtsheer & O. Feldman (eds.) *Beyond public speech: Explorations of the symbols used by politicians and the media* (pp. 165–91). Westport, Conn.: Praeger.

Feldman, O. & Kawakami, K. (1989). Leaders and leadership in Japanese politics: Images during a campaign period. *Comparative Political Studies*, 22, 265–90.

Feldman, O., & De Landtsheer, C. (eds.) (1998). *Politically speaking: A worldwide examination of language used in the public sphere.* Westport, Conn.: Praeger.

Feldman, O., & Watts, M. W. (2000). Autoritat und politische autoritat in Japan [Authority and political authority in Japan]. In S. Rippl, C. Seipel, & A. Kindervater (eds.), *Autoritarismus [Authoritarianism]*, (pp. 147–71). Opladen, Germany: Leske & Budrich.

Gamson, W. A., & Stuart, D. (1992). Media discourse as a symbolic contest: The bomb in political cartoons. *Sociological Forum*, 3, 55–86.

Gombrich, E. H. (1982). *The image and the eye.* Ithaca, NY: Cornell University Press.

Goss, B., & Williams, M. L. (1973). The effects of equivocation on perceived-source credibility. *Central States Speech Journal*, 24, 162–67.

Hackett, R. F. (1973). Political modernization and the Meiji Genro. In R. E. Ward (ed.), *Political development in modern Japan* (pp. 65–97). Princeton: Princeton University Press.

Hamada, K. (1994). *Hamako no yo no naka machigattoru* [Hamako cries out: Everything is wrong in society]. Tôkyô: Yomiuri Shimbunsha.

Hamilton, M. A. & Mineo, P. J. (1998). A framework for understanding equivocation. *Journal of Language and Social Psychology*, 17, 3–35.

Harris, S. (1991). Evasive action: How politicians respond to questions in political interviews. In P. Scannell (ed.), *Broadcast talk* (pp. 76–99). London: Sage.

Heritage, J. (1985). Analyzing news interviews: Aspects of the production of talk for an overhearing audience. In T. van Dijk (ed.), *Handbook of discourse analysis*, vol. 3. (pp. 95–117). New York, NY: Academic Press.

Hook, G. D. (1986). *Language and Politics*. Tôkyô: Kuroshio Shuppan.

Imai, M. (1981). *16 ways to avoid saying no: An invitation to experience Japanese management from the inside*. Tôkyô: Nihon Keizai Shimbunsha.

Inoguchi, T. (1995). *Karaoke seiji kara no datshitsu* [Away from *karaoke* politics]. *This is Yomiuri*, 2, 62–71.

Itô M. (1982). *Jimintô sengokushi: Kenryoku no kenkyû* [History of the LDP's wars: Research on authority]. Tôkyô: Asahi Sonorama.

Iwami, T. (1995a). Seiji genron: Kaikenronsha daga, ima wa tsuyoku shuchô shinai [Political talk: I support the revision of the Constitution but for the time being I would not emphasize this strongly]. *Sandae Mainichi*, April 16, 21.

—— (1995b). Seiji genron: Nidai seitô ga nozomashi ga, dômo jishin ga nai [Political talk: Two party system is preferred yet I am not confident about it]. *Sandae Mainichi*, September 24, 21.

—— (1998). *Seiji ni hitsuyo na no wa, kotoba to sozôryoku to honno sukoshi no okane* [All politics requires are words, imagination, and a bit of money]. Tôkyô: Mainichi Shimbunsha.

Johnson, C. (1980). *Omote* (Explicit) and *ura* (Implicit): Translating Japanese political terms. *Journal of Japanese Studies*, 6, 89–115.

Jucker, L. (1986). *News interviews: A pragmalinguistic analysis*. Amsterdam, The Netherlands: John Benjamins.

Kawano, N. (1999). *Shushô ni totte no 'heiwa' no imi* [The meaning of 'peace' for Japanese prime ministers]. *Kokusai kyôryoku kenkyûshi*, 5, 31–43.

Kawano, N., & Matsuo, M. (2002). Political outcomes of the slip of the tongue of Japanese ministers. *Hiroshima Peace Science*, 24, 197–221.

Kioi, S. (1967). *Wan man hyôka hensenshi* [Chronicles of the changing evaluations toward "one-man"]. *Bungei Shunjû*, 12, 154.

Kishima, T. (1991). *Political life in Japan: Democracy in a reversible world*. Princeton, NJ: Princeton University Press.

Kissinger, H. (1985). Threat to US–Japan Relations (reprinted from Los Angeles Times). *Seattle Times*, October, 13.

Kitao, K. & Kitao, S. K. (1989). *Intercultural communication: Between Japan and the United States*. Tôkyô: Eichosha Shinsha.

Kobayashi, T. (1998). On air: *Tôshuzô no PR sakusen wo* [On air: The PR strategy of parties' leaders]. *Asahi*, August 8, 6.

Kôdansha Encyclopedia of Japan. (1983). Tôkyô: Kôdansha.

Koike, Y. (1995). *Watakushi ga ozawa-san ni nori kaeta riyû* [The reason I became pro-Ozawa]. *Sandae Mainichi*, December 31, 29–31.

Lakoff, G. (1991). Metaphor and war: The metaphor system used to justify war in the Gulf. *Journal of Urban and Cultural Studies*, 2, 59–72.

Lakoff, G. & Turner, M. (1989). *More than cool reason: A field guide to poetic metaphor*. Chicago, IL: University of Chicago Press.

Langeveld, W. (1981). Political cartoons as a medium of political communication. *International Journal of Political Education*, 4, 343–71.

Masumi J., (1988). *Gendai Seiji: 1955 nen ikô* [Contemporary Politics: From 1955]. Tôkyô: Tôkyô Daigaku Shuppankai.

McCargo, D. (1996). The political role of the Japanese media. *The Pacific Review*, 9, 251–64.

Medhurst, M. J. & Desousa, M. A. (1981). Political cartoons as rhetorical form: A taxonomy of graphic discourse. *Communication Monographs*, 48.

Mio, J. S. (1997). Metaphor and Politics. *Metaphor and Symbol*, 12, 113–33.

Mitchell, D. D. (1976). *Amaeru: The expreession of reciprocal dependency needs in Japanese politics and law*. Boulder, Col: Westview.

Mizutani, O. (1981). *Japanese: The spoken language in Japanese life* (trans. J. Ashby). Tôkyô: Japan Times.

Mooy, J. (1976). *A study of Metaphor: On the nature of metaphorical expressions with special reference to their reference*. Amsterdam, The Netherlands: North Holl.

Nihon Shimbun Kyôkai. (2002). *Nihon shimbun nenkan* [Japanese newspapers yearly]. Tôkyô: Nihon Shimbun Kyôkai.

Nonaka, N. (1995). *Jimintô seikenka no seiji eriito* [Political elite under LDP rule]. Tôkyô: Tôkyô Daigaku Shuppankai.

Oxford English Dictionary II. CD Rom.

Read, S. J., Cesa, I. L., Jones, D. K., & Collins, N. L. (1990). When is the federal budget like a baby? Metaphor in political rhetoric. *Metaphor and Symbolic Activity*, 5, 125–49.

Ryan, T. A., & Schwartz, C. B. (1956). Speed of perception as a function of mode of representation. *American Journal of Psychology*, 69, 60–69.

Saikawa, T. (1999). *Renritsu seiji no butaiura: Seikai saihen, ryûsa no rokunenkan* [The back stage of the coalition politics: Six years of quicksand during the reorganization of the political world]. Tôkyô: Bungeisha.

Sakonjo, N. (1983). *Nakasone 'fuchin kûbo' ron wo toku* [Solving the dispute over prime minister Nakasone remark on 'unsinkable aircraft carrier']. *Chûô Kôron*, 3, 152–56.

Samejima, M. (1994). *Tonosama to sanjûrokunin no samurai* [A feudal lord and the 36 samurai]. Tôkyô: Jitsugyôno Nihonsha.

Schlesinger, J. M. (1999). *Shadow shoguns: The rise and fall of Japan's postwar political machine*. Stanford, CA: Stanford University Press.

Schlesinger, M., & Lau, R. R. (2000). The meaning and measure of policy metaphors. *American Political Science Review*, 94, 611–26.

Schodt, F. L. (1986). *Manga, manga: The world of Japanese comics*. Tôkyô: Kôdansha International.

Semino, E., & Masci, M. (1996). Politics is football: Metaphor in the discourse of Silvio Berlusconi in Italy. *Discourse & Society*, 7, 243–69.

Seymour-Ure, C. (1986). Drawn and quartered: The election in cartoons. In I. Crewe & M. Haroop (eds.), *Political communications: The general election campaign of 1983* (pp. 160–76). Cambridge: Cambridge University Press.

Sheppard, A. (1977). Developmental levels in explanations of humor from childhood to late adolescence. In A. J. Chapman & H. C. Foot (eds.), *It's a funny thing, humour* (pp. 225–28). New York, NY: Pergamon.

Shiota, M. (1980). *Zenkôsan ni aimashita ka* [Did you meet Mr. Zenkô?]. *Bungei Shunjû*, 9, 134–45.

Shitsugen ô nintei iinkai (ed.) (2000). *Daishitsugen* [Slip of tongue]. Tôkyô: Jôhô Sentâ Shuppan Kyoko.

Spellman, M. (1997). *Senryû: Haiku reflections of the times*. Altanta: Mangajin.

Stone, D. A. (1988). *Policy paradox and political reason*. Glenview, IL: Scott, Foresman.

Suzuki, T. (1989). *Words in Context: A Japanese Perspective on Language and Culture* (5th printing), (trans. A. Miura). Tôkyô & New York, NY: Kôdansha International.

Takemura, M. (1994). *Chiisakutomo kirari to hikaru kuni nippon* [Small but glittering nation—Japan]. Tôkyô: Kôbunsha.

Tanaka S. (1995). Interview with Komiya Etsuko. *Sandae Mainichi*, January 1, 52–57.

Tase, Y. (1994). *Seiji janarizumu no tsumi to batsu* [The crime and punishment of political journalism]. Tôkyô: Shinshosha.

van Teeffelen, T. (1994). Racism and metaphor: The Palestinian-Israeli conflict in popular literature. *Discourse & Society*, 5, 381–405.

Williams, M. L., & Goss, B. (1975). Equivocation: Character insurance. *Human Communication Research*, 1, 265–70.

Weekly and Daily Newspapers

Aera (May 24, 1988). *Okuno jinin* [On Okuno's resignation], 61.

—— (May 9, 1989). *Nagatachô ronri ga ikizumaru toki* [When the logic of *Nagatachô* will be stuck], 62.

—— (July 11, 1989). *Josei sukyandalu de doromamire* [Troubled by the woman's scandal], 14.

—— (March 6, 1990). *Gôtanna nata no otoko: Ozawa ichirô no shôri* [Man of a bold ax: The victory of Ozawa Ichirô], 22.

—— (September 10, 1991). *Namekuji sôsaisen* [Slugish presidential election], 66.

—— (October 27, 1992). *'Don kanemaru shin' yabure kokyô ni kaeru* [Going back home defeated, Don Kanemaru Shin], 13.

—— (March 23, 1993). *'Seijika' to iu na no yamishôbai* [Dark business named 'Politician'], 6.

—— (May 25, 1993). *Boku wa sekando: Kamisori wo togu gotôda fukusôri* [I am the second: Sharpening the razor Gotôda vice prime minister], 10.

—— (August 10, 1993). *Kôno shi eranda jimin no keiryaku, shushô ni narenai 16 dai sôsai* [LDP's plot in choosing Kôno as the party's president: The sixteenth president who would not become prime minister], 13.

—— (January 3, 1994). *Watakushitachi wa donna kuni wo mezasubeki ka: Riidâ ga kataru nihon no shinro, kokka kan* [What type of country do we have to look for:

Leaders' talk about the course of Japan and the country's views], 18.

—— (February 28, 1994). *Kantei mitsugetsu kappulu no hakyoku* [The end of the honeymoon at the prime minister's office], 18.

—— (January 23, 1995), *'Shôwa no yôkai' no jitsuzô: Kishi nobusuke gokuchû nikki* [The real image of 'Shôwa Ghost:' Diary in the jail of Nobusuke Kishi], 13.

—— (July 24, 1995). *Taishô dôshi ni onnen wa nakatta: Kaku fuku sensô hiwa wo ryô sokkin ga kataru* [No hate was between the generals: Aids of Tanaka and Fukuda talk about things behind of the war between the two], 18.

—— (December 30, 1996). *Moto naikaku sôri daijin: Nakasone yasuhiro (gendai no shozô)* [Former prime minister: Nakasone Yasuhiro (contemporary portrait), 7.

—— (August 10, 1998). *Katô kôichi shi ga hikaseta bimbôkuji: Miyazawa kiichi shi zôshô ni* [Miyazawa Kiichi was forced to become the least lucky of all by Katô Kôichi as he was appointed as a minister of finance], 17.

—— (December 7, 1998). *Jiji renritsu de warau shôchô no na: Obuchi ozawa gôi no mikata* [On the LDP-Liberal Party Coalition: Views on the agreement between Obuchi and Ozawa], 18.

—— (January 25, 1999). *Kitaitchi zero ga umu obuchi majikku? Jiji renritsu seiken stâto* [Expecting nothing of Obuchi: The starting of the coalition government], 18.

Asahi (October 7, 1979). *Tensei jingo* [Vox populi vox dei], 1.

—— (October 22, 1984). *Shiteki shimon kikan: Kasumigaseki ni hanazakari* [An advisory body: Kasumigaseki in Full Bloom], 9.

—— (November 1, 1984). *Teiryû ni 'kakubanare' no kôzu* [Keeping distance from the influence of Tanaka is at the bottom of the political composition], editors' debate, 3.

—— (July 1, 1986). *Nyû riidâ 'kyôen' no hazu ga . . .* [. . . And we expected a 'contest' between the new leaders], 3.

—— (July 15, 1986). *Fukuda ha 'abeha' ni koromogae: Tônai no sedai kôtai wo unagasu* [Changing the clothes in Fukuda faction to Abe faction: Encouraging generation change in the LDP], 1.

—— (December 18, 1986). *Tanakaha no 'mochidai' fukkatsu* [The revival of 'mochidai' in Tanaka's faction], 2.

—— (December 22, 1986). *Mochidai no kôzô* [The structure of *mochidai*]. Evening edition, 1.

—— (January 6, 1987). *Abe jimin sômukaichô ('87 seiji, butai, shûyaku)* [Abe the LDP's executive chairman (1987—politics, stage, role)], 2.

—— (August 7, 1987). *Shushô erabi no kijun: Nagatachô no soto kara no chûmon* [Criteria for selecting the prime minister], editors' debate, 4

—— (August 8, 1987). *Kishi moto shushô no shi* [On the death of former prime minister Kishi], 27.

—— (May 19, 1989). *Nyôbô yaku nakasone senryaku no shichû* ["Prime Minister's wife" supports Nakasone's strategy], 1.

—— (August 6, 1989). *Jimin sôsaisen, kazu kazu no dorama enjite 34 nenkan ni 20 kai* [LDP presidential election: Twenty dramas during 34 years], 2.

—— (September 3, 1989). *Kaifu shushô no kôken yaku no kômoto toshio shi* [Komoto Toshio's guardianship role of prime minister Kaifu], 2.

—— (October 5, 1989). *Daihyô shitsumon kakikesu yaji* [Scratching out during interpellation in the Diet's plenary session], 2.

—— (March 12, 1990). *Tanaka moto shushôtei, keibi toku: Imataikô, yami shôgun . . . yume no ato* [Former prime minister Tanaka residence: '*Imataikô*,' shugun in the dark . . . the end of the dream], 31.

—— (May 14, 1990). *Shushô to 'isshin dôtai' no kokorogamae de* [Being of one flesh with the prime minister], 2.

—— (May 16, 1990). *Gyôkaku wo dô saishuppatsu saseru ka* [How to restart administrative reforms?], editorial, 5.

—— (August 20, 1990). *Jimina seisakutsû ni mo shiren no aki jimin, hata tsutomo shi* [Facing tough time: LDP's Hata Tsutomu], 2.

—— (January 14, 1991). *Saihen shikakeru 'mura' no bantô* [Clerk of the 'villge' setting up the plan for reforms], 2.

—— (May 21, 1991). *'KK sensô' shûketsu?* [The end of KK war?], 4.

—— (July 16, 1991). *Hashimoto zôshô yoritsuron, kyûsoku ni shibomu sedai kôtai ni hanpatsu* [Support for finance minister Hashimoto shrinking rapidly as a result of generational change], 4.

—— (August 7, 1991). *Butai no uragawa* [Back stage], 4.

—— (October 30, 1991). *Odôron to gôrishugi: Tenken miyazawa kiichi* [King-road and rationalism: Examining Miyazawa Kiichi], 4.

—— (November 9, 1991). *Katô kôichi kanbô chôkan* [Katô Kôichi, the new chief cabinet secretary], 4.

—— (February 4, 1992). *Miyazawa shushô ga bei rôdôkan 'baburu mo onaji'* [Prime Minister Miyazawa remarks on American's work ethic], 2.

—— (April 24, 1992). *PKO hôan seiritsu e nankan 3 hâdoru* [Three hurdles as obstacles in establishing the PKO bill], 2.

—— (March 19, 1993). *'Kokujin to akushu. . . kuroku naro kanji' giin, hyôgo kengi iinkai de hatsugen* ["Shaking hands with black people . . . feeling like the hands turn black"], Western Japan edition, 30.

—— (May 28, 1993). *Sei, kan, gyô wa tetsu no sankakukei* [The iron triangle of government, bureaucracy, and the industry], 3.

—— (June 10, 1993). *Senkyo kaikaku, shubutai wa jimin sômukai ni* [Election reforms, turning the spot light toward the LDP's executive board], 2.

—— (July 4, 1993). *Kakutô tôshu no kihon shisei* [The basic attitude of the parties' leaders], 7.

—— (August 2, 1993). *Shinro sadamaranu funade, naigai ni kadai* [Uncertain route: Problems on the domestic and international arenas], 1.

—— (August 11, 1993). *Saki no sensô, shinryaku sensô to meigen* [An explicit declaration that the war was a "war of aggression"], 1.

—— (August 15, 1993). *'Hosokawa karâ' jiwari* [Emerging 'Hosokawa color'], 2.

—— (September 15, 1993). *Ano kinken taishitsu, aratamarimasu ka* [Can money oriented political attitude be changed], 1.

—— (November 3, 1993). *Ryôtei de kaigô, makarinaran kantei shusai wa hiru mo dame: Hosokawa shushô ga shiji* [Prohibiting meetings of officials in fine restaurants and even lunch time meetings hosted by the prime ministers' office: Prime minister Hosokawa's indication], 7.

—— (December 2, 1993). *Nakanishi boeichôkan, kempô minaoshi shuchô* [Nakanishi, the director general of the Defense Agency, claims for revision of the Constitution], 1.

—— (December 17, 1993). *'Tanaka seiji' no kage, ima mo 'kazu to kane' de shihai*

[The shadow of "Tanaka style of politics:" Controlling through "numbers and money" even today], 7.

—— (February 23, 1994). *Soredemo naikaku kaizô nanoka* [Is this a reshuffle of government?], editorial, 2.

—— (March 30, 1994). *Seiren: Yosan motomete 'kankan settai'* [Honesty: Meeting with officials for requesting budget], 1.

—— (May 17, 1994). *Ima no ronchô ga tsuzuku nara kuni no shôrai ayauku suru, Ozawa shi ga masukomi wo hihan* [Ozawa criticises the news media: Continuing the present tone of the arguments is dangerous for the country's future], 22.

—— (August 15, 1994). *'Shinryaku, kokoro kara owabi' murayama shushô danwa* [Prime Minister Murayama expressed his "sincere apology" for Japan's aggression], evening editon, 1.

—— (September 9, 1994). *Seikai saihen, futokoro ni mo henka* [Reorganization of the political world and the change of the financial status], 9.

—— (February 21, 1995). *'Murayama kantei' kage usushi nemawashi nigatena 'ôbantô' fuku chôkan wo zenmen ni* [The vice chief cabinet secretary at the front of the negotiations in Murayama's cabinet], evening edition, 1.

—— (April 19, 1995). *'Genrô' no yû-utsu kensei ni kageri* [Melancholy of 'genrô'], 7.

—— (July 6, 1995). *Zôgo no tatsujin: Fukuda moto shushô goroku* [A master of word coinage: The collection of former prime minister Fukuda], 9.

—— (July 12, 1995). *Onna ga ugoku* [Women start moving], 7.

—— (November 3, 1995). *Motsureru kunigae, jiban onzon* [Being entangled with changing the constituency, keeping the constituency], 7.

—— (March 28, 1996a). *Kanemaru shin, moto fuku sôri ga shikyo* [The death of former vice prime minister Shin Kanemaru], evening edition, 1.

—— (March 28, 1996b). *Yamanashi kara fuhô hissori kanemaru shin moto jimintô fukusôsai shikyo* [The death of the LDP vice-president Kanemaru Shin], evening edition, 19.

—— (September 23, 1996). *Seiken shiya, renkei saguru 'senkyogo' e jimin mo shin-shin mo 'minshutô' hataage* [Seeking coalition with the intention to achieve political power], 2.

—— (November 8, 1996). *Gyôsei kaikaku, ôkura kôsei ga shikinseki* [The ministry of finance and the ministry of health and welfare as touchstones of the administrative reforms], 3.

—— (April 18, 1997). *'Hôhô' e kyûhandoru wa kiken: Taiyô tô no tôtaikai de okuda saikô komon ni kiku* [Dangerous of changing the route: Questions to Okuda, the supreme advisor of the Sun Party's], 7.

—— (June 10, 1997). *Zoku giin no jitsuryoku, kokkai no hiriki* [Real power of "tribe" politicians, powerless Diet], 7.

—— (July 2, 1997). *Ippon zuri chakuchaku: Senkyoku akete mate imasu* [Single-hook fishing: Giving you the chance to run in the constituency], 7.

—— (July 4, 1997). *'Shôwa no kômonsama' fukuda moto shushô wo shinobukai* [After the death of former prime minister Fukuda], 7.

—— (September 12, 1997). *Nagatachô ronri ni ikari: Jimin kankeisha wa kuchi tsugumu satô kôkô shi nyûkaku* [Anger at *Nagatachô* logic: LDP Diet members shut up their mouth when Satô Kôkô enters the new cabinet], 30.

—— (September 20, 1997). *'Gyôkaku no dai ippo wa seijika kara' zaishoku 25 nen no hyôshô, koizumi kôshô ga kyohi* [Koizumi, the minister of welfare rejects the award for 25 years of service in the Diet: 'Reforms start from politicians,' he said], 2.

—— (October 1, 1997). *Watakushi wa kazamidori* [I am a weathervane], 7.

—— (October 12, 1997). *Fufu de ken nai angya* [The couple that go together in the prefecture]. Niigata edition, 4

—— (December 27, 1997). *Zokugiin wa 'kan shudô' wo koeta ka* [Do 'tribe Diet members' exceed bureaucracy oriented system?], 4.

—— (June 5, 1998). *'Ozawa shushô' wa 'kodomo' shidai?* [Will the 'children' decide if Ozawa becomes a prime minister?], 7.

—— (June 11, 1998). *Giin no 'kôridai' 200 man en uwanose: Jimintô senkyo katsudô hi kubaru* [Diet members' "ice-money" additional 2 million yen: Money distributed for election campaign in the LDP], 7.

—— (July 13, 1998). *Kôkei erabi nankô hanshikkôbu ha no dôkô kagi* [Difficulty in selecting the successor: Observing the tendency of the executives], 3.

—— (August 16, 1998). *Shinan yaku tayori no obuchi seiken* [The dependency of Obuchi administration on instructers], 2.

—— (August 21, 1998). *Shôten sairoku: Yosan iinkai, sanin hatsuka* [Refocusing the observation: The day of the upper house' budget committee], 6.

—— (September 4, 1998). *Piza to bonjin: Seiji wo osou mediya kôzui* [Pizza and ordinary man: Media flood attacking politics], 6.

—— (September 8, 1998). *Kantei no kokui wa tatakiage* [The 'stage assistant' from the Prime Minister's Office struggles his way up], 7.

—— (September 21, 1998). *'Tamamushi-iro gôi' setten tesaguri* [Blind search for assessment of '*tamamushi-iro* agreement'], 2.

—— (December 26, 1998). *'Shinkû shushô' shissoku sezu: 'Bonjin' buki ni toshikoshi obuchi keizô shushô* [The vacuum prime minister does not slow down: Prime minister Obuchi Keizô armed as 'ordinary person'], 6.

—— (January 4, 1999). *Kanreki wa aseri no kisetsu? Jimin, habatsu de susumu sedai kôtai* [Is sixty years old the period of impatience? LDP, the progress of generation change in the factions], 2.

—— (January 14, 1999). *'Jiji' renritsu funade ni nokoru hidane: Anpo seisaku gôi* [The tinder that still remains in the coalition between the LDP and the Liberal Party: Agreement on security policy], 3.

—— (February 10, 1999). *Obuchi sôri, tombogaeri chômon gaikô* [Prime Minister Obuchi's funeral diplomacy: Dragonfly turning backward somersaults], 7.

—— (February 25, 1999). *Kage no shireitô wa 'hidari senkai' min'i bunseki ni 'waza' hime* [The conning tower behind the scene is 'turning to the left:' Concealing "skill" of the analysis of public opinion], 7.

—— (July 7, 1999). *Zahyô: Shinku shushô to jijikô seiji* [Coordinates: Vacuum prime minister and the coalition politics], 7.

—— (August 13, 1999). *Minshu, sonzaikan saguri kunikuno gyûho* [Democratic Party of Japan: Winning recognition by using the 'ox-walk'], 2.

—— (October 8, 1999). *'Kage no naikaku' nexto kabinetto de no hatoyama minshu ga yotô ni idomu* [Challenging the ruling parties by the "shadow cabinet" of Hatoyama's Democratic Party], 6.

—— (November 16, 1999). *'Posto obuchi' shôjun* [Aiming at 'post Obuchi'], 6.

—— (December 22, 1999). *Yaburete kiba migaku 'ippikki ôkami' saitôban kake habatsu kessei* [The loser lonely wolf polishing its teeth: forming factions for the purpose of regaining positions], 7.

—— (December 26, 1999). *2000 nen seikyoku no kii pâson* [Key person in the politics of the year 2000], 2.

—— (May 15, 2000), *Tensei jingo* [Vox popoli vox dei], 1.

—— (June 4, 2000). *Hatsugenroku* [Records of utterances], 5

—— (June 21, 2000). *Kimeteinai hito netete kurereba* [The undecided people can stay asleep], 2

—— (July 25, 2000). *Ichinensei giin mo daihyô shitsumon* [First grade Diet members will also ask questions during Diet deliberations], 4

—— (October 26, 2000). *Tensei Jingo* [Vox populi, vox dei], 1.

—— (March 1, 2001). *'Waga kuni no shoshô' shibashi jôkigen* [Our prime minister's mood is well only for a short time], 38.

—— (April 18, 2001). *Obuchi zen shushô ni 'odabutsu-san'* [Calling former prime minister Obuchi "odabutsusan"], 4

—— (April 20, 2001). *Yudayajin ga sumitai kuni ni* [In the country Jews would like to live], 4

—— (November 9, 2002). *Hatano Akira san shikyo* [On the Death of Hatano Akira], 39.

Bungei Shunjû (October 1986). *Hôgen daijin ôini kataru* [The outspoken minister's abuse of language], 122–33.

Daily Yomiuri (December 7, 1999). Diet members face winds of political change, 7.

Mainichi (April 24, 1988). *Ôsaka wa tantsubo. . . kitanai machi* [Ôsaka is spittoon . . . a dirty city], 4.

—— (September 22, 1990). *Kajiyama hôshô ga hôgen* [The careless remark of Kajiyama, the Minister of Justice], 2

—— (July 2, 1995). *Murayama seiken ichi nen* [The first year of Murayama's administration], editorial, 5

—— (September 13, 1997). *Hashimoto kaizô naikaku: Arashi no funade* [Hashimoto's reshuffled cabinet: Stormy departure (of a ship)], 2.

—— (May 11, 1999). *Teichaku suru 'takeshita noboru fuzai' Obuchi shushô 'hitori-dachi'* [On the absence of Takeshita Noboru and the growing independent of Prime Minister Obuchi]. 2.

—— (May 17, 2001). *Kanbô kimitsuhi mondai* [The problem regarding the classified funds of the Chief Cabinet Secretary], 2.

Sandae Mainichi (May 7/14, 1995). *Murayama shushô ni hôchô hanamichi-ron* [Prime minister Murayama's farewell road following the visit to China], 151–53.

Shûkan Asahi (December 29, 2000). *Hashimoto Ryûtarô moto shushô, hitori maia-gattete ii no* [It is not the time for former Prime Minister Hashimoto Ryûtarô to soar high into the sky], 35.

Yomiuri (January 21, 1992). *Sakurauchi hatsugen wo issei hihan* [Total criticism over Sakurauchi's remarks], evening edition, 2.

—— (June 9, 1992). *Kankoku 'mori hatsugen' chôsa e* [Inquiring into Mori's remarks on Korea], 2.

Index